# STAR WARS®

## THE ESSENTIAL CHRONOLOGY

**THE**
**STAR WARS**®
**LIBRARY PUBLISHED BY DEL REY BOOKS**

*STAR WARS: THE ESSENTIAL GUIDE TO CHARACTERS*
*STAR WARS: THE ESSENTIAL GUIDE TO VEHICLES AND VESSELS*
*STAR WARS: THE ESSENTIAL GUIDE TO WEAPONS AND*
  *TECHNOLOGY*
*STAR WARS: THE ESSENTIAL GUIDE TO PLANETS AND MOONS*
*STAR WARS: THE ESSENTIAL GUIDE TO DROIDS*
*STAR WARS: THE ESSENTIAL CHRONOLOGY*

*STAR WARS ENCYCLOPEDIA*
*GUIDE TO THE STAR WARS UNIVERSE*
*STAR WARS TECHNICAL JOURNAL*
*STAR WARS: SECRETS OF SHADOWS OF THE EMPIRE*
*I'D JUST AS SOON KISS A WOOKIEE:*
  *THE QUOTABLE STAR WARS*

*THE ART OF STAR WARS: A NEW HOPE*
*THE ART OF STAR WARS: THE EMPIRE STRIKES BACK*
*THE ART OF STAR WARS: RETURN OF THE JEDI*

*STAR WARS: A NEW HOPE SCRIPT FACSIMILE*
*STAR WARS: THE EMPIRE STRIKES BACK SCRIPT FACSIMILE*
*STAR WARS: RETURN OF THE JEDI SCRIPT FACSIMILE*

*STAR WARS: A NEW HOPE ILLUSTRATED SCREENPLAY*
*STAR WARS: THE EMPIRE STRIKES BACK*
  *ILLUSTRATED SCREENPLAY*
*STAR WARS: RETURN OF THE JEDI ILLUSTRATED SCREENPLAY*

*STAR WARS: A NEW HOPE—*
  *THE NATIONAL PUBLIC RADIO DRAMATIZATION*
*STAR WARS: THE EMPIRE STRIKES BACK—*
  *THE NATIONAL PUBLIC RADIO DRAMATIZATION*
*STAR WARS: RETURN OF THE JEDI—*
  *THE NATIONAL PUBLIC RADIO DRAMATIZATION*

*THE MAKING OF STAR WARS: EPISODE I THE PHANTOM MENACE*
*STAR WARS: EPISODE I THE PHANTOM MENACE*
  *ILLUSTRATED SCREENPLAY*
*THE ART OF STAR WARS: EPISODE I THE PHANTOM MENACE*
*STAR WARS: EPISODE I THE PHANTOM MENACE*
  *SCRIPT FACSIMILE*

# STAR WARS®

# THE ESSENTIAL CHRONOLOGY

TEXT BY
## KEVIN J. ANDERSON
### AND DANIEL WALLACE

ORIGINAL ILLUSTRATIONS BY
## BILL HUGHES

THE BALLANTINE PUBLISHING GROUP
NEW YORK

A Del Rey® Book
Published by The Ballantine Publishing Group

www.starwars.com
www.randomhouse.com/delrey/

Library of Congress Catalog Card Number: 99-65085

ISBN 0-345-43439-0

Interior and cover design by Michaelis/Carpelis Design Assoc. Inc.
Cover illustration by Bill Hughes

Manufactured in the United States of America

First Edition: April 2000

10  9  8  7  6  5  4  3

*To George Lucas, without whose imagination and vision this history never would have been created, much less written down.*

# TABLE OF CONTENTS

INTRODUCTION FOR STUDENTS
OF HISTORY                                      xiii

NOTE ON DATING CONVENTIONS        xiii

## PART I—TALES OF THE ANCIENT JEDI KNIGHTS                               1

### EMERGENCE OF THE SITH                    2
The Golden Age of the Sith (5000 B.B.Y.)     2
The Great Hyperspace War (5000 B.B.Y.)       5

### LEGACY OF THE SITH                       7
The Shadow of Freedon Nadd
    (4400 B.B.Y.)                            7
Trials of the Jedi (4000 B.B.Y.)             8
The Naddist Revolt (3998 B.B.Y.)            10
The Coming Ruin (3997 B.B.Y.)               11
The Sith War (3996 B.B.Y.)                  15
The Devastation of Ossus (3996 B.B.Y.)      16
The Redemption of Ulic Qel-Droma
    (3986 B.B.Y.)                           17
Repercussions through the Republic
    (4000–3000 B.B.Y.)                      18
The New Sith (2000–1000 B.B.Y.)             18
Jedi Valiancy (600–400 B.B.Y.)             20

## PART II—THE EMPIRE AND THE NEW ORDER                               21

Birth of the Empire
    (approx. 50–18 B.B.Y.)                  21
Dawn of Dissent
    (approx. 18–0 B.B.Y.)                   25

## PART III—PROFILES IN HISTORY                                  27

### HAN SOLO                                 27
Ylesia (10 B.B.Y.)                          27
The Academy (10–5 B.B.Y.)                   28
The Life of a Smuggler (5–2 B.B.Y.)         29
Corporate Sector Blues (2–1 B.B.Y.)         31
Destitute in the Tion (1–0 B.B.Y.)          32
Return to Ylesia
    (0 B.B.Y., months before
    the Battle of Yavin)                    33
The Last Spice Run
    (0 B.B.Y., immediately prior
    to the Battle of Yavin)                 34

### LANDO CALRISSIAN                         35
The Sharu Awaken (4 B.B.Y.)                 35
The Battle of Nar Shaddaa (3 B.B.Y.)        37
Back to the Oseon (3 B.B.Y.)                38
Fortune Won, Fortune Lost (3 B.B.Y.)        39
To Save the ThonBoka (3–2.5 B.B.Y.)         39
Entrepreneurism (2.5–0 B.B.Y.)              41
"The Respectable One" (0–3 A.B.Y.)          42

### THE SKYWALKERS                           43

## PART IV—REBELLION AGAINST THE EMPIRE                               45

### THE REBELLION BEGINS                     45
The Death Star Construction (3–0 B.B.Y.)    45
Preparations for Battle (0 B.B.Y.)          47
The Capture of Princess Leia (0 B.B.Y.)     48
A New Hope (0 B.B.Y.)                       49

| | |
|---|---|
| Impact and Consequences | |
| (0–0.5 A.B.Y.) | 50 |
| Rebel Trap (0–0.5 A.B.Y.) | 52 |
| Imperial Counterstrike (0.5–2 A.B.Y.) | 53 |
| Circarpous Joins the Resistance (2 A.B.Y.) | 54 |
| Home in the Ice (2–3 A.B.Y.) | 55 |

**A LIGHT ECLIPSED** — 55

| | |
|---|---|
| The Battle of Hoth (3 A.B.Y.) | 55 |
| A New Jedi (3 A.B.Y.) | 56 |
| Prince Xizor and Black Sun (3.5 A.B.Y.) | 58 |

**ALLIANCE TRIUMPHANT** — 60

| | |
|---|---|
| The Rebellion Regroups (4 A.B.Y.) | 60 |
| The Battle of Endor (4 A.B.Y.) | 60 |
| The Truce at Bakura (4 A.B.Y.) | 63 |
| Onward to Ssi-ruuvi Space (4–5 A.B.Y.) | 65 |

**PART V—BIRTH OF THE NEW REPUBLIC** — 67

| | |
|---|---|
| Imperial Fragmentation (4–4.5 A.B.Y.) | 67 |
| Black Nebula (4–4.5 A.B.Y.) | 68 |
| Isard's Ascension (4.5–5 A.B.Y.) | 68 |
| General Skywalker (5–5.5 A.B.Y.) | 71 |
| The Last Grand Admiral? (6 A.B.Y.) | 72 |
| The Battle for Coruscant (6.5–7 A.B.Y.) | 72 |
| The Krytos Virus (7–7.5 A.B.Y.) | 73 |
| The Bacta War (7.5 A.B.Y.) | 75 |
| The Hunt for Zsinj (7.5–8 A.B.Y.) | 76 |
| The Hapans and the | |
| Dathomir Nightsisters (8 A.B.Y.) | 78 |
| The Death of Zsinj (8 A.B.Y.) | 80 |
| Picking up the Pieces (8.5 A.B.Y.) | 82 |

**PART VI—EMPIRE RESURGENT** — 83

**THE DEPREDATIONS OF GRAND ADMIRAL THRAWN** (9 A.B.Y.) — 83

| | |
|---|---|
| Talon Karrde and the | |
| Smugglers (9 A.B.Y.) | 84 |
| The Noghri Switch Sides (9 A.B.Y.) | 85 |
| The *Katana* Fleet and the | |
| Clone Troopers (9 A.B.Y.) | 86 |
| Thrawn's Fall (9 A.B.Y.) | 88 |

**THE RETURN OF ISARD** (9–10 A.B.Y.) — 89

**THE RESURRECTION OF EMPEROR PALPATINE** (10 A.B.Y.) — 90

| | |
|---|---|
| Operation Shadow Hand (10 A.B.Y.) | 94 |
| Palpatine Vanquished (11 A.B.Y.) | 96 |
| Jax, Kanos, and the | |
| Interim Council (11 A.B.Y.) | 97 |

**PART VII— THE RETURN OF THE JEDI KNIGHTS** — **99**

**SKYWALKER'S JEDI ACADEMY** (11 A.B.Y.) — 99

| | |
|---|---|
| Maw Installation (11 A.B.Y.) | 100 |
| Political Troubles (11 A.B.Y.) | 101 |
| Exar Kun's Revenge (11 A.B.Y.) | 102 |
| The Recapture of Maw | |
| Installation (11 A.B.Y.) | 104 |
| The Emperor's Hand and the | |
| Senex Lords (12 A.B.Y.) | 106 |
| The *Eye of Palpatine* (12 A.B.Y.) | 109 |

**THE DARKSABER THREAT** (12 A.B.Y.) — 110

| | |
|---|---|
| The Hutt Plan (12 A.B.Y.) | 111 |
| Admiral Daala Returns (12 A.B.Y.) | 113 |
| Durga's Folly (12 A.B.Y.) | 113 |
| Assault on Yavin 4 (12 A.B.Y.) | 115 |
| The Empire Regroups (12–13 A.B.Y.) | 117 |
| Mission to Adumar (13 A.B.Y.) | 118 |

**THE DEATH SEED PLAGUE** (13 A.B.Y.) — 118

**PART VIII—UPRISINGS AND INSURGENCIES** — **123**

**THE EMPIRE REBORN MOVEMENT** (14 A.B.Y.) — 123

| | |
|---|---|
| The Power of Waru (14 A.B.Y.) | 124 |

**THE BLACK FLEET CRISIS** (16–17 A.B.Y.) — 127

| | |
|---|---|
| Master Skywalker and the | |
| Fallanassi (16–17 A.B.Y.) | 130 |
| The Teljkon Vagabond (16–17 A.B.Y.) | 131 |

**UPRISING AT ALMANIA** (17 A.B.Y.) — 132

| | |
|---|---|
| Smuggler's Run (17 A.B.Y.) | 136 |
| Imperial Skirmishes (17–18 A.B.Y.) | 137 |

THE CORELLIAN INSURRECTION
(18 A.B.Y.)                                        138

**PART IX—A LASTING PEACE    143**

The Caamas Document (19 A.B.Y.)        143
The Hand of Thrawn (19 A.B.Y.)          147

**PART X—GENERATIONS OF JEDI
KNIGHTS                              151**

THE GOLDEN GLOBE AND KENOBI'S
LIGHTSABER (22 A.B.Y.)                 151

THE SHADOW ACADEMY AND THE SECOND
IMPERIUM (23 A.B.Y.)                   154

THE DIVERSITY ALLIANCE (23–24 A.B.Y.)     158

THE RESURGENCE OF BLACK SUN
(24 A.B.Y.)                            161

AFTERWORD                             165

MAP                                   166

TIME LINE                             169

INDEX                                 181

# ACKNOWLEDGMENTS

A work like this involves so many details and so many careful readers.
We especially would like to thank Rebecca Moesta Anderson, Catherine Sidor,
Steve Saffel, Sue Rostoni, Lucy Autrey Wilson, Allan Kausch...and, of course,
all of the writers of the original works included here.

# INTRODUCTION FOR STUDENTS OF HISTORY

After the fall of the Empire, many archives were opened, and hidden information came to the attention of scholars across the galaxy. It was discovered that, over the course of only a few decades, the Imperial propaganda machinery had done a thorough and astonishing job of rewriting the past, casting events in an uncertain light, and portraying history from a warped point of view.

Teams of learned historians have spent years sifting through files found in the Imperial Information Center. Students of Jedi lore and history have studied the few extant Jedi Holocrons (repositories of Jedi knowledge), while others have compiled and compared folktales, legends, and songs to weave the tapestry of "a thousand generations" of Jedi Knights.

Because we are living in tumultuous times, we have also taken care to speak with many of the primary players themselves, living legends who were at the core of significant events. We are at a crux point in history, and while the actual personages remain with us, we have recorded their statements, remembrances, and opinions. We intend to leave a thorough and objective chronicle for the future.

This document is most assuredly a work in progress, leaving many gaps and sketchy descriptions as scholars continue to discover new and compelling data. Such a work—by its very nature—can never really be finished. Nonetheless, the chief of state and the New Republic Senate have issued instructions to publish this draft of *The Essential Chronology* as it stands, secure in the knowledge that further expanded editions will be forthcoming.

Citizens of the New Republic must know their foundation in history. We have a rich and glorious tradition behind us, as well as a legacy of dark mistakes. We must learn from both.

—*New Republic Historical Council*

# NOTE ON DATING CONVENTIONS

We have chosen to mark the years in this document with the emerging dating standard, one that establishes the true significance of the Empire's decline and the Rebellion's unstoppable triumph. We have taken as our calendar "zero point" the date of the Battle of Yavin, the destruction of the first Death Star, and the first overwhelming victory of the Rebel Alliance. We see this as the primary beginning of our time and way of life. Thus, events that precede the historic Battle of Yavin are indicated B.B.Y., while those occurring after are A.B.Y. Future generations will recognize these years as the genesis of a golden age for the galaxy.

## PART I

# TALES OF THE ANCIENT JEDI KNIGHTS

The complete history of the Old Republic would fill a thousand libraries. Some events and some sacrifices have become legend, passed from generation to generation.

As with any history that extends back for millennia, details and facts become blurred by time. Events that took place so long ago become shrouded in contradictions and myth. The exact sequence and some of the names may not be entirely accurate, but without question the overall conflicts are real.

Pre-Republic history is incredibly ancient and notoriously difficult to research. At some point in this ancient era the Corellian system was artificially created, providing evidence that our region of space was once visited by stunningly powerful alien architects, who may also have been responsible for the unlikely cluster of black holes near Kessel known as the Maw. On Coruscant, prime planet of what would later be known as the Core Worlds, two armies—the Taungs and the Battalions of Zhell—clashed in a legendary battle. The Zhell were defeated when a sudden volcanic eruption smothered their encampment, and the towering plume of black ash loomed over the Taung army for two years. The awed Taungs took the name Warriors of the Shadow—or, in the ancient tongue, Dha Werda Verda. Their story is recounted in the epic poem of the same name. The original site of this battlefield is now buried beneath the skyscrapers of Imperial City.

Xim the Despot is the most celebrated pre-Republic conqueror of all. In the remote region now known as the Tion Hegemony, Xim gathered vast armies under his banner, including a legion of unstoppable war droids—the earliest-known combat automatons. Xim's glorious empire spread to encompass hundreds of thousands of worlds in the vicinity of the Tion. The warlord miscalculated, however, when he tried to expand into Hutt Space. The Hutts had built up their own formidable star empire, and they fiercely opposed Xim for possession of the Si'klaata Cluster. Two exhausting but inconclusive battles were fought on the planet Vontor. In the third such confrontation, Xim's war droids were opposed by the Hutts' latest conscripts—a horde of fighters from the Nikto, Vodran, and Klattooinan species. Xim was utterly vanquished, and Kossak the Hutt declared victory in the Third Battle of Vontor.

Approximately twenty-five thousand years before the New Republic, the widespread use of faster-than-light hyperspace travel brought the galaxy together as a single community, giving birth to a democratic union of star systems known as the Galactic Republic. From the time of its inception, the Republic grew, over many millennia, to encompass vast numbers of inhabited worlds.

The mystical energy field known as the Force, as represented by the order of Jedi Knights, made up the fundamental underpinnings of the Republic. The earliest Jedi were philosophers, studying the Force's light, dark, living, and unifying aspects, and prophesying that one day a Chosen One would arise and bring balance to the Force. Later generations took a more active role in the galactic community, wielding the Force in defense against the legions of evil. In those glorious days, many Force-sensitive individuals entered arduous training under accomplished Jedi Masters, taking up the weapons, the knowledge, and the powers of the Jedi way. Some say the order of Jedi Knights began on the planet Ossus, though that claim has never been verified.

# EMERGENCE OF THE SITH

## *The Golden Age of the Sith*
## 5000 B.B.Y.

The Great Hyperspace War was a conflagration that swept across the galaxy, a clash between distant and near-forgotten Sith Lords and an unsuspecting and vulnerable Republic. This struggle between good and evil occurred in the high period of the Old Republic, and its outcome affected galactic civilization for thousands of years.

From the years preceding the war, the background and origins of the Sith Empire hold only a murky place in the annals of recorded history. We know of an ancient struggle of light side versus dark side, the first great schism within the Jedi Knights. After a century of bloodshed, the dark Jedi were defeated, and the survivors took their battered ships into exile, leaving known space behind and crossing the galaxy into uncharted territory. Eventually, the vanquished dark Jedi found a primitive civilization—a new people to dominate—the Sith.

The dark Jedi were treated as gods by these powerful yet malleable people. With unlimited resources and willing human slaves, the Jedi exiles forged the Sith civilization into a new empire, bringing about a golden age of evil that was separated from the Republic, in the wilds of the galaxy, thousands of light-years from the Perlemian Trade Route that was the Republic's outermost border at the time. Over millennia, the dark rulers of the Sith Empire lost their charts and hyperspace maps, so they no longer even knew how to find the Republic.

On the other side of the galaxy, records of the Jedi revolt faded, and the overthrow of the evil Force wielders fell from memory. Only folktales remained.

Five thousand years before the reign of the Emperor, the Old Republic was riding high and expanding. The great Jedi Knights and dedicated explorers tamed a significant portion of the galaxy, though many distant sectors remained uncharted.

It was a time of rugged frontiers: pioneers established homes on harsh new colony worlds; alien races encountered humans for the first time. Small-scale battles were fought and won as the galactic government continued to unify scattered systems. Convoluted paths through the incomprehensible wilderness of hyperspace were still being mapped, which made long-distance travel often treacherous and uncertain.

Gav and Jori Daragon, brother and sister, were hyperspace mappers whose desperate voyage of discovery altered the history of the galaxy. Intrepid risk takers—some called them crazy—they played the high-stakes game of seeking safe trade routes through unmapped and dangerous hyperspace. In their ship *Starbreaker 12*, they would pick a random

*Gav and Jori Daragon*

course and roar off, hoping to arrive someplace useful—hoping to survive the journey.

Like many explorers, smugglers, and colonists, Gav and Jori were a bit rough around the edges. Earlier in their lives, Gav and Jori had learned that they possessed Force potential, but neither had the patience or the drive to endure the rigorous mental training required to become a Jedi Knight. Instead, they used their "luck" and their blind faith to avoid running into stars or black holes. Always strapped for credits, they kept hoping to blaze a new trail that would earn them a substantial fee from the Brotherhood of Navigators.

After one particular near disaster, the destitute Gav and Jori could not even afford to pay for repairs to their ship, and the *Starbreaker 12* sat unclaimed in a repair dock within the iron-walled metropolis of Cinnagar. With nothing but threats and creditors waiting for them, the two stole their own ship and shot off into the skies. They hoped that, by taking one more chance, they could map out a valuable new run, farther than ever before. With such information as collateral, they could pay off their debts and buy back their lives. As Cinnagar security forces shot at them, Gav and Jori spun the navicomputer dials and headed off into the unknown.

On the far side of the galaxy, the Sith Empire— cut off from the Republic by vast distances and unexplored pathways—had grown powerful over the centuries, dabbling in its own brand of sorcery and dark Force wielding. And it had reached a time of crisis.

After a century of ironhanded rule, the greatest Dark Lord of the Sith Empire, Marka Ragnos, had died. The ensuing power vacuum sparked a great struggle, a brewing civil war that could tear apart the ancient empire. Hungry factions convened on the mausoleum planet of Korriban as Ragnos was laid to rest among the towering tombs. Even under the shadow-filled skies, the funeral held great pomp and splendor, as the sacrifice of Sith slaves heralded completion of a spectacular new tomb.

At the grave site, the two strongest Sith opponents confronted each other. Naga Sadow, eager to expand Sith powers, dabbled with unproven magical and alchemical techniques, while his rival Ludo Kressh, content with the existing foundations of their empire, was loath to risk any folly that might cost them everything.

At the doorstep of the new tomb, Sadow and Kressh engaged in a bloody duel, until to their astonishment the image of the fallen Dark Lord appeared as a spectral herald, the last gasp of his life force. Cryptic and ominous, the departing shade of Marka Ragnos announced that the fate of the Sith Empire would depend on the outcome of their conflict.

In the middle of this confrontation, the *Starbreaker 12* arrived at Korriban. Lost and curious, Gav and Jori Daragon had barely survived their headlong plunge through hyperspace, and now they needed to gather information on the newly discovered world. Without trade possibilities and resources, their expedition would be useless.

The feuding Sith Lords showed no interest in peaceful trade with the Republic, though. Gav and Jori were captured as alien spies and taken off to the bleak planet Ziost, where they were held prisoner and interrogated by the Sith rulers.

The Dark Lords remembered little of the distant Republic. The conservative Ludo Kressh thought the Daragons were precursors to an invasion, while his ambitious rival Naga Sadow viewed the unsuspecting Republic as a vast new field to conquer. Secretly, Sadow also believed that a new outside enemy, such as the Republic, could bring together the strained factions of the Sith Empire and distract the populace from political weaknesses closer to home.

After a tribunal of Sith Lords sentenced Gav and Jori to death, Naga Sadow helped the two escape, taking advantage of his Massassi warriors, members of a specially bred soldier species. He took Gav and Jori to his own isolated fortress, leaving behind provocative evidence that other agents of the Republic had freed the prisoners.

At the next Sith council meeting, Naga Sadow exploited doubts and fears about the Republic. He used Gav and Jori as scapegoats to galvanize the empire, convincing the other lords of an impending invasion. He insisted that the Sith must strike first.

Back at his fortress, Sadow began to initiate Gav into the ways of Sith sorcery. During the rigorous training, he kept Jori Daragon away from her brother, manipulating them both. Knowing their

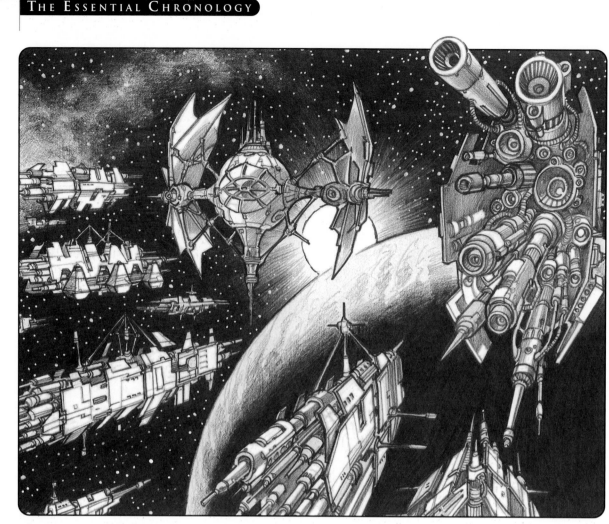

*Naga Sadow's invasion fleet*

dire and uncertain straits, Jori demanded their ship back: it was their only way home. Because of the random route by which they had discovered the Sith Empire, the only safe return course was stored in the *Starbreaker 12*'s computer. Without it, she and her brother could never find their way home. After Sadow continued to make excuses for keeping them in his fortress, Jori began to wonder if the Sith Lord was really their ally.

When Ludo Kressh uncovered evidence that Sadow might have been behind the prisoners' escape, he gathered loyal Sith forces to raid Sadow's fortress and expose him as a traitor and schemer; in this way, Kressh planned to assume the leadership of the empire.

All of this occurred exactly as Naga Sadow had planned, and he prepared to crush his rival's "surprise" attack. During the chaos of the attack, Sadow convinced Jori Daragon that her only

chance was to make good her escape; he also arranged it so that at the last moment, Gav would not be able to join her, and she had to depart alone. It was a terrible moment of choice for her, as Ludo Kressh's ships arrived and unleashed a destructive cannonade.

Devastated, Jori abandoned her brother to the promised protection of Naga Sadow, vowing to come to his rescue as soon as she could. But she also knew that the Sith Empire was gearing up to attack the Republic, and only she could sound the alarm back home.

As soon as the *Starbreaker 12* disappeared into hyperspace, Naga Sadow unleashed his *real* military reserves, and his forces crushed Kressh's fleet, destroying his rival's flagship and, presumably, Kressh himself. With the opposition in shambles, Sadow seized the moment to crown himself Dark Lord of the Sith.

## The Great Hyperspace War
### 5000 B.B.Y.

Though Jori Daragon did not realize it, her ship carried a homing beacon that would lead Naga Sadow and his forces right to the heart of the unsuspecting Republic. She arrived back in the Teta system and sounded her alarms, sending out a call to arms—but Jori was immediately arrested and charged with fraud, felony, and theft of her ship. She spoke frantically about the Sith threat, but nobody believed her, thinking it a ruse concocted by a desperate criminal. She was sentenced to a harsh colony world, unable to rescue her brother from the Sith Empire, but before long, Jori escaped. She stowed away on a cargo transport that took her to the Tetan primary world. After a desperate chase, Jori managed to slip in to meet the Empress of Teta herself. Jori spilled out her story, begging to be heard.

A few of the Republic's great Jedi Knights, upon hearing the tale, were perplexed. Those included the young Odan-Urr, his master Ooroo, and Teta's adviser Memit Nadill. When Jori furnished details of Naga Sadow's ambitions, they recalled legends of outcast dark Jedi who had vanished into obscurity long ago. Their suspicions aroused, they convinced the empress to prepare for a possible invasion.

While the Jedi Knights spread the word around the Republic, the empress traveled to Coruscant to rally support among other political leaders. After speaking at the capital, though, Teta could not convince the rest of the allied worlds to take action; only a few Jedi listeners heeded her warnings.

Back in the Sith Empire, Naga Sadow consolidated the remaining Sith forces and his blood-thirsty Massassi soldiers. Taking his pliable protégé Gav, Sadow set off on a huge surprise raid against the vulnerable Republic. They launched, following the coordinates transmitted by the *Starbreaker 12*. Naga Sadow's entire battle fleet arrived in the Teta system, weapons blazing.

The unexpected conflict spread across the Republic like a storm: a succession of battles that pitted war fleets and loyal Jedi Knights against Sith sorcery and firepower. One of the young heroes of these battles was the alien Jedi Odan-Urr, who again became a pivotal figure in the Sith War a thousand years later.

During these struggles, the Empress Teta proved to be a talented commander, but the Sith enemy was relentless—and unpredictable, since Naga Sadow had only sketchy knowledge of this new sector of the galaxy. The battles did not fare well for the Republic.

Finally, the combined Republic fleet made a major stand around the flare-active red-giant star Primus Goluud, where Sadow duped Gav Daragon one final time and left him to face the combined retaliation fleet. Sadow used his own terrible Sith technology to trigger an explosion in the core of the star.

Though Jori Daragon had no military training, she did know a lot of tricks for flying a starship. In the course of battle, Jori clashed head-on with her brainwashed brother, Gav. He ultimately redeemed himself, realizing what he had done—and what Sadow had done to him—and so he turned back to help his sister and the Republic. He asked for Jori's forgiveness just before the red-giant star went supernova, destroying him.

With the changing tides of battle, the Republic rallied against the invaders, decisively trouncing the Sith fleet. Memit Nadill and his team of Jedi Knights defeated the enemy on Coruscant itself, while Odan-Urr won an important skirmish on the outlying planet of Kirrek, a victory that cost the life of the great Jedi Master Ooroo.

Naga Sadow called a rapid retreat, taking his surviving warriors back to the Sith Empire. Limping home with tattered forces, Sadow found that his old enemy Ludo Kressh was not dead after all. Kressh had cultivated spies of his own and had escaped the assassination attempt.

With his loyalists, Kressh lay in wait for Sadow's already battered forces. Giving no quarter, Kressh mercilessly attacked Sadow's "traitors" before they could recover. Naga Sadow fought back with wild abandon; at this point he had nothing to lose. Both sides were devastated in the battle.

The pursuing Republic forces arrived in the middle of the fray to vanquish the Sith threat once and for all. The fleets of Sadow and Kressh were decimated in the cross fire.

*The defense of Coruscant*

Staging an all-or-nothing diversion, Naga Sadow took his most faithful followers and escaped in his damaged flagship, sacrificing the rest of his forces. Republic ships chased him, but Sadow chose one last sorcerous gambit: He flew his warship between a tight binary star, the Denarii Nova, using Sith powers to manipulate solar flares and destroy pursuing Republic ships in his wake. He left no trace of himself behind.

Of all his former glory, Naga Sadow retained only a single ship and his Massassi crew. The Dark Lord went to ground on a little-known jungle moon that orbited the gas giant Yavin. There on Yavin 4 he made his camp, entombed his warship, and left the Massassi behind as guardians.

Naga Sadow vowed to let the fires of conflict die away before he would return again. Using Sith technology and sorcery, he managed to cocoon himself in a chamber that placed him in suspended animation—this in anticipation of a later day, when someone would pick up the dark teachings and bring about the new Sith golden age that the fallen Dark Lord Marka Ragnos had foretold.

Ragnos wasn't the only one whose prophecies rang true. With his final words as he died on the battlefield of Kirrek, Master Ooroo had prophesied that his studious trainee, Odan-Urr, would found a vast library and would live to a great old age, eventually to die among his beloved scrolls and books. Beginning with Master Ooroo's collection of arcane artifacts, and gathering numerous items found among the wreckage of the defeated Sith invasion fleet, Odan-Urr did indeed establish the greatest library and learning center of the Old Republic, the grand museum city on Ossus. And, as his master had predicted, Odan-Urr died a thousand years later, among his books, at the beginning of the Sith War.

## LEGACY OF THE SITH

The Sith Empire crumbled, and victorious Republic observers could be forgiven for the rosy optimism that ensued. For new star systems were explored, and new species were discovered and taken into the fold as the galactic government learned better ways to rule over diverse cultures and across vast distances.

Centuries passed. No further contact occurred involving the dark leaders or remnants of the Sith, but the evil influence returned in a different and more insidious form than before—a cancer from within.

### The Shadow of Freedon Nadd
**4400 B.B.Y.**

Six centuries after Naga Sadow exiled himself on the jungle moon, after Sadow's Massassi servants built the great temples, an ambitious Jedi Knight, Freedon Nadd, followed rumors and intuition to the isolated Yavin system.

In the centuries since the defeated Dark Lord had sealed his preserved essence beneath the focusing chamber of a primary temple, the Massassi refugees had degenerated into powerful but primitive savages. Nadd came to them, fought with them—but his use of the Force awed the Massassi into remembering their past. They showed him where the Dark Lord had gone to sleep, waiting for another evil hero to come, waiting for someone like Freedon Nadd.

Nadd awakened the ancient Sith Lord, who taught him sorcerous ways, dark twistings of the Force, giving him skills and weapons that other Jedi Knights could not withstand. The fate of the resurrected Naga Sadow is not known, but Freedon Nadd left Yavin 4 and set about making himself a king on the primitive world of Onderon, outside the boundaries of the Old Republic.

For centuries the peaceful people of Onderon had been beset by horrible creatures that crossed over from the erratic moon Dxun. The vicious predators had taken a terrible toll on the population until the people constructed a walled city, Iziz, for their protection.

Freedon Nadd, with his knowledge of Sith magic and his willingness to use the dark side, easily made himself the leader of these people. Over the

*The Beast Wars of Onderon*

decades the walled city grew, implacably driving back the jungle. Nadd helped his subjects develop destructive technology so they could better fight the monsters—and, later, their own internal enemies, rebels against the Sith Lord's rule.

One of the policies Nadd instituted was to banish criminals, including anyone who spoke out against Nadd himself. They were sent beyond the walls of Iziz, where they would be devoured by the voracious predators. However, some of these exiles survived and banded together, even learning how to capture the beasts and domesticate them. Riding flying beasts and carrying handmade weapons, the survivors struck back against the city that had exiled them, thus beginning centuries of unrest and rebellion—a scattered guerrilla war that even Freedon Nadd's powers could not crush.

After Nadd's death, the sarcophagus containing his body became a focus of dark-side energy used by his descendants. Nadd's legacy passed from generation to generation, but the unending civil war continued, with a cost in blood nearly as high as the early attacks from the beasts of Dxun. Centuries later, as the Republic expanded its territory and other Jedi Knights encountered the Onderon system, the crisis was ready to explode.

## Trials of the Jedi
### 4000 B.B.Y.

The survival of the Republic depended on two factors: wise governing by administrators and lawmakers, and the preservation of harmony and justice by a heroic warrior society—the Jedi Knights. It was a practice for Jedi to become guardians of new systems, overseeing transitions and assisting with local difficulties.

Jedi Master Arca Jeth of Arkania received the stewardship and responsibility for the Onderon system. Instead of becoming the watchman himself, though, he sent his three students—the good-natured and impetuous brothers Ulic and Cay Qel-Droma and a gruff Twi'lek named Tott Doneeta. It seemed a simple assignment, to smooth over a local conflict on a backwater world, but in reality this set the stage for one of the greatest events in the history of the Old Republic.

Arriving on the untamed world, the three Jedi Knights were greeted by ancient Queen Amanoa, ruler of Iziz. She described the depredations of the beast riders, who came to the walled city to ravage, kill, and kidnap. The old queen asked for the Jedi to help end the years of pain and suffering. When the beast riders next attacked the palace itself, they abducted Queen Amanoa's daughter, Galia, taking her out to the jungle strongholds.

The Qel-Droma brothers and Doneeta set out to rescue her, but found that all was not as they had been led to believe. Galia and the warlord leader Oron Kira had planned this together: they would marry and unify the two groups, which would stop the endless bloodshed.

Acting as mediators, the Jedi presented the proposal to Queen Amanoa, only to learn that she had no interest in peace. For years the old queen had tapped into Freedon Nadd's power, and in her outrage she called upon the dark side to destroy Oron Kira's people. She summoned all the armies of Iziz and commanded them to crush the outsiders.

The Jedi fought back, but they were outclassed. In the struggle Cay Qel-Droma lost his arm, which he later replaced with a droid prosthetic. Master Arca himself was called, and when he arrived, the tide of the battle turned. The beast riders overcame the evil soldiers of Queen Amanoa. With the combined forces of light, Arca drove back Amanoa's evil and vanquished the shadows that had long festered at the heart of the city. Galia and Oron Kira worked to restore their world to peace and the benefits of civilization.

Though her path had not yet crossed Ulic's, another Jedi Knight—Nomi Sunrider—went through an ordeal that would prepare her, too, to become one of the greatest leaders and warriors of her age.

The young woman was married to a newly trained Jedi, Andur Sunrider, and they had an infant daughter, Vima. Nomi had a strong affinity for the Force, but lacked the self-confidence and the drive to become a Jedi herself.

Andur and his family made a pilgrimage to the Stenness system to give a gift of precious Adegan crystals to the Jedi Master Thon. En route, though, a group of thugs murdered Andur and attempted to steal the Adegan crystals. In her shock and grief, Nomi saw the Jedi image of her slain husband, who told her to take up his lightsaber and defend herself and their daughter. Guided by the Force, Nomi slew most of the attackers—and then listened to Andur's parting words, instructing her to

*Ulic Qel-Droma
and Arca Jeth*

go to Master Thon herself, to learn to be a Jedi Knight.

Despite her reluctance ever to wield a deadly lightsaber again, Nomi found herself driven down a path to learn the ways of the Force. On the bleak world of Ambria, she found Master Thon: an awesome, armor-plated Tchuukthai of savage countenance but great wisdom. Nomi agreed to accept Jedi training from the Jedi Master, so long as she never needed to use a lightsaber, though Thon claimed that the lightsaber was her own destiny.

However, fate placed her in a position where she had no choice but to defend herself and Vima. When pirates attacked Ambria, she fought alongside Master Thon to protect their world. Nomi overcame her doubts and reluctance and learned that a lightsaber wasn't the only weapon a Jedi could use. Nomi Sunrider became an undisputed master at the technique of Jedi battle meditation, in which she used the Force to manipulate enemies to fight one another.

After training Nomi for some months, Master Thon brought her to the Jedi learning center on Ossus, where he gave her over to Master Vodo-Siosk Baas. There, with other Jedi trainees, Nomi Sunrider learned even more of the Force and finally built her personal lightsaber.

## The Naddist Revolt
### 3998 B.B.Y.

Back on Onderon, despite two years of relative peace, unrest continued, sparked primarily by a grim sect that revered the memory of Freedon Nadd.

Master Arca remained with his students Ulic and Cay Qel-Droma and Tott Doneeta. All were affected by the oppressive shadows of the dark side that still remained—Master Arca most of all. In an attempt to eliminate the cancerous evil, they prepared to move the sarcophagus containing Freedon Nadd, as well as the coffin of Queen Amanoa, far away to the monster-filled moon of Dxun.

During the funeral procession, however, the followers of Freedon Nadd launched an unexpected attack from beneath the city of Iziz. During the assault, Master Arca was struck by a blow of dark

Force, which allowed the Naddist rebels to capture the royal sarcophagi.

Recovering, Arca learned that Queen Galia's ancient father, King Ommin, had been kept alive. Though frail and decrepit, Ommin resided in a secret life-support facility. Suspicious, Arca visited the dying old man, with Galia and Ulic Qel-Droma at his side. He discovered that Ommin himself was the source of the great shadow, that he had been a follower of Freedon Nadd. Ommin's dabblings released the spirit avatar of Nadd, who joined forces with Ommin. The crippled old king lashed out at Arca with blistering bolts of dark-side energy, subduing him. Though Ulic fought bravely to save his Master, Ommin fled with the paralyzed Arca to another dark-side stronghold, where the stolen sarcophagi had been taken.

Devastated by his failure and his weakness, Ulic Qel-Droma called for assistance from the Galactic Republic and the coalition of Jedi Knights. Republic military ships converged on the Onderon system, while another team of Jedi were hand-picked and dispatched from the library world, Ossus. The group included now-confident and well-trained Nomi Sunrider. Under fire, the Jedi reinforcements encountered the siege of Iziz and battled through to join Ulic and his companions. Together and strong, the Jedi Knights descended into the lower levels of the city to find and rescue Master Arca.

In the midst of the chaos on Onderon, two other figures arrived, oblivious to the danger: Satal Keto and his cousin Aleema, heirs to the now-corrupt Empress Teta system. Spoiled, bored, and rich, Satal, Aleema, and their friends had dabbled in Sith magic, amusing themselves with artifacts recovered by the scholar Jedi Odan-Urr immediately after the Great Hyperspace War a thousand years before. This group of bored aristocrats named themselves the Krath, after a fearsome childhood legend.

Satal Keto, egged on by the beautiful and ambitious Aleema, had stolen an ancient book of Sith secrets from a museum on Coruscant. They departed to Onderon, having heard about the Freedon Nadd Uprising and the Sith practitioners there. War or no war, Satal and Aleema were determined to find someone who could translate the mysterious book and teach them more Sith sorcery.

Using their novice dark-side skills, as well as plain luck, the two aristocrats made their way through the battle-ravaged city and down to the stronghold where King Ommin held Master Arca prisoner. Delighted to see the arcane book of Sith secrets, Ommin gave Satal Keto a Sith amulet and promised to translate the book.

While a scribe diligently worked to reproduce the tome, the specter of Freedon Nadd appeared. With Republic troops pounding the city and the unified Jedi Knights on their way, Nadd realized King Ommin had lost; instead, he threw his lot with the two aristocrats, convincing Satal Keto and Aleema that they alone held the key to the rebirth of the Sith golden age—and that he would guide them.

The Jedi Knights fought their way into Ommin's stronghold just as Master Arca was about to be crushed by the dark side. Nadd withdrew his power and support from the ancient king, and Ulic charged forward, unrestrained, to kill the old man and rescue Arca.

As Satal Keto and Aleema fled Iziz, bearing a wealth of Sith artifacts back to the Empress Teta system, Freedon Nadd appeared to taunt Arca, Ulic, and the Jedi Knights, saying that the dark side would claim others.

Republic forces finally imposed order and martial law on the devastated Iziz. The sarcophagus of Freedon Nadd was finally taken to an armored tomb on the beast moon of Dxun, sealed behind slabs of Mandalorian iron—which the Jedi hoped would last for millennia.

## The Coming Ruin
### 3997 B.B.Y.

Armed with their Sith knowledge and artifacts, Satal Keto and Aleema marshaled their Krath forces for a coup of the Empress Teta system. However, killing the old-guard aristocratic leaders proved far easier than subjugating the people, and the seven worlds revolted against the new barbaric despots. Nonetheless, Keto and Aleema delighted in the chance to make use of their new Sith powers to crush the resistance.

Word of the revolt and the alarming use of Sith sorcery made its way to Onderon, where Ulic and Cay Qel-Droma, Tott Doneeta, and Nomi Sunrider worked with Master Arca to restore peace to the war-torn world. Nomi and Ulic had grown close during the reparations, and Master Arca decided to send them both to deal with the situation in the Empress Teta system.

Republic military forces were also dispatched by Coruscant to the ferocious battles around the seven worlds. Ulic and Nomi joined them and assisted in the struggle, using their Jedi abilities, but Aleema countered with powerful Sith illusions. In a suicide attack, one of the Krath ships nearly destroyed the bridge of the Republic flagship. Ulic received a terrible wound, but Nomi saved his life. The rebuffed Republic fleet retreated.

Simultaneously, on distant Dantooine, Jedi Master Vodo-Siosk Baas trained three students: the Cathar mates Crado and Sylvar, and his most talented apprentice, Exar Kun. In the course of their training, Kun proved himself Crado's superior with the lightsaber. Tensions escalated, and during one-to-one combat, Sylvar slashed Kun across the face with her claws. Master Vodo stepped in, and Kun met the challenge. Showing no restraint, he defeated his own teacher and brashly claimed he had learned all the Jedi Master could teach him. Vodo was disturbed at the shadow he saw in his student, the potential for evil.

Ambitious and curious, Kun surreptitiously studied ancient legends, learning much about the ancient Hyperspace War and the golden age of the Sith. Consumed by his interests, Exar Kun went to Onderon to learn more of the Freedon Nadd Uprising and the resurgence of ancient ways. He posed as a Jedi archaeologist sent to uncover Sith artifacts. Cay Qel-Droma and Tott Doneeta offered their assistance, but Master Arca recognized Kun's arrogance and told him they would offer no help.

On his own, Kun hired a pair of mercenaries and traveled to the Dxun moon to break into the sealed tomb of Freedon Nadd. After battling guardian beasts, he used his lightsaber to cut through the Mandalorian iron. In the vault, he cracked open the sarcophagus, stared down at the skeletal corpse clothed in black armor—and was astonished to see Nadd's specter appear.

The ominous dark Jedi revealed precious metal scrolls that had been hidden in a compartment under his remains. He told Kun that a great future awaited him in the dark side, but Kun dismissed the ghost's prophecy. When he left the tomb, his two mercenaries tried to rob him. Exar Kun responded with sudden and unthinking violence. He drew his lightsaber and killed the men. Horrified at his bloody outburst, Kun left the system, taking the scrolls with him.

His path led him to Korriban, the tomb world of the ancient Sith Empire, where Gav and Jori Daragon had first encountered Naga Sadow a thousand years earlier. From the scrolls, Kun learned more about Freedon Nadd's connection to the legendary Sith. Among the ruins, Kun explored a spectacular crypt, but as he went deeper, the crumbling ceiling collapsed, crushing him.

As he cried out for help, the spirit of Freedon Nadd appeared, promising rescue—but only if Kun surrendered to the dark side. Kun made an empty promise just to save his life, but the vow sent him sliding farther down the slippery slope. He uttered the fateful words, unleashing a flood of power that blasted away the rubble, knitted his broken bones, and left him lying naked on the dry clay of Korriban.

Exar Kun let out a tremendous shriek that echoed across the galaxy, calling in despair upon Master Vodo, whom he had abandoned.

When the anguished cry reached him through the Force, Vodo was en route to Deneba, the site of a great Jedi convocation called to discuss the strife in the Empress Teta system, and the greater darkness it presaged. When Vodo was stricken by Kun's psychic outcry, Crado and Sylvar rushed to his side. Not quite understanding what he had experienced, but dreading the implications, Vodo hurried on to the convocation.

The historic meeting was called to order by the ancient librarian Odan-Urr, who had spent centuries building Ossus into the foremost center of Jedi learning. The premier Jedi Knights of the period had come, including Master Arca and Master Thon, Nomi Sunrider, and the recovered Ulic Qel-Droma. Jedi witnesses spoke of the dangerous Sith sorcery unleashed by the Krath, the growing foothold of the dark side, and the need to stop such evil from spreading.

In the middle of the assembly, automated pods rained down through the atmosphere, unleashing hordes of Krath war droids that attacked the Jedi Knights. The Jedi defended themselves in a furious fight, destroying the droids, but the battle left one tragic legacy. Master Arca, one of the greatest Jedi Masters of his age, was killed by a projectile even as he saved the life of his student Ulic Qel-Droma. Ulic despaired, convinced he had failed Arca once again. This broke his spirit and left him open to the influences of the dark side. His vulnerability would one day bring tremendous devastation to the galaxy.

As the Jedi Knights recovered from the onslaught, an anguished Ulic made a fateful decision. Discovering that the assassin droids were of Tetan manufacture, he vowed to go to the Empress Teta system, infiltrate the Krath, and destroy them from within. Concerned that the brash young Jedi was engaging in this reckless action for the wrong reasons, Master Thon warned him about the temptations of the dark side. But Ulic would not be swayed. His brother, Cay, begged to go with him, insisting that they stick together as brothers should, but Ulic refused. He needed to do this himself, he said, for Master Arca. So Ulic bade farewell to Nomi Sunrider, barely admitting his growing love for her, and departed for Cinnagar.

Healed and "reborn" in the Sith ruins on Korriban, Exar Kun deluded himself into thinking he had tricked Freedon Nadd with his feigned promise—but Nadd knew better. The specter told Kun to make his way to Yavin 4, the last resting place of Naga Sadow, who had instructed Nadd himself centuries before.

On that isolated jungle moon, Exar Kun discovered an ancient, mysterious temple, where the degenerate descendants of the Massassi captured him. One of their high priests still wore the trappings of Sith magic, though he didn't entirely know how to use the sorcery. The Massassi chained Kun and tried to sacrifice him to a gigantic monster beneath the main temple, forcing Exar Kun to call once again upon the dark side in order to save himself.

The specter of Freedon Nadd reappeared, delighted with Kun's victory and claiming him as an ally and protégé—but Kun would hear none of it. Still simmering with the Sith powers he had mastered, Kun lashed out and obliterated Nadd for

*Reawakening of evil*

all time. Using the dark side seemed much easier.

Exar Kun proclaimed himself the Dark Lord of the Sith, the only surviving practitioner of the ancient arts. He subjugated the Massassi and had them construct more temples, huge structures based on Sith architecture and designed to focus dark forces. When the new slaves dug deep beneath the sites of the ancient ruins, he found the great Sith battleship, long ago entombed by Naga Sadow. Exar Kun took it as his own.

Disguised as a grim "fallen Jedi," Ulic Qel-Droma infiltrated the iron-walled city of Cinnagar, where the Krath usurpers had crushed all dissent. When a scuffle broke out and an assassin tried to kill the beautiful Aleema, Ulic saw his chance to be taken into the Krath, and accepted this terrible act as part of the cost for ultimate victory. He protected Aleema, killing the would-be assassin. Blood stained his hands, and Ulic had taken the next great step on the road to damnation.

As a reward, Aleema took Ulic into the palace, intending to keep him as her lover, though Satal Keto was highly suspicious—and jealous. Keto interrogated and tortured Ulic, insisting he was a Jedi spy, which Ulic repeatedly denied. Finally, Keto injected Ulic with Sith poison; Ulic managed to counteract it, though the poison continued to affect his mind and actions. Finally, Ulic was inducted into the Krath as a general of the military forces—and a personal pet of the evil Aleema.

As months passed with no word from Ulic, Nomi Sunrider joined Cay Qel-Droma and Tott Doneeta in an attempt to rescue him. While Cay Qel-Droma and Doneeta remained in orbit, Sunrider dropped down to Cinnagar, seeking news. Reluctant to kill with her lightsaber, she was captured by Krath forces and dragged before Satal Keto and Ulic. Testing Ulic, Keto asked him what they should do with the Jedi spy. At such a critical point in his plans, Ulic could not allow his cover to be exposed. Pretending not to know her, he nonchalantly ordered Sunrider's execution.

Despairing that she had lost Ulic forever, Sunrider used her Jedi meditation techniques to escape the dungeons of Cinnagar, even as Ulic prepared a secret message for her, telling her his plans. Unfortunately, Sunrider fled back to her ship

before learning the truth, firmly believing that Ulic had turned against them—and Satal Keto intercepted the message. Knowing Ulic was an infiltrator after all, Keto sent his men to kill the Jedi spy, but in a great duel Ulic unleashed his fury over the murder of Master Arca and killed Satal Keto instead. With Keto slain, Ulic Qel-Droma took his place beside Aleema, declaring himself the new ruler of the Krath.

In his ornate meditation chamber under the largest temple on Yavin 4, Exar Kun, a very powerful figure now, studied Sith teachings. He dabbled in dark-side alchemy, creating freakish two-headed avians to serve as watchbeasts and inventing a glowing golden sphere that trapped the children of the Massassi and allowed him to feed off their energies. With his mind he reached across the galaxy and detected other users of Sith magic in the Empress Teta system. Knowing his destiny—to bring about a new Sith golden age—Kun traveled to Cinnagar, determined to destroy Ulic as an unwanted rival.

Meanwhile, despite grave cautions from the older Jedi Masters, the brash Jedi Knights Cay Qel-Droma, Nomi Sunrider, and Tott Doneeta put together a rescue mission to drag Ulic away from the treachery of the Krath.

Corrupted by the Sith poison and the dark consequences of his actions, Ulic responded to the Jedi attack with all the military might at his disposal. When Nomi confronted him in the throne room, Ulic hesitated, but made his choice to cast her away. Convinced he had important work to do in the Empress Teta system, and blind to his own delusions, he refused to join the Jedi. In despair and defeat, the Jedi Knights withdrew.

Then Exar Kun marched into the palace, drawing his lightsaber. He and Ulic fought in a blazing clash of Jedi blades—and during the conflict the Sith amulets both men wore began to shimmer. Before them appeared the image of the long-dead Dark Lord of the Sith, Marka Ragnos, the Sith ruler whose death had triggered the civil war between Naga Sadow and Ludo Kressh a thousand years before. Ragnos commanded the two men to join forces, claiming that the alliance of Ulic Qel-Droma and Exar Kun could bring about the long-predicted return of Sith glory. Kun and Qel-Droma clasped hands and vowed to do whatever was necessary to create such a future.

## The Sith War
### 3996 B.B.Y.

While the Republic remained unsuspecting, Exar Kun and Ulic Qel-Droma consolidated their forces. Kun worked to create numerous Sith converts among the weaker-willed Jedi. He traveled to Ossus. A charismatic and powerful speaker, Exar Kun spread his insidious Sith teachings throughout the Jedi learning center, acting as if he were some sort of prophet. And young Jedi students began listening to him, students such as his Cathar training companion Crado, who idolized Kun. Crado's mate, Sylvar, refused to be swayed.

Kun knew that the ancient Jedi librarian Odan-Urr kept an original Sith holocron that had been used by Naga Sadow during the invasion a millennium before. He stole the dark artifact and killed old Odan-Urr when the ancient librarian tried to stop him, thus fulfilling the prophecy made centuries earlier by Master Ooroo.

Finding the librarian dead, the other students were told by Exar Kun that Odan-Urr had sacrificed himself to give Kun even more knowledge. He took his group of converts back to the Massassi temples on Yavin 4, where he unleashed a powerful Sith spell that bound the Jedi to him. Kun made the hapless Crado, desperately eager to please, his second-in-command.

Ulic Qel-Droma, meanwhile, took charge of the strategic war. He used the Krath military and Aleema's Sith illusions in lightning strikes launched to gather supplies and weaponry from outposts and shipyards. Next, he launched a brash, all-out attack on Coruscant itself, hoping to take down the seat of the Republic government and impose Sith rule upon the galaxy. However, the loyal Jedi—including Nomi Sunrider, Cay Qel-Droma, Tott Doneeta, and Masters Vodo and Thon—joined together against the threat. Surrounded by light and the Force, Ulic was captured and the invading forces were driven back, while Aleema escaped. Stripped of his power, Ulic was taken to face trial for his crimes against the Republic.

The trial was held in the great Senate Chamber on Coruscant, where the extent of Ulic's crimes and depredations were revealed. Though independent, the Jedi Knights had sworn to uphold the laws of the Republic. For a Jedi Knight, betrayal of the Republic was an unforgivable crime. Nomi Sunrider and Cay Qel-Droma begged for leniency on behalf of their wayward Jedi friend. Ulic, however, displayed no repentance. Master Vodo also arrived for the trial, suspecting that Ulic wasn't acting alone; he sensed the dark hand of his lost student Exar Kun.

When Ulic was about to be sentenced, however, the doors crashed open and Exar Kun strode in, flanked by bestial Massassi bodyguards. Before the whole assembly, the new Dark Lord of the Sith used his twisted powers to hypnotize the observers and manipulate the president of the senate. When Nomi and Cay tried to resist, Ulic—still showing a vestige of his old self—begged his friends not to interfere. Overconfident, Kun announced that no one would stop his plans.

But Master Vodo-Siosk Baas stepped onto the floor: the diminutive Jedi would stand against him. Exar Kun battled his old Master, using a double-bladed lightsaber and all the Sith tricks he had learned. He tried to lure Vodo to join his Sith cause, but the Jedi Master refused. As the fight continued, Vodo grew weaker and Kun gained strength. Finally, just as Vodo vowed that he *would* defeat Exar Kun, the Dark Lord struck with his lightsaber and killed his teacher. Walking away from their resounding victory in the Senate Hall, Ulic and Kun left the other Jedi and the senators behind, returning to their stronghold on Yavin 4.

Vodo wasn't the only Jedi to die. Before departing to retrieve Ulic, Exar Kun had sent out his Sith-possessed converts on an insidious mission to assassinate their own Masters. Many of the converts died, but the bloodbath of slaughtered Jedi Masters made the Republic reel. Crado tried to kill Master Thon, but did not succeed; instead, Crado fled.

When Crado confessed his failure to Exar Kun back on Yavin 4, he begged for another chance to impress his Dark Lord. Ulic and Kun allowed the Cathar a new job: he and Aleema would retrieve a powerful weapon from the ancient Sith flagship, the craft buried by Naga Sadow. Kun showed them

*The tragedy that turned the tide*

how to use the weapon to create a gigantic starstorm by destroying the Cron cluster.

Crado and Aleema departed, eager to crush their enemies—not suspecting that Kun and Ulic had chosen to let them be victims of their own ambitions. Crado was to be punished for his incompetence, Aleema for her treachery; she had tried to take over Ulic's forces while he was imprisoned. When these two triggered the ancient Sith weapon, they lost control. Both vanished in a sweeping conflagration that spread out to destroy entire star systems. The blazing shock wave from the exploding stars streaked toward Ossus, the library world—exactly as Kun had hoped.

## The Devastation of Ossus
### 3996 B.B.Y.

During the frantic evacuation of Ossus, Jedi scrambled to retrieve as many of the irreplaceable artifacts as possible. Amidst this chaos, Exar Kun and

Ulic brought their forces to the library world to raid what remained and take huge stockpiles for their own use. A treelike Jedi Master, Ood Bnar, had taken on the mantle of librarian after Odan-Urr. Knowing he could not protect every precious item from the oncoming blast wave, he was burying a priceless collection of ancient lightsabers when Exar Kun and his Massassi warriors marched in to take them. Just when he seemed to have lost his battle with Kun, Ood called upon the Force inside the soil of Ossus, transforming himself into a gigantic tree that protected the treasure and drove back the Dark Lord of the Sith. Taking his other plunder, Exar Kun departed from Ossus.

As the waves of supernova fire came closer to the doomed world, Ulic Qel-Droma fought against the rallying Republic and Jedi forces. Leaving her daughter, Vima, under the protection of Master Thon, Nomi Sunrider joined Tott Doneeta and Cay Qel-Droma to find Ulic to bring him back with them. Cay and Ulic engaged in an aerial dogfight in their ships, and Cay was shot down. Ulic unleashed his anger and attacked Cay. Cay defended himself, unwilling to harm his own brother, but Ulic had no such compunctions. In a devastating fury, Ulic Qel-Droma struck down his own brother, his friend, his ally. Then, staring at the body and seeing what he had done, Ulic collapsed in horror.

Nomi Sunrider and Tott Doneeta arrived too late to help Cay, but a distraught Nomi unleashed a wild Force ability, a blocking technique that blinded Ulic to the Force, effectively stripping him of his powers. Utterly crushed, no longer even a Jedi Knight, Ulic Qel-Droma reeled, realizing how much pain and suffering he had caused. He had gone down the dark path with the intention of avenging Master Arca, but instead he had grown worse even than his enemies.

Knowing how the Sith War must end, Ulic offered to take Master Thon and the remaining Jedi in a coordinated strike against the Yavin 4 headquarters of Exar Kun. The Jedi Knights bade farewell to the implanted tree Jedi Ood Bnar, leaving him to face the oncoming stellar shock wave, and they traveled to the isolated jungle moon.

Kun knew the Jedi forces were coming. Alone, he could not possibly withstand the combined Force powers of the Jedi—but he had one last plan to launch. Kun gathered the remaining Massassi into the Great Temple and chained himself at the focal point of the pyramids. As the Jedi forces in orbit generated a wall of light that bombarded the thick jungles, Exar Kun drained the power from all of his loyal Massassi slaves, triggering a final wave of Sith sorcery that liberated his spirit and preserved it inside the giant structures. Trapped, unable to escape the prison he had created for himself, he remained entombed in the temples for four thousand years, until students at Luke Skywalker's Jedi academy unknowingly released him to cause more havoc ...

The Jedi attack caused an immense conflagration in the jungles, obliterating the trees and scorching the temple complex so that nothing could survive. Fully victorious, the Jedi Knights departed and worked to pick up the pieces of their damaged Republic. The Sith War was over.

## The Redemption of Ulic Qel-Droma
### 3986 B.B.Y.

Ulic Qel-Droma, a disgraced war criminal, never regained his Jedi powers. A ruined man, he wandered from world to world and hid from history, haunted by the ghosts of his own guilt. Ten years after the Sith War, he went to the frozen world of Rhen Var to make his final home in the ruins of an abandoned fortress.

Nomi Sunrider, too, was scarred by the loss of Ulic, the second man she had ever loved. Both romances had ended in tragedy. She devoted much of her life to politics and rebuilding the order of the Jedi Knights. Focused on her duties, though, Nomi Sunrider had never paid sufficient attention to her impressionable daughter, Vima, who had been handed off to caretakers while Nomi did the work of a Jedi. Though the child of two powerful, Force-sensitive people, Vima did not receive sufficient training, and so she ran away from a great Jedi convocation Nomi had called at Exis Station. Vima set out to find Ulic Qel-Droma, convinced that the legendary man would train her as a Jedi.

The young girl did track down Ulic and, despite his grave reluctance, convinced the bitter man to teach her what he knew of the Force. Even without

*Vima Sunrider*

the use of his powers, he taught Vima much about honor and duty, and his heart softened to the girl; Vima came to love him like the father she'd never had.

Sylvar, the Cathar Jedi, had never overcome her anger at the death of her mate, Crado, for which she partly blamed Ulic. She went on a frantic hunt for the runaway young girl, enlisting the aid of a down-on-his-luck scavenger, Hoggon. She vowed to find Vima—and make Ulic pay for his crimes.

When Sylvar, Nomi Sunrider, and Hoggon finally arrived, crying out for Ulic's blood, Vima defended her teacher. Sylvar and Nomi were forced to overcome their anger and pain, forgiving the man who had already paid so much for his crimes. But Hoggon—eager to make his mark on history—shot Ulic in the back and killed him.

To everyone's astonishment, though he had been blinded to the Force, Ulic Qel-Droma vanished into the light. His luminous being demonstrated that, despite everything, he had finally reached the mental and spiritual point where he had become a true Jedi Master.

With such a beginning to her career as a Jedi Knight, Vima Sunrider learned much and eventually became one of the greatest Jedi of her age.

## Repercussions through the Republic
### 4000-3000 B.B.Y.

Years of consolidation and recovery followed in the aftermath of the Sith War. These were filled with more strife and more Jedi heroism. One tragic outgrowth was a regional conflict known as the Kanz Disorders, which ultimately cost five billion lives.

Provisional Governor Myrial of Argazda used the chaos of the Sith War to cover her attempts at establishing a military dictatorship throughout the Kanz sector on the frontier. With the Jedi preoccupied, Myrial's armies bombed recalcitrant planets, including Lorrd, and sold their inhabitants into slavery. The Lorrdians, forbidden by their slave masters from speaking aloud, developed into geniuses at nonverbal communication, a trait still exhibited today. The Kanz sector eventually seceded from the Republic and existed as a totalitarian state for three centuries, until Jedi efforts toppled the regime.

Concurrent with the Sith War came the rise of the matriarchy in the Hapes Consortium. A few decades before Ulic Qel-Droma and Exar Kun nearly toppled the Republic, a band of Jedi Knights—including Master Arca Jeth—traveled into the densely packed Hapan worlds and eliminated the barbaric Lorell Raiders, who had preyed on Republic shipping for generations. The women of the Hapes Consortium, freed from their servitude to the Raiders, established a female-dominated society and placed all power in a single monarch, the queen mother. Centuries later, the Hapan queen mother sealed the borders to the star cluster, and the Consortium developed in near-total isolation for three millennia until Princess Leia Organa broke down the barriers in a historic diplomatic achievement for the New Republic.

Three thousand years before the current era, the legendary pioneer woman Freia Kallea blazed an impressive new hyperspace route—the astonishing Hydian Way, which spanned nearly the width of the galaxy. The Hydian Way finally opened up the galaxy to widespread colonization beyond the narrow wedge of space known as the Slice and fundamentally altered the scale of galactic civilization.

## The New Sith
### 2000-1000 B.B.Y.

The original race of beings known as the Sith disappeared into the fog of history and haven't been seen since the Sith golden age. But the ancient teachings of Sith Lords and the tangible evil they wrought continued to plague the stability of the Republic. Over time, the term *Sith* took on its current meaning, that of a cult dedicated to the dark side of the Force.

Two thousand years before the rise of the Empire, a rogue Jedi Knight broke away from the teachings of the Jedi Council and founded a new order of the Sith, much as Exar Kun had done. Over time, other Jedi Knights joined the renegade, and soon the Republic had a serious threat on its hands. The followers of the Sith grew in power over the next millennium and eventually made war against the Republic. The Jedi opposed them, but in the end the Sith were felled by their own internal schisms: unwilling to share power, the Sith disciples destroyed each other in a violent bloodbath.

One of the few survivors was the Sith Lord Kaan, who gathered twenty thousand devoted followers under his dark banner and sought to establish a galaxywide dictatorship of "rule by the strong." A makeshift army was hastily assembled to oppose him, led by the great Jedi Master Lord Hoth. The Army of Light steadily pushed back the Brotherhood of Darkness, finally cornering them on Ruusan, where seven titanic battles were fought.

The Brotherhood of Darkness lost all but two of the battles, reducing their once-fearsome army to a tenth of its original size. Lord Hoth expected his enemy's unconditional surrender. Instead, the evil Kaan and his disciples barricaded themselves in underground chambers and used their dark powers to create a "thought bomb"—a volatile cauldron of seething Force energy.

That next morning, Lord Hoth and the Army of Light entered the enemy encampment marching past rows of severed heads and bodies dangling from poles—grisly trophies of virtuous Jedi who had fallen in the conflicts. The Lord of Darkness and the Defender of Light met in a great valley

*The Battle of Ruusan*

above the underground chambers; there, Kaan triggered the thought bomb. A furious explosion of energy annihilated every last member of the Army of Light and the Brotherhood of Darkness. The vacuum at the center of the blast sucked in thousands of the disembodied spirits and trapped them in an unbreakable state of equilibrium. The spirits were doomed to remain until a powerful Force user arrived at the Valley of the Jedi and upset the natural balance. The natives of Ruusan made a prophecy: "A Knight shall come, a battle will be fought, and the prisoners go free." That prophecy would remain unfulfilled until a year after the Battle of Endor.

After Ruusan, the Jedi mistakenly believed the Sith order had been exterminated at last. One Sith Lord, Darth Bane, escaped. He sought a new apprentice to keep the Sith knowledge alive. This time, he would value stealth and secrecy above all else. For the Sith to call attention to themselves would be to invite their own destruction.

Over the next thousand years the Sith remained in hiding. Following the strict dictate of Darth Bane, there were never more than two Sith Lords at one time—a master and an apprentice. The Sith meditated on the dark side and codified their teachings. Like monks in a hermitage, they waited in isolation for a chance to strike at the Jedi Knights.

## Jedi Valiancy
### 600–400 B.B.Y.

Even without the influence of the Sith, some Jedi Knights were seduced by evil. The Jedi Council rarely executed these fallen Jedi, preferring instead to banish the offenders in the hopes that, in primitive isolation, they might focus on their Masters' teachings and return to the light.

Six hundred years before the ascension of Palpatine, a fallen Jedi named Allya was exiled to the savage forests of Dathomir, a rugged planet that had long served as a prison colony for some of the Republic's worst criminals. Allya used the Force to subjugate the prisoners and tame Dathomir's feral rancors. Over time Allya had many daughters, all of whom she taught to use the Force. A female-dominant society eventually took shape, led by "witches" who viewed the Force as a form of atavistic magic.

Dathomir's witches came to the Republic's attention two hundred years later when the great Jedi training vessel *Chu'unthor* crashed on the planet's surface. A triumvirate of famous Jedi Masters—Gra'aton, Vulatan, and Yoda—along with many Jedi Knights and acolytes, attempted to rescue the *Chu'unthor's* passengers and were attacked by the native spellcasters. The Jedi suffered substantial losses and retreated, but their return visit was far more successful. Master Yoda used his insight to negotiate a peaceful settlement with the leader of the witches.

Other Jedi, continuing their work across the Republic, laid the foundations for events that would become significant in later centuries. A Hutt Jedi, Beldorian the Splendid, traveled to Nam Chorios and discovered that the planet's crystal energy magnified his Force powers. Beldorian set himself up as a petty local dictator.

Another Jedi, a tiny Kushiban named Ikrit, journeyed to Yavin 4 and discovered the golden sphere Exar Kun had created thousands of years earlier with alchemical magic. Realizing he was incapable of freeing the Massassi spirits trapped within the orb, Ikrit placed himself in a Jedi trance to await the arrival of one who could break the curse, even if it would take centuries.

# PART II

## THE EMPIRE AND THE NEW ORDER

**T**hose who remember the dark days of the Empire know that the tyranny of Palpatine appeared absolute and unshakable. Emperor Palpatine himself boasted that his Empire would last for a thousand years or more.

But the Empire was so corrupt and amoral that internal resistance sprang up shortly after Palpatine took control, growing stronger with each brutal atrocity. The conflict of Empire and Rebellion is known as the Galactic Civil War, and it is the single most important era of our history.

### Birth of the Empire
#### APPROX. 50–18 B.B.Y.

A history of the Empire should not simply begin with the dark day on which Palpatine declared himself Emperor. Rather, students must consider the circumstances that led to an atmosphere in which such an event was possible in the first place. The Old Republic existed for a thousand generations; how could it have been overthrown so suddenly?

The Republic fell victim to its own success. The sprawling representative government sought to oversee territory spanning a large portion of the galaxy, and a cumbersome set of checks and balances made simple decisions impossible. Too many senators and planetary governors began to adopt the view that the existing system of government, nearly as old as history itself, would continue through sheer force of inertia. They no longer put their best efforts into enacting legislation and meeting the needs of their constituents. The Republic grew stagnant. Laziness and complacency became the rule, and with laziness came corruption.

Nevertheless, certain officials still attempted ambitious and grandiose projects. One example was the *Katana* fleet, named after its flagship. This armada of two hundred slave-rigged Dreadnaughts promised to be the pride of the Republic navy. Unfortunately, a hive virus caused the crew of the flagship *Katana* to go mad. They jumped their ship into random hyperspace coordinates, and the slave rig brought the other 199 vessels along for the ride, where they would remain undiscovered for over half a century. The fiasco further eroded the public's already waning confidence in the Republic's leadership.

The crafty Senator Palpatine of Naboo watched the government's decay with a practiced eye and a knowing smile. Palpatine, a sectorial senator representing many star systems, was one of the Senate's most experienced and respected members. He saw the time drawing near when the disgusted citizenry would cry out for stronger leadership, and he set his plans in motion behind the scenes. Perhaps the greatest obstacle to his dreams of glory would be the Jedi Knights.

The Jedi were still the Republic's guardians and defenders, but over the centuries they became intertwined with politics and government. The Republic's supreme chancellor was able to request assistance from the Jedi Knights, whereupon they would act as ambassadors, investigators, and peace officers. The Jedi headquarters was located on Coruscant, not far from the seat of government. Perhaps unfairly, the image of the Jedi became tainted by the dishonesty of politicians.

It seems almost absurd that the momentous shift from Republic to Empire grew out of something as trivial as a taxation dispute, but the most injurious evil is rarely accompanied by tremors and thunderclaps. The seemingly mundane senate resolution BR-0371 introduced a tariff on major hyperspace trading routes throughout the Outer and Mid Rims, with revenue going to the Republic to pay off its burgeoning fiscal debt.

Predictably, the act was met with resistance by shippers both small and large, and no party was larger than the Trade Federation—a massive conglomeration of member corporations that dominated Rim commerce. Palpatine's enthusiastic support of the taxation measure may have been deliberately intended to spur the Trade Federation to action, since their rash response played perfectly into his long-term plans. On advice from a shadowy Sith Lord, Darth Sidious, the Trade Federation blockaded Naboo.

The Trade Federation, mere pawns in a Sith scheme, pushed matters past the breaking point by invading Naboo with a deadly droid army. News of the shocking event was revealed to the senate by Naboo's Queen Amidala, who followed up by dropping an even bigger bombshell—calling for a vote of no-confidence in Supreme Chancellor Finis Valorum, whom she felt had abandoned her people.

In an earlier era, such a sudden and divisive matter as forcing a chancellor's resignation would never have made it to a vote. But Valorum, embroiled in an embarrassing corruption scandal, had few friends in the senate. He was swiftly voted out of office and several possible successors were named. Thanks to a groundswell of sympathy for Palpatine and his embattled homeworld, the crafty senator was soon elected the next—and ultimately, the last—chancellor of the Old Republic.

Concurrent with these events was a mystical discovery that had galactic consequences. While helping Queen Amidala escape the Trade Federation blockade and make her plea to the Senate, Jedi Master Qui-Gon Jinn encountered a nine-year-old slave boy on the desert planet Tatooine. The boy, Anakin Skywalker, existed at the epicenter of a potent vergence in the Force. Everything indicated that young Skywalker was the Chosen One of ancient Jedi prophecy, the one

*The invasion of Naboo*

foretold to bring balance to the Force. Master Jinn won Anakin's freedom and brought him to the Jedi Temple on Coruscant for testing and verification.

The Jedi Council members, while impressed with Skywalker's skill, refused to allow the boy to be trained as Qui-Gon Jinn's Padawan. At nine, Skywalker was well past the age limit for Jedi instruction. Master Windu was far more concerned over the possible reappearance of the Sith. On Tatooine, Qui-Gon Jinn had battled a warrior with Jedi-like skills—a thousand years after the Sith Order's presumed extinction at the Battle of Ruusan. Master Jinn returned to Naboo with instructions to draw his mysterious attacker into the open once more.

The mission ended in tragedy. The warrior, later identified as Darth Maul, killed Master Jinn in a lightsaber duel, but was himself slain. Over Master Yoda's objections, the Jedi Council honored Qui-Gon Jinn's dying request and permitted Anakin

*Darth Maul*

Skywalker to join the ranks of the Jedi Padawans. Qui-Gon's former student Obi-Wan Kenobi accepted the boy as his apprentice and vowed to train him to the best of his ability. (Kenobi's eventual failure culminated years later when Anakin Skywalker embraced the dark side, allied himself with Palpatine, and assumed the name and title Darth Vader, Dark Lord of the Sith.)

When a Jedi exploration mission called the Outbound Flight Project was announced following the Naboo crisis, Chancellor Palpatine seized the opportunity. The Jedi Masters aboard the Outbound Flight vessel intended to use the Force to breach the sphere of hyperspace turbulence surrounding the galaxy and search for life in other corners of the universe, but they were never given the chance. As the Jedi research ship made a slow swing through the Unknown Regions on its way to the galactic edge and beyond, Palpatine's agents intercepted and destroyed it. There is substantial evidence that Thrawn, later to become the Empire's greatest grand admiral, was involved in the incident. The destruction of Outbound Flight dashed all hopes of contacting life in nearby galaxies.

After the debacle, two years after the Battle of

*Qui-Gon Jinn*

*Palpatine, the new Emperor*

Naboo, the Jedi Knight Vergere mysteriously vanished after being sent by Master Mace Windu on a scouting mission to the strange and bewildering planet of Zonama Sekot. One year later, Obi-Wan Kenobi and his new Padawan apprentice, Anakin Skywalker, explored Zonama Sekot and learned that Vergere might have been captured by an unknown alien species.

The Clone Wars were a dark time for the galaxy. The thousand-thousand worlds of the Old Republic were swept up in a furious conflagration that rendered entire planets uninhabitable. Many historical archives were destroyed, while other archives covering this period were wiped clean in the years fol-

lowing the Emperor's ascension. Not even the library planet of Obroa-skai can provide accurate details on the Clone Wars, the extermination of the Jedi, or the crowning of the Emperor, though it is hoped that new information on this era will soon come to light. We would be remiss as historians if we did not qualify these dark decades with a caveat, bearing in mind that only independent corroboration can place these events in the proper context and sequence.

The chaos of the Clone Wars triggered a violent Dark Jedi insurrection on Bpfassh. Nejaa Halcyon and several other Jedi Knights destroyed another Dark Jedi enclave on Susevfi, eliminating the danger but alienating the Dark Jedi's followers, the *Jensaarai*. The *Jensaarai* would develop their teachings in secret until discovered by Luke Skywalker decades later.

Palpatine continued the systematic annihilation of his enemies, though at this point he wasn't secure enough in his power to do it openly. After the Clone Wars, he engineered the devastation of the planet Caamas. The respected Caamasi preached "peace through moral strength," and Palpatine saw their influence as a threat. A group of Bothan saboteurs helped Palpatine's agents sabotage Caamas's shield generators, paving the way for a sudden, violent attack that sent destructive firestorms raging across the world. In a separate incident, Seti Ashgad, one of Palpatine's most vocal opponents in the senate, was abruptly arrested and exiled to the dismal planet Nam Chorios.

The greatest threats to Palpatine's power were the Jedi Knights, and he crushed them swiftly and mercilessly. The bloody crusade, often called the Jedi Purge, resulted in the deaths of thousands of Jedi Knights and Masters and caused the survivors to go underground. The Emperor's assistant, Darth Vader—who as Anakin Skywalker had been raised as a member of the Jedi Order—was allegedly responsible for the greatest atrocities of the Purge.

Eventually the ineffectual fumblings of the Old Republic's government became too obvious to ignore. Secure in his power, Palpatine declared himself Emperor, spelling out his clear vision to a citizenry starved for leadership. The New Order, Palpatine promised, would trade strength for frailty, order for chaos, and decisiveness for uncertainty. The public was excited and overwhelmingly enthusiastic.

The Empire had begun.

## Dawn of Dissent
### APPROX. 18–0 B.B.Y.

At first, the Empire proved an unknown variable. Some senators embraced the New Order while others watched cautiously to see what might develop.

Palpatine, however, wasted no time in consolidating his rule. Besides his urge to exterminate the Jedi, the Emperor also possessed a passion for warships and superweapons. He combined the two

when he commissioned a gargantuan, asteroid-shaped battlemoon dubbed the *Eye of Palpatine*. The *Eye* was constructed in secret for the purpose of wiping out a Jedi enclave on Belsavis. Fortunately, the Emperor's death engine was disabled by Jedi saboteurs, and the refugees on Belsavis fled to parts unknown.

When the Jedi were slaughtered, some citizens cheered, while others shook their heads in distress. Noble-minded senators believed they could curb the worst of the new Emperor's excesses through the time-honored bureaucratic system of checks and balances. The Ghorman Massacre proved them wrong.

In the Sern sector, near the Core Worlds, a peaceful antitax demonstration on Ghorman was broken up when a warship callously landed on top of the protesters—crushing and injuring hundreds. Palpatine praised the action and promoted the ship's captain, Tarkin, to the lauded position of moff.

The Ghorman Massacre convinced Senator Bail Organa of Alderaan that the ideals of the Old Republic were finally and truly dead. Organa and another senator, Mon Mothma of Chandrila, began meeting in secret to discuss an organized rebellion against the New Order.

Meanwhile, the Emperor continued remaking the galaxy according to his own desires. Coruscant was renamed Imperial Center. Nonhuman races were cruelly persecuted, and antislavery laws were repealed. Palpatine restricted civilian access to the HoloNet communications system, preventing planets from receiving any news that wasn't Imperial propaganda. The Commission for the Preservation of the New Order (COMPNOR) was formed and began administering ideological purity tests to Imperial citizens.

Above all else, Palpatine expanded the military. The Imperial Navy commanded thousands of *Imperial*-class Star Destroyers, each one capable of subjugating an entire planet. The Imperial Army became known for their terrifying AT-AT and AT-ST armored walkers. The Emperor even created a specialty branch of the armed forces, the storm-troopers. The ubiquitous white-armored troopers became the ultimate symbol of Imperial might.

Bail Organa and Mon Mothma continued to

plot against the Imperial war machine. Mon Mothma was far more outspoken in her opposition and was accused of treason. To escape a certain death sentence, she went underground, visiting oppressed planets and speaking to fledgling insurgent movements. Sedition spread from world to world, though it remained disorganized and unfocused.

Less than two years before the Battle of Yavin, the Corellian Treaty was signed—a landmark moment in the history of the revolution. The Corellian Treaty merged the three largest revolutionary groups into a single unified party, the Alliance to Restore the Republic. The document was signed by Bail Organa, Mon Mothma, and Senator Garm Bel Iblis of Corellia.

The Alliance to Restore the Republic, more commonly known as the Rebel Alliance, maintained a clear command hierarchy with Mon Mothma at its head. It also possessed an enthusiastic and growing military. Mon Mothma negotiated a secret arrangement with the Mon Calamari shipyards that gave the Rebels access to top-of-the-line capital ships, while a team of defectors from the Incom Corporation provided the Alliance with prototypes and blueprints of a new precision attack craft—the T-65 X-wing starfighter.

Though the Alliance utilized countless cells on thousands of planets, a single command headquarters was established as a place for the leadership to group and plan strategy. The first of these top secret bases was located on a tiny planetoid in the Chrellis system, though the headquarters was designed for continual relocation. From Chrellis the base moved to Briggia, Orion IV, and several other worlds before relocating to Dantooine, which itself had an ancient connection with the great Jedi Knights of the past. This was the quiet world where Master Vodo-Siosk Baas trained many powerful students.

Alarmed at the growing opposition, the Emperor initiated Operation Strike Fear to crush Mon Mothma and her followers. However, the Alliance fleet distinguished itself with hard-fought victories, including the capture of the frigate *Priam*

*Mon Mothma*

and the demolition of the Star Destroyer *Invincible*.

The Imperial culture that spawned Operation Strike Fear led to a terrible outrage on Ralltiir, one of the Empire's most prosperous and stable member worlds. In response to an allegation of Rebel sympathizers among the Ralltiir High Council, Imperial shock troops seized control of the planet and rounded up prominent citizens for interrogation and torture. Lord Tion, a toady within Tarkin's political sphere, presided over the breaking of Ralltiir.

Although the Rim planets had been systematically brutalized for years, not since Ghorman had a Core World been the subject of such a violent atrocity. Of course, the Alderaan tragedy would soon far overshadow Ralltiir's agony, but at the same time it was a galvanizing event. More and more planets joined the revolution against the Empire with each passing day.

The Rebel Alliance had taken shape.

## PART III

# PROFILES IN HISTORY

Galactic history is more than the epic sweep of battles and conquerors, of grand armies and dread discoveries. On its most basic level, history is the story of individual people. Emperor Palpatine and Mon Mothma are so revered and reviled by various segments of the population that they appear as archetypes in the modern consciousness, not as human beings at all. Nevertheless, it's important to remember that even the highest heroes have humble beginnings, and that the actions of a single person can affect billions of lives.

Without the contributions of "scoundrels" such as Han Solo and Lando Calrissian, as well as the youthful heroism of Luke Skywalker, Princess Leia Organa would have died in Imperial captivity and the second Death Star would have destroyed the Alliance fleet at Endor. As a service to future historians, we have interviewed these key figures, chronicling their early years and elusive histories to better understand what made them into the heroes they are today.

## HAN SOLO

Han Solo never knew his parents. His earliest memory was being lost and alone on Corellia, until a venal con man named Garris Shrike took the abandoned child under his wing. Solo spent his youth aboard the ancient troopship *Trader's Luck* as a member of Shrike's well-organized trading clan, who earned their keep through begging, pickpocketing, and grand larceny. If the children failed, they were beaten to near death.

The only bright spot in Solo's early life was a kindly female Wookiee named Dewlanna, who worked for Shrike as a cook and acted as the human boy's surrogate mother. She taught Solo to speak and understand the Wookiee language of Shyriiwook.

He desperately wanted to learn more about his parents, but that door remained closed to him. The only Solo relative he found was Thrackan Sal-Solo, a cruel bully who appeared to be Han Solo's cousin. After an unpleasant encounter, Sal-Solo disappeared from sight, then eventually rose to a leadership position with an antialien organization called the Human League. More than three decades would pass before Sal-Solo would torment the New Republic, during the Corellian insurrection.

Over the years, Han Solo became an expert thief and street fighter. His skill at piloting swoop racers earned plenty of prize money for Shrike, and his mastery of alien languages served him well when the *Trader's Luck* went from system to system on moneymaking scams. At seventeen, Solo was captured by law-enforcement officials and forced to fight in Regional Sector Four's All-Human Free-for-All Extravaganza on Jubilar. He won the contest by defeating three much larger opponents, but Shrike mercilessly beat him for insubordination when he returned to the *Trader's Luck*.

### Ylesia
### 10 B.B.Y.

At nineteen, Solo escaped from the *Trader's Luck* by stowing away in a robotic cargo freighter. The freighter deposited its passenger on Ylesia, a

*Bria Tharen*

tropical world within the lawless borders of Hutt Space. Though Ylesia advertised itself to the galaxy as a religious retreat, it was actually a brutal spice-processing planet controlled by the Besadii Hutt crime family. Weak-minded converts, attracted by the empty promises of a pseudoreligion, were shipped to Ylesia and put to work toiling in the glitterstim and ryll factories.

Han Solo began piloting ships carrying spice cargoes for the Hutts and their t'landa Til underlings. Though the pay was good and the work interesting, the attentions of a beautiful woman shook Solo from his complacency.

He fell in love with Pilgrim 921, also known as Bria Tharen, and vowed to rescue her from slavery. During the escape, Solo and Tharen destroyed the primary glitterstim factory and plundered the t'landa Til high priest's priceless art collection. They fled Ylesia aboard a stolen yacht after staging a daring rope-ladder rescue of a Togorian prisoner from a neighboring colony.

## The Academy
### 10–5 B.B.Y.

The Besadii Hutts placed a sizable bounty on Han Solo's head, but they knew him only under the alias Vyyk Drago. Solo planned to sell the Ylesian loot, use the money to alter his retinal patterns, and enroll in the Imperial Academy to start a new life as a naval officer. He suffered a great blow when a suspicious Imperial Bank manager placed a freeze on Solo's questionable account—and another when Bria Tharen left him.

Bankrupt and despairing, Solo was able to scrape together enough credits to obtain a forged set of ID credentials and have his retinas surgically altered. Since the Besadii clan was looking for him under an alias, he used his true identity on an application to the Imperial Academy. His last night before enrollment was spoiled by an ugly figure from the past—Garris Shrike, who had been lured by the Hutt bounty. Unlike the other bounty hunters on the trail, Shrike was the only person in the galaxy who knew Solo's alias.

Fortunately, a rival bounty hunter shot Shrike down, and Solo killed the second man in a brutal bare-knuckled brawl. He then switched clothes and ID, and shot the corpse in the face—thus confounding forensic identification. As far as the Besadii Hutts would know, Vyyk Drago was dead.

Free and clear for the first time in his life, Cadet Solo boarded a troop transport for Carida, home of the most respected military academy in the Empire. Over the next four years, Solo proved to be extremely talented, but not a model Imperial student. During one infamous exercise, he landed a malfunctioning U-33 orbital loadlifter with suicidal flair, earning himself the nickname Slick from Lieutenant Badure, his piloting instructor. In another incident, Solo's classmate Mako Spince destroyed Carida's mascot moon with a gram of antimatter.

Despite the misadventures, Solo graduated at the top of his class, beating out Cadet Soontir Fel for the title of valedictorian.

Graduation was followed by eight months of commissioned service in the Imperial Navy. A promising career in the Corellian sector fleet was cut short when Solo rescued a Wookiee slave from ill-treatment at the hands of a superior officer. This earned him a dishonorable discharge, which would prevent him from obtaining any civilian piloting job. However, the Wookiee—Chewbacca—swore a life debt to Solo and promised to follow him everywhere. Solo initially tried to discourage Chewbacca, but gradually realized that a two-and-a-half-meter-tall fanged Wookiee wasn't a bad ally to have at one's side during firefights and cantina brawls.

With no hope of lawful employment, Solo and Chewbacca headed into Hutt Space to work for the criminal syndicates.

## *The Life of a Smuggler*
### 5–2 B.B.Y.

Hutt politics seethed with intrigue. On Nal Hutta, the two most powerful clans—Besadii, headed by Aruk and his offspring Durga; and Desilijic, led by Jiliac and his nephew Jabba—vied for dominance. The Besadii clan controlled the spice operation on Ylesia, but Desilijic possessed important holdings on Tatooine and elsewhere. Their discreet maneuverings would inevitably be replaced by deadly conflict.

On Nar Shaddaa, the smugglers' moon, Solo and Chewbacca were introduced to illicit Hutt activities by Mako Spince, Solo's old friend from the

*Chewbacca*

Academy. They formed a partnership and, as the months passed, met dozens of offbeat individuals such as smuggler-mechanic Shug Ninx, the beautiful and exotic technician Salla Zend, and the female con artist Xaverri. They visited hideaways and hellholes like Smuggler's Run and Kessel, and Solo learned how to fly the dangerous Kessel Run cargo route by skirting the Maw black hole cluster. Solo's piloting skills came to the attention of Jabba the Hutt, and soon he was making regular smuggling runs for the Desilijic clan.

Rubbing elbows with high-level Hutts was a risky game, since Solo still had a price on his head from the rival Besadii clan. On Ylesia, the colony's high priest uncovered astonishing evidence that Vyyk Drago—reported dead five years earlier—had resurfaced under the name Han Solo. The galaxy's best bounty hunter was hired to bring in Solo's hide.

The bounty hunter Boba Fett tracked Solo to Nar Shaddaa, but his capture was spoiled by the impromptu rescue by a charming stranger: Lando Calrissian, owner of a banged-up YT-1300 freighter called the *Millennium Falcon*. Calrissian proved somewhat lacking as a pilot, so Solo taught his rescuer the basics of flying, and Calrissian soon took off in the *Falcon*, headed for the Rafa system and some adventuring of his own.

Meanwhile, Solo stayed largely out of sight, working as a magician's assistant on Xaverri's six-month illusionist tour. Upon his return, he purchased a shoddy, cut-rate SoroSuub Starmite, which he christened the *Bria*, after his lost love, Bria Tharen.

Sudden scrutiny from the Empire brought all normal life on Nar Shaddaa to a screeching halt. Moff Sarn Shild proclaimed that the Hutts' lawless territory would greatly benefit from stricter Imperial control. As a public-relations stunt, Shild was authorized to blockade Nal Hutta and turn the smugglers' moon into molten slag.

The Hutts responded in typical fashion: They sent a messenger to Shild's offices to bribe him. When the moff refused to bend, the Hutts shifted their attentions to Admiral Greelanx, the officer in charge of executing the assault. Greelanx proved to be considerably more accommodating and agreed to sell his battle plan. The Hutts organized a defense and placed their ships in precise locations

*The Battle of Nar Shaddaa*

dictated by the admiral's plan, hoping to inflict enough damage on the Imperial fleet to force a strategic withdrawal.

The scheme worked perfectly. The Battle of Nar Shaddaa remained a localized conflict involving no ship larger than a Dreadnaught, and today is considered little more than a historical footnote. But for the desperate smugglers who banded together to protect their adopted home, it was a life-or-death struggle against staggering odds. Though he didn't realize it at the time, Han Solo was pitted against his former Academy classmate Soontir Fel, then serving as captain of the Dreadnaught *Pride of the Senate*. The battle came to a premature end when one of Greelanx's three Dreadnaughts was destroyed. Unable to justify further losses, the admiral retreated into hyperspace.

After distinguishing himself in the Battle of Nar Shaddaa, Han Solo lost the *Bria* in a mishap. To raise funds for a new starship, Solo entered the annual championship sabacc tournament, held that year in Cloud City's Yarith Bespin casino. Lando Calrissian, freshly returned from his adventures in the ThonBoka, was one of his many opponents. The roster of players steadily dwindled until the two men faced each other across a card-strewn table. Solo took the final hand, winning the sabacc championship and earning his pick of any vessel on Calrissian's used-starship lot. Solo chose the *Millennium Falcon*.

Celebrating their new ship, Solo and Chewbacca visited Kashyyyk, the Wookiee homeworld, where Chewbacca was married to his love, Mallatobuck. At about the same time, Solo became involved in a serious relationship with fellow smuggler Salla Zend, but spooked by commitment phobia, he abandoned Zend and fled Hutt Space entirely, heading out with Chewbacca for the Corporate Sector in the hopes of striking it rich.

## Corporate Sector Blues
### 2–1 B.B.Y.

The semi-independent Corporate Sector Authority was, in many ways, worse than the Empire. The ruling CSA cared little for ideology and ruthlessly rolled over individuals who stood in the way of pure profit. Prior to Solo's arrival, the CSA completed construction on the Stars' End prison complex on the desolate rock Mytus VII. Dissidents, agitators, smugglers, and other troublemakers were quietly rounded up and imprisoned in Stars' End stasis cells.

Solo accepted small-time smuggling commissions for Big Bunji and Ploovo Two-For-One, but he also fell in with a covert team of independent dissidents investigating the disappearances. Team members included Bollux, a labor droid, and Blue Max, a positronic processor hidden in Bollux's chest cavity. Chewbacca was captured, and Solo became more determined than ever to scuttle the CSA's top secret prison.

Posing as a troupe of entertainers, Solo and his team landed on the airless planetoid and were escorted to the dagger-shaped prison tower. On Solo's orders, Blue Max triggered an overload in the prison's reactor core. During the chaos, as the team tried to free their friends and escape, Stars' End's power plant exploded—much more than the simple distraction Solo had hoped for. The blast, contained by the prison's anticoncussion field, was funneled downward against the surface of the planet. Facing negligible gravity and no atmospheric friction, the entire tower rocketed into near orbit.

The structure reached the top of its arc and fell back toward the rocky face of Mytus VII. It was a race against time as the *Falcon* docked against the tower so that Chewbacca and other prisoners could be rescued, then detached just as Stars' End smashed back into the surface. According to unconfirmed reports, the CSA salvaged the molecularly bonded structure and erected it on a different world, a rumor that has soured negotiations between the New Republic and the Corporate Sector Authority to this day.

Solo and Chewbacca continued their association with Bollux and Blue Max. They inspired the Cult of Varn on the arid planet Kamar by showing the holofeature *Varn, World of Water* to the desert-dwelling native insectoids. When Solo replaced the bland documentary with a toe-tapping musical comedy, the water-worshipping Kamarians angrily chased away the false prophet and his great flying chariot. Since that time, Varn cultists have established evangelical religious orders on Mon Calamari, Bengat, and Varn itself, much to the consternation of the locals.

*Solo and Fiolla in a hair-raising escape*

Heading back to the Corporate Sector, Solo was promised ten thousand credits to make a pickup on Lur. When he learned that the pickup consisted of slaves, he turned the tables on the slavers and freed their captives. Nonetheless, Solo stubbornly insisted that *somebody* still owed him ten thousand credits, and he doggedly followed the slavers' trail to Bonadan, where he met Fiolla of Lorrd, an assistant auditor-general of the CSA who enlisted Solo's help, hoping his smuggler connections might prove useful. When the slavers tried to jump them, Solo hopped aboard a swoop and used the racing skills Garris Shrike had taught him to throw off pursuit.

They followed the next link in the slaving chain to the planet Ammuud. En route, Solo and Fiolla booked passage aboard a luxury liner, while Chewbacca and the droids, accompanied by a CSA territorial manager named Odumin, took the *Falcon*.

Odumin was working to crack the slaving ring on his own and had an agent already in place on Ammuud. That agent was the legendary gunman Gallandro, who is still remembered in gunfighting circles for his blinding speed-draw. In the events that followed, Gallandro challenged one of the clan leaders to a duel. The clan leader chose Han Solo as his champion—and Gallandro backed down. Grateful at having averted the conflict, the ruling clan of Ammuud turned over all records they had relating to the slaving ring and their operations. Solo and Fiolla fought against the vengeful slavers and were rescued through the timely arrival of a CSA *Victory*-class Star Destroyer.

Territorial Manager Odumin, while grateful to the two smugglers for their help, fully intended to prosecute them for their numerous violations of the CSA legal code. With a fast maneuver, Solo managed to take both Odumin and Fiolla hostage;

then he successfully negotiated his unconditional release—and managed to have his ten thousand credits thrown in, to boot.

## Destitute in the Tion
### 1–0 B.B.Y.

All CSA naval patrols were issued holographs of the *Millennium Falcon* and orders to "destroy on sight." Realizing that their days in the Corporate Sector were over, Solo, Chewbacca, and the droids Bollux and Blue Max hopped through the Outer Rim for months, squandering their ten thousand credits on repairs, celebrations, and far-fetched, disastrous schemes. Bankrupt, they eventually wound up in the backwater Tion Hegemony, working as starship mechanics for Grigmin's Traveling Airshow.

Solo parlayed this embarrassing vocation into a slightly better job running cargo for the University of Rudrig. While there, he bumped into his old friend "Trooper" Badure, formerly a respected piloting instructor on Carida but now a desperate fortune hunter searching for the fabled lost ship, *Queen of Ranroon*. Built during the glory days of Xim the Despot, the *Queen of Ranroon* had once hauled the plunder of a thousand conquered worlds. Xim had constructed a vault on the planet Dellalt to house the treasure, but according to legend, the ship had vanished—along with all her wealth.

Accompanied by Badure and Skynx, a multilegged Ruurian academic, Solo landed on primitive Dellalt. The *Falcon* was promptly stolen by rivals of Badure's, who parked it on the opposite side of a mountain range. With no other ships available for hire on the uncivilized world, Solo and his companions were forced to head over the mountains on foot. During one fight for survival, Solo was slashed across the chin with a primitive hunting knife. The wound never healed properly and left a scar that is noticeable to this day.

Marching through the snowy highlands, they were captured by a strange cult called the Survivors. The inbred, backward descendants of the *Queen of Ranroon*'s honor guard, the Survivors had existed on Dellalt for more than a thousand generations, maintaining Xim the Despot's war-droid army in their secure mountain keep. Solo and the others escaped the Survivors and located the

*Millennium Falcon* at a contract-labor mining camp. The fast-gun mercenary Gallandro, anxious for a rematch with Solo, was waiting for him.

Before either party could make a move, rank on rank of the war droids of Xim marched into the clearing where they stood. Despite their antiquity, the droids followed their orders with ruthless efficiency and began to raze the camp. Bollux and Blue Max saved the day by transmitting a rhythmic frequency to the automaton army. At a point where the killer droids paraded over a rickety suspension bridge, the signal caused them to march in a pounding lockstep. Beneath their shaking, vibrating footfalls, the bridge bounced, swayed—and collapsed.

Gallandro, one of the few survivors, claimed that he would forget his enmity with Solo—in exchange for a full share of Xim's treasure. The *Falcon*'s quad laser cannons made short work of the vault gates, and when the group reached the hidden treasure chambers, Gallandro showed his true, traitorous stripes.

In a one-on-one blaster duel, Gallandro outdrew Solo and incapacitated the Corellian with a blaster wound to the shoulder. He then pursued the fleeing Skynx, but the multilegged Ruurian tricked the gunman into entering a lethal no-weapons zone. Dozens of laser bolts fried Gallandro to cinders.

It was the end of the gunman's legendary career, though he was survived by his infant daughter Anja, who lived on the colony world of Anobis. Anja Gallandro would cause new problems for Han Solo more than a quarter century later.

Even though they had located Xim the Despot's treasure, instead of the priceless jewels Solo had expected, they found only kiirium and mytag crystals—valuable war matériel in Xim's day, but worthless in the modern era. Skynx stayed behind on Dellalt to translate and catalog the vault's many historical artifacts, and Bollux and Blue Max remained with the Ruurian, rather than accompany Solo and Chewbacca back to Hutt Space.

Skynx eventually became the lead researcher on the Dellalt Project, as it came to be known in archaeological circles. After ten years of study, he succumbed to the life cycle of his species and metamorphosed into a mindless chroma-wing, though his offspring Amisus grew up to become the leader of the Unified Ruurian Colonies. Amisus

*The* Millennium Falcon

pledged the Ruurians' loyalty to Grand Admiral Thrawn during the Hand of Thrawn incident fifteen years after the Battle of Endor.

## Return to Ylesia
### 0 B.B.Y., MONTHS BEFORE THE BATTLE OF YAVIN

Han Solo and Chewbacca were welcomed back to Nar Shaddaa as returning heroes. But much had occurred in their absence. The Desilijic clan had surreptitiously poisoned Aruk the Hutt, ancient leader of the Besadii clan. During the two years that had followed, Aruk's offspring Durga had assumed control of Besadii with under-the-table help from Prince Xizor and the Black Sun criminal syndicate. When Durga uncovered the truth about his father's death, he slithered over to the Desilijic palace and challenged Clan Leader Jiliac to single combat under the Old Law. The opponents met, and the two Hutts crashed into each other with the full force of their mammoth bodies, using their huge tails as massive bludgeons. After an exhaust-

ing contest, Durga emerged victorious.

The death of Jiliac made Jabba the ruler of the Desilijic clan. Jabba immediately began to implement a scheme that would devastate the Besadii clan by eliminating their primary source of income—the spice-processing facilities on Ylesia. To do this, he contacted Han Solo's ex-love Bria Tharen.

Tharen had become an undercover operative in the growing resistance movement opposed to Emperor Palpatine. She had helped lay the groundwork for Mon Mothma's orchestration of the Corellian Treaty, which merged various dissident groups into a unified Rebel Alliance. Jabba agreed to help Tharen fund a full-scale Ylesian assault that would destroy the spice factories and leave Besadii with nothing. The Rebels would then be free to sell the spice on the open market to fund their growing insurgency.

On Nar Shaddaa, Han Solo and Bria Tharen fell in love all over again. Accompanied by Lando Calrissian, Solo agreed to join in the Ylesian assault with his fellow smugglers for half of the spice profits. While Jabba's assassins killed the Ylesian priests, the smugglers and Rebels landed on the steamy planet and assaulted the colonies on foot. Casualties were high, but before long the invaders had eliminated all opposition and secured the spice factories. In the aftermath, however, Commander Tharen and the Rebel troops double-crossed their smuggler allies and took all the spice for themselves.

The betrayal was a double blow for Solo. He and Tharen parted on the worst of terms, yet Solo's comrades assumed he'd been in on the whole operation from the beginning. And Lando Calrissian proclaimed that he never wanted to see Solo's face again as long as he lived.

## The Last Spice Run
### 0 B.B.Y., IMMEDIATELY PRIOR TO THE BATTLE OF YAVIN

Betrayed and rejected, Han and Chewbacca agreed to make a Kessel Run for Jabba on their way back to Nar Shaddaa. They were pursued by Imperial customs vessels tipped off by the spice supplier Moruth Doole, and the *Millennium Falcon* skimmed closer to the Maw black hole cluster than anyone had thought possible. Unfortunately, Solo was forced to dump his load of spice to avoid detection; the loss of such a valuable shipment angered Jabba greatly.

Since none of his former friends would loan money to a man they considered a traitor, Solo was forced to go to Tatooine in the hopes of earning enough credits to pay off Jabba. There, a bounty hunter from the past made an unexpected reappearance. Boba Fett wasn't interested in Solo's head this time; he wished only to relay a message. Fett had once crossed paths with Bria Tharen and had agreed to notify the woman's father in the event of her death. His sources had confirmed Tharen's demise during the Rebel Alliance's Operation Skyhook on Toprawa. Solo agreed to convey the tragic information to Tharen's surviving family.

With his first love dead, one chapter of Han Solo's life closed forever. But a new one was about to begin. The Corellian smuggler strode into the smoky darkness of the Mos Eisley cantina for a fateful rendezvous with two local desert dwellers, who needed passage to Alderaan. Soon Solo would have a large bounty placed on his head by Jabba the Hutt, for the subsequent tangle of events prevented him from paying back the crime lord. He was to be kept very busy indeed.

# LANDO CALRISSIAN

Unlike most reluctant heroes, Lando Calrissian has always been extremely forthcoming with details about his early entrepreneurial career. Unfortunately, each of the stories is more outlandish than the last, and they often conflict with each other. As a result, much about Calrissian remains a riddle.

One can only guess at the environment that spawned this ambitious man and the forces that shaped him into a charming gambler who always placed his biggest bet on the underdog. Luckily, Calrissian entered a high-profile career phase in his late twenties, so that his accounts began to be verified via independent eyewitnesses, historical records, and interviews with contemporaries such as Han Solo.

Approximately four years prior to the Battle of Yavin, Calrissian was already separating fools from their money as a professional sabacc gambler and con artist. Calrissian lost quite often, but when he won, he won big. His profits allowed him to indulge his tastes in clothing, fine cuisine, and members of the opposite sex.

He hopped around the galaxy in style aboard luxurious pleasure liners such as the *Star of Empire*, and so when he won a dilapidated Corellian freighter, the *Millennium Falcon*, from a sabacc player on Bespin who couldn't cover his debt, Calrissian had mixed feelings. It would be an expensive and time-consuming process to learn how to fly, but having his own mode of transportation would come in handy whenever he needed to make a quick getaway. Besides, the ship could always be sold for ready cash.

To learn the art of piloting, Calrissian hired a tutor—Han Solo, a smuggler, a fair sabacc player, and one of the best star jockeys in all of Hutt Space. He caught up with Solo at just the right time. The bounty hunter Boba Fett had Solo at gunpoint, but Calrissian intercepted the pair and turned the tables on Fett. He injected the bounty hunter with an obedience drug and ordered him to fly off to the rim of the galaxy. A grateful Solo offered to teach Calrissian how to pilot, at no charge.

## The Sharu Awaken
### 4 B.B.Y.

Calrissian was a quick study, but learning to single-pilot a freighter was a tricky proposition. Thus, he was still an abysmal aviator when he decided to pack up and leave Hutt Space for someplace—anyplace—else. He assumed that Boba Fett would be back looking for revenge, and Nar Shaddaa wasn't an easy place for a con man to find gullible marks.

So Calrissian headed for a wealthy asteroid field in the Oseon system, stuck in the outback Centrality region. Normally the Oseon was a gambler's paradise, but Calrissian encountered poor luck at the tables. He did win ownership of a droid, though it remained in storage in the neighboring Rafa system. Calrissian prepared to leave the Oseon immediately to collect his prize on Rafa IV.

Remembering the difficulty he'd had landing the *Millennium Falcon* on Oseon 2795, Calrissian rented an unnamed Class Five pilot droid to handle the much more difficult task of an atmospheric touchdown on Rafa IV.

Every planet in the Rafa system was covered with colossal plastic pyramids built by the ancient Sharu. At the time of Calrissian's visit, the Sharu were considered a long-vanished aboriginal species; their impregnable pyramids had never been opened or explored. The present natives of the sys-

*An ancient secret revealed*

tem were referred to as the Toka, or "Broken People." To all appearances the Toka were primitive and simpleminded, and they were exploited by the human colonists as cheap slave labor.

When Calrissian arrived in the Rafa system to pick up his newly won droid, the robot turned out to be a strange, starfish-shaped construction named Vuffi Raa, boasting five detachable limbs and a perky personality; immediately, Calrissian recognized there was more to this unusual droid than was readily apparent.

Calrissian was soon arrested on charges trumped up by the colonial governor. He and his new droid were forcibly enlisted on behalf of Rokur Gepta, the Sorcerer of Tund. The mysterious gray-cloaked wizard was a disciple of ancient Sith teachings and eager to get his hands on a fabulous artifact known as the Mindharp of Sharu.

Calrissian was given a transdimensional key designed to unlock the Mindharp's pyramid. Unfortunately, no one knew exactly which pyramid that was, and the Rafa system was choked with thousands of the plastic ziggurats. Calrissian decided to start on the neighboring world of Rafa V, home to the largest Sharu structure of all, but was ambushed by an army of Toka archers. The hostile primitives tied Calrissian to a crystalline lifetree, hoping he would freeze to death during the night.

But Vuffi Raa rescued his master, and the two of them investigated the most massive pyramid. There, they discovered the Mindharp—it was a strange object that constantly changed form as it shifted through dimensions—and removed it from its eons-old place of rest.

Calrissian discovered that the ancient Sharu once had been threatened by an unimaginably powerful alien entity. To ensure their own survival, the Sharu had gone underground, hiding their cities beneath the plastic pyramids and using crystalline life-orchards to temporarily drain their own intelligence. They had also spread rumors of a fabulous treasure—the Mindharp of Sharu. When another civilization proved advanced enough to reactivate the Mindharp, the Sharu would know it was safe to come out of hiding.

Rafa IV's colonial governor greedily took the Mindharp and sentenced the gambler to a lifetime of hard labor in a penal colony. Vuffi Raa freed him again, but the planet began to rock with violent quakes and tremors.

The colonial governor had activated the Mindharp, and the artifact's subharmonic emanations stimulated a complete reversal of the social order throughout the entire planetary system. The pyramids crumbled, and bizarre new cities emerged from the dust. Intelligence and memories were restored to the primitive Toka, making them into the legendary Sharu once again.

For weeks the Rafa system was completely blockaded, and when the inexplicable interdiction field suddenly vanished, the first visitors beheld an utterly changed society. The new cities were frighteningly alien, and the Sharu appeared to care little for the concerns of "lesser" sentients. Many of the human cities had been damaged beyond repair in the quakes, and the surviving colonists chose not to remain behind in a place where they were the objects of scorn. Trade with the Rafa system dried up virtually overnight.

On the other hand, the event was a boon to scientists, who descended on Rafa in droves. For his part in the transformation, Calrissian was hailed as a hero. While the Sharu did not shoo the researchers away, neither did they choose to cooperate. Detailed information on Sharu history and technology is still an elusive unknown.

Apparently, Emperor Palpatine felt threatened enough by the Sharu to post a permanent picket guard on the system's outer fringes, though he never made a military move against the advanced race. The New Republic has limited its involvement with the Sharu to a five-hundred-member, government-funded research team, staffed by the Obroan Institute for Archaeology.

### The Battle of Nar Shaddaa
3 B.B.Y.

Calrissian and Vuffi Raa fled the system mere hours after the Mindharp's activation, escaping to the safety of hyperspace with a full cargo of rare life crystals in the *Falcon*'s hold. When worn around the neck, life crystals were rumored to increase a person's life span; thus, they were a highly profitable Rafa export. After the Sharu reemergence, life crystals were suddenly in limited quantity.

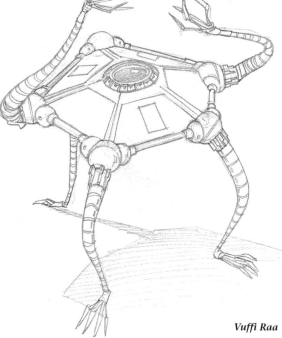

*Vuffi Raa*

Calrissian acquired the last load of life crystals before the Sharu locked down all trade—which meant he could set his own price. The gambler cleared nearly a quarter of a million credits on the deal.

He returned to Nar Shaddaa and, with a portion of his credits, purchased a used-starship lot from a dissatisfied Duros salesman. But running the business proved more difficult and expensive than he had anticipated, despite the able assistance of Vuffi Raa. Calrissian was already considering cutting his losses—when the Empire invaded the system.

Along with hundreds of other smugglers, Calrissian took to the sky and successfully blunted the Imperial offensive in the Battle of Nar Shaddaa. Like a born maestro, Vuffi Raa piloted the *Millennium Falcon* through the blaster barrages.

But the Battle of Nar Shaddaa signaled the end of Lando's used-starship lot. Calrissian, feeling a sense of obligation to his fellow outlaws, had donated his entire inventory for the space skirmish. When the dust cleared, less than a tenth of his stock remained spaceworthy. Privately, Calrissian sold his old friend Roa 90 percent ownership in the lot, at a considerable loss, then puzzled over how to salvage his career.

He turned his sights toward Cloud City's Yarith Bespin casino, which shortly would be hosting the regional sabacc championships. It was the perfect opportunity for Calrissian to recoup his losses. Unfortunately, the entry fee was ten thousand credits. Having paid off his creditors, Calrissian didn't even have a tenth that amount. Discouraged, he decided to return to the Centrality with Vuffi Raa.

There, Calrissian used the *Falcon* for its original cargo-hauling purpose, but he was a washout as an interstellar trader. Tariffs, import fees, and sales licenses sucked his credit account dry. Thus, when he received an invitation to play sabacc in the Oseon system, Calrissian jumped at the chance.

## Back to the Oseon
### 3 B.B.Y.

Calrissian and Vuffi Raa arrived just in time for the annual Flamewind. For three weeks each year, stellar flares interact with ionized vapors to create a stunning visual feast in brilliant pulsing hues of green, yellow, blue, orange, and every color between.

The Oseon asteroid belts are infamous playgrounds for the wealthy and powerful, but things get even more decadent during the Flamewind. Since it's impossible to navigate during the event, guests are stuck in the system until the breathtaking light show subsides.

Upon his arrival, Calrissian was apprehended by the administrator senior of the Oseon system and forced to participate in a dangerous drug bust. The trillionaire industrialist Bohhuah Mutdah, drug addict and sole owner of Oseon 5792, had made some powerful enemies in the upper echelons of the Imperial law-enforcement community. The administrator was authorized to arrest him in a sting operation.

Posing as Mutdah's drug dealer, Calrissian ferried two drug-enforcement agents to Oseon 5792, through the heart of the Flamewind. It was almost impossible to navigate through the blinding sheets of color, and the accompanying radiation storms nearly drove them all mad. Eventually, however, they reached Oseon 5792. As Calrissian made the drug exchange, the two agents burst in to place Mutdah under arrest.

Ten seconds later, both agents were dead.

As Calrissian looked on in astonishment, Mutdah set down his blaster and began to shimmer and fold in a mindbending display. The disguise melted away, revealing a familiar figure—Rokur Gepta, the Sorcerer of Tund, whom Calrissian had outwitted with the Mindharp of Sharu.

In hindsight, the fact that Gepta took the time to insinuate himself into this affair is remarkable, given that his only motive was a deep-seated hatred of Lando Calrissian. Gepta blamed the rogue gambler for the loss of the Sharu artifact, and he was spiteful enough to carry a grudge across light-years. He also enjoyed an amicable relationship with Emperor Palpatine, who had given the sorcerer a decommissioned Republic cruiser and granted him near-total autonomy within the confines of the Centrality. Gepta could command Imperial naval units and call in TIE bomber airstrikes on recalcitrant worlds. It is a testament to Calrissian's notoriety that this power was completely subverted to making his life miserable.

Calrissian was saved when a squadron of starfighters bearing Renatasian markings appeared outside the asteroid's canopy, lasers blazing. The transparisteel dome shattered, and Calrissian narrowly reached his ship through the swirling air and

*A gambler and his nemesis*

debris. The *Falcon* escaped just as the Renatasians hurled a towed Dreadnaught engine straight into the asteroid, destroying it utterly.

The timely intervention was a happy coincidence; the starfighters hadn't been gunning for either Calrissian or Rokur Gepta, but rather for the harmless but mysterious droid Vuffi Raa: Thirteen years prior to the Battle of Yavin, Renatasia, one of many "lost" human colonies, had been rediscovered in a seldom-visited pocket of the Centrality. Obeying his programming, Vuffi Raa had landed on Renatasia and paved the way for an Imperial takeover. While just as brutal as the devastation of Caamas, the invasion of Renatasia received little outside attention and failed to inspire outrage in the senate. Nevertheless, a group of handpicked natives had commandeered twelve aging starfighters and vowed to kill the "Butcher of Renatasia."

Calrissian, while sympathetic to the Renatasians, was unwilling to help them annihilate his closest friend. He flew away, leaving them behind in the Oseon, using the Flamewind radiation to mask his escape. Nonetheless, the Renatasians soon teamed up with Rokur Gepta, who also had escaped the destruction of Oseon 5792. Together they continued their search for Calrissian and Vuffi Raa.

## Fortune Won, Fortune Lost
### 3 B.B.Y.

The aftermath of the Mutdah drug bust turned out to be the most fortuitous turn of events Lando Calrissian *ever* experienced. During the chaos of his escape, Calrissian lifted the case containing Mutdah's drug payment. In one day, he went from insolvency to being a millionaire twenty times over.

Like all things with Calrissian, though, it didn't last. He deposited the money in small lump sums across numerous bank accounts, to reduce suspicion and the risk of a financial audit. Fifty thousand credits—more than enough to cover the sabacc tournament entry fee—went into the bank first, then were electronically transferred to a numbered account on Aargau. Calrissian then departed in the *Millennium Falcon* for Dela, the Centrality's financial hub, to deposit the rest of his money.

Through sheer dumb luck, he arrived at Dela

*The Oswaft versus the Empire*

during the middle of a pirate attack by Drea Renthal's gang. Renthal, the infamous "pirate queen," possessed one of the largest freebooter fleets in the galaxy and had fought against the Imperials in the Battle of Nar Shaddaa.

The *Falcon* was captured and boarded. When the pirate raiders discovered the astonishing sum stashed in Mutdah's lockbox, Calrissian was brought before Renthal. The queen was an attractive woman, and Calrissian turned his charm up to maximum wattage in the hope of convincing her to leave him at least a token portion of the cash. He failed, but it wasn't to be the last time Calrissian and Renthal would cross paths.

## To Save the ThonBoka
### 3–2.5 B.B.Y.

With the sabacc tournament mere months away, Calrissian and Vuffi Raa made a new and unusual friend—Lehesu of the Oswaft. The Oswaft are an extremely reclusive species of gigantic vacuum-breathers who resemble a cross between a Corellian sea ray and an Arkanian jellyfish. The Oswaft communicate via an intense, information-dense language and possess the ability to make natural hyperspace jumps.

The Centrality had known of the Oswaft's existence for generations, but the aliens hadn't come to the attention of the Emperor until just before Calrissian's debacle at Dela. Mistrustful of an intelligent species that could traverse hyperspace at will, Palpatine issued orders to exterminate the Oswaft. Five hundred capital ships blockaded the "mouth" of the creatures' home, a sack-shaped nebula known as the StarCave or the ThonBoka. The fleet's *Carrack*-class cruisers were modified to emit electric charges that would contaminate the interstellar plankton that drifted inside the nebula. With their sole source of nutrients poisoned, the Oswaft began to starve.

Lehesu's desperate pleas spurred Calrissian and Vuffi Raa to action. The *Millennium Falcon* ran the Imperial blockade, and Calrissian met with the besieged Oswaft elders—each colossal creature nearly a kilometer in diameter. Since the Oswaft had no conception of warfare, Calrissian was forced to improvise a desperate plan of survival. The alien defenders synthesized Oswaft-shaped excretions through their pores, so that the Imperial gunners shot at false targets and inflicted friendly fire on their own ships. Simultaneously, many Oswaft "shouted" at the warships; their powerful voice-streams destroyed many enemy vessels.

The fighting abruptly ceased when a vengeful Rokur Gepta arrived in his battleship and ordered the fleet to stand down. He delivered a startlingly bitter ultimatum: he would fight Lando Calrissian, one on one, in the zero-gravity vacuum between the ships. If Calrissian refused, he would fire an electromagnetic torpedo and lethally irradiate everything in the nebula.

The holographic log recorder aboard the Star Destroyer *Eminence* recorded the single combat, much to the gratitude of future historians. Zipped up in spacesuits, Calrissian and the Sorcerer of Tund faced off in the middle of the watching fleet. They shot at one another while maneuvering for position with jet packs. One of Calrissian's wild shots caught Gepta in the ankle. With a shriek, the sorcerer's form withered and disappeared.

It is unknown whether Emperor Palpatine had been aware that Rokur Gepta was actually a Croke, a tiny snail-like creature from the Unknown Regions. The Emperor had long been interested in the Sorcerers of Tund, since their religious teachings were based on an archaic interpretation of original Sith doctrine. Gepta had used his Croke powers of illusion to infiltrate that secret society, co-opt its Sith teachings, and then annihilate it; Tund is now an uninhabited, irradiated wasteland. The death of Gepta marked an end to the Sorcerers of Tund.

The Imperial fleet responded to Gepta's demise with a hail of laser fire. Suddenly, a booming cry burst across all comm channels: *"Cease fire or be destroyed!"* Thousands of gargantuan, fifty-kilometer-wide metallic spheres rapidly surrounded the armada on all sides. The new arrivals were self-aware droids, hailing from deep in the Unknown Regions. They had come for Vuffi Raa, their "child."

Vuffi Raa had been constructed by the mechanical beings for the purpose of recording new experiences throughout the galaxy. Now that his purpose had been fulfilled, Vuffi Raa departed with his progenitors. The Imperial fleet quietly withdrew, abandoning their mission of Oswaft genocide.

The mysterious droids disappeared into the vastness of the Unknown Regions. Though there is no proof that they have ever reappeared, numerous eyewitness reports tell of massive objects roughly matching the droids' appearance. These have been compiled from all over the New Republic, including a hundred-thousand-person mass sighting documented during the Priole Danna festival on Lamuir IV. While many of these anecdotes may have commonplace explanations, it remains possible the entities have been observing galactic civilization from a distance, for their own purposes.

## Entrepreneurism
## 2.5–0 B.B.Y.

Calrissian was sorry to see his companion go, but through the strange droid's tutelage, he had learned a great deal about starship piloting. Furthermore, the grateful Oswaft had given him a full cargo hold of precious gemstones as a generous farewell gift. He invested the gemstones in a berubium mine in the Borgo asteroid belt and then lost the fortune again when the mine proved to be worthless. Down to nothing, Calrissian withdrew the fifty thousand credits from his numbered account and waited for the sabacc tournament.

Two things made the waiting easier. The first was his old used-spaceship lot on Nar Shaddaa. Calrissian picked up the pieces of the struggling business and hired several new managers. The second was Drea Renthal, the pirate queen. Though he had good reason to carry a grudge against her, Calrissian realized that he and Renthal shared a similar outlook on life. Against all odds, the two became romantically entangled—at least for a few weeks.

The sabacc tournament on Cloud City proved a crushing disappointment for Calrissian, however. The gambler made it to the final championship round and found himself facing his old friend Han Solo—a fair sabacc player, but far from a master of the game. When the final card-chips were played, though, Solo had won an impressive stack of credits and sole ownership of the *Millennium Falcon*.

After the match, Calrissian was so impoverished that he was forced to swallow his pride and ask Solo for a fifteen-hundred-credit loan. Over the next year, he turned the small sum into hundreds of thousands of credits by gambling with the galaxy's high rollers. He also carried out several masterly con jobs against the Imperials, including a scam on Pesmenben IV that was similar to the berubium mine scenario that had ruined him.

Calrissian's second run-in with Boba Fett occurred aboard a luxury liner, where Fett had come to capture Rebel Alliance commander Bria Tharen. He picked up Calrissian for use as an expendable hostage, but fortunately, a chance attack by Drea Renthal's star pirates saved both their lives. Renthal put up a substantial sum to buy Calrissian's and Tharen's freedom.

Bria Tharen eventually joined forces with the Desilijic Hutts to coordinate a massive attack on the spice-processing planet Ylesia. Lando Calrissian participated in the assault, fighting alongside Han Solo. But when the combined Rebel and smuggler armies had wiped out all resistance, Bria Tharen swindled her allies. The Rebels departed with all the spice, leaving the smugglers with nothing.

Lando Calrissian, like many others, blamed Solo for the double cross. When Solo came to Calrissian to ask for a loan to pay off Jabba the Hutt, Calrissian threw him against the wall and declared their friendship to be a thing of the past.

## "The Respectable One"
### 0–3 A.B.Y.

The Rebels won the Battle of Yavin not long afterward, but Lando Calrissian was busy with larger and larger escapades. Five months after Yavin, Calrissian shipped a denta bean cargo to the agricultural planet Taanab and was caught on the surface during a pirate raid. Instead of huddling and waiting for the squall to blow over, Calrissian accepted the wager of a drunken cantina patron and flew an unnamed freighter against the notorious Norulac freebooters. The battle was short and one-sided—Calrissian smashed and humiliated the pirate fleet, even dumping his outgoing cargo of electrified netting in order to tangle the enemy ships into one helpless, immovable lump.

He was a hero on Taanab, but his fame didn't extend past the sector's borders. That changed, however, when TriNebulon News picked up the story months later and broadcast it across the newsnets. Calrissian became a minor celebrity and the subject of endless "can you believe it" barroom banter. Years later, this notoriety is precisely what would convince Alliance High Command to promote Calrissian to the rank of general, just prior to the Battle of Endor.

Calrissian briefly investigated Hologram Fun World as a possible investment opportunity and got caught up in the Imperials' Project Starscream. (Calrissian would assume ownership of Hologram Fun World one year after the Battle of Endor; this also led to his interest in investing in a large family amusement center on Cloud City, the SkyCenter Galleria.)

Calrissian's greatest coup, however, came in a sabacc game held in the Trest casino on Bespin. His opponent was Dominic Raynor, Cloud City's baron administrator. By the time Raynor folded his cards in frustration, Calrissian had won the title of baron administrator—and all the power that came with it.

To his credit, Calrissian took his new political assignment very seriously. He charmed the citizenry of Cloud City and won over the Exex business administration board. He established an excellent working relationship with the city's computer coordinator, a cyborg named Lobot. He staved off the advances of the Mining Guild and deflected the attention of the Empire, allowing business to continue as usual, despite the growing Rebellion.

He hired a squadron of commando pilots to protect the city from pirate raids. When the droid EV-9D9 went psychotic and dismantled a quarter of the city's droid population, he salvaged the situation and enacted new security procedures. He increased net Tibanna gas mining profits by over 35 percent and turned Cloud City into a stable, prosperous center of industry. Millions of sentients looked to him for their well-being.

Which is why the arrival of two intruders—Han Solo and Darth Vader—along with a third unwelcome interloper, Boba Fett, threw Calrissian into a moral quandary. He balanced the life of Solo against the welfare of an entire city and found his friend wanting. But Calrissian wasn't so foolish that he would keep on playing when the Empire had stacked the deck.

Fortunately for the fate of the galaxy, the gambler made the right decision in the end.

## THE SKYWALKERS

Like a ray of hope in the darkest night, the Skywalker twins emerged from one of the galaxy's most turbulent periods to reverse a generation of injustice and genocide. Luke Skywalker and Leia Organa were destined for great things from the moment of their birth and have arguably influenced modern history more than any other duo.

Luke Skywalker, now a Jedi Master, brought the Jedi Knights back from extinction and presided over a new generation of Force-strong galactic guardians. Leia Organa, the second chief of state of the New Republic, helped overthrow the Empire and shepherded the civilized galaxy through some of its bleakest years.

The two grew up in different foster homes on opposite sides of the civilized galaxy and consequently know very little of how they came to be placed in the care of their guardians. Historians have pieced together this critical chronicle as precisely as possible, though the end result contains an inevitable amount of speculation and supposition.

The lineage of the Skywalker twins is, quite simply, epic. Their father was Anakin Skywalker, one of the most powerful Jedi Knights in history, whose dark actions under the name Darth Vader nearly brought an end to that order. Their mother was a queen, who bestowed upon her children a royal birthright despite their adopted upbringings.

Both infants were amazingly strong in the Force. Emperor Palpatine, who feared rival Force users so much that he had overseen the Jedi Purge, realized that Anakin Skywalker's heirs could possess

enough latent power to pose a serious threat to his reign. The great Jedi Knight Obi-Wan Kenobi is believed to have recognized this danger and hidden the newborns, both from the Emperor and from their own father. In the care of others, he hoped, the twins would develop into finely honed weapons that would doom the Emperor in the long run.

Kenobi placed Luke with Owen and Beru Lars, hardworking moisture farmers on the sun-seared

*The Skywalker twins*

planet Tatooine. The harsh desert world had been Anakin Skywalker's boyhood home, and a remote possibility did exist that Vader could uncover his son's hiding place. Owen and Beru Lars, however, were low-profile isolationists, and Kenobi remained behind on Tatooine as added insurance. In his sparse hermitage in the Jundland Wastes, "Old Ben" Kenobi hid from Emperor Palpatine and watched over young Luke, waiting for the day when the boy would reach manhood and fulfill a destiny.

Leia's upbringing was the polar opposite of her brother's. Raised on the pacifist planet Alderaan by Bail Prestor Organa, Obi-Wan Kenobi's commander in the Clone Wars, Leia lived a life of privilege and responsibility. House Organa was the royal family of Alderaan, and Leia was accorded all the prerogatives due a princess.

Like her mother, Leia became a confident, poised young woman and a quick political thinker. In the ruling city of Aldera, Leia studied diplomacy, government, and languages, and played in the palace corridors with her best friend Winter. Senator Bail Organa often brought his adopted

daughter on trips to other worlds, including the Republic capital planet of Coruscant, and attended to her physical development by hiring weapons master Giles Durane to instruct Leia in the arts of self-defense and marksmanship. While still in her teens, Leia became the youngest representative ever elected to the Imperial Senate.

The general public did not learn of Luke and Leia's sinister lineage until years after the Battle of Endor. In fact, due to their having been raised apart, the two siblings did not even realize they were brother and sister until four years after Leia's rescue from the Death Star battle station.

In the wake of the public revelation regarding Darth Vader's ancestry, some partisan politicians have accused Leia Organa of following in her father's footsteps. However, most citizens have been surprisingly conciliatory toward the offspring of Vader, holding the view that children should not be punished for the transgressions of their parents. In any case, the good that Luke and Leia have accomplished over the decades weighs heavier than any shadow legacy.

# PART IV

# REBELLION AGAINST THE EMPIRE

## THE REBELLION BEGINS

### The Death Star Construction
### 3-0 B.B.Y.

After the turmoil in the Republic Senate, after Palpatine had risen to power, after the slaughter of the Jedi Knights, the Emperor then decided to create weapons as great in stature as his Empire itself. He saw this as a way to consolidate his strength and add more iron to his hand. Thus, Palpatine set about gathering the best minds, whose technical knowledge could be turned to destruction.

Because of concerns expressed by certain senators, the Emperor chose to have this work performed in secret. Once the weapons were completed and placed at the disposal of his Imperial space fleet, he felt he would never again need to worry about the objections voiced by the weak parasites of the dying Republic.

Palpatine found ways to divert funds, appropriate the resources of entire planetary systems, and bury any questions in a maze of bureaucratic paperwork; the corrupt government excelled at such loopholes. He enlisted the aid of one of his greatest military strategists, Grand Moff Tarkin, who searched for the perfect isolated place where he would build a guarded and hidden facility that would be secure and inaccessible from rebellious ears.

In the vicinity of Kessel, an exotic grouping of black holes formed an extreme navigational hazard known as the Maw. This provided a backdrop for the famed Kessel Run, a dangerous high-speed route used by smugglers. At the exact center of the gravitational trap lay an island of stability, where the deadly singularities canceled each other. After several suicide scouts attempted to map the interior of the Maw, a safe though convoluted route was found. Tarkin chose this place, the universe's own fortress, as the site for his new top secret weapons installation.

Construction slaves and droid-controlled equipment hauled a group of small asteroids inside and joined them together. Buildings and vacuum facilities were erected and laboratories stocked. Personnel were assigned permanently, and their records were altered to indicate that they had died in the line of duty. Next, Tarkin gathered the best researchers in secret from across the Empire. Some came willingly—such as the driven and partially insane weapons designer Umak Leth and the ambitious engineer Bevel Lemelisk, both of whom were eager to use the best facilities and unlimited funding that Tarkin could arrange for them.

Other researchers included the great Dr. Ohran Keldor and a small group of Mrlssi who excelled at designing life-support systems for extremely large inhabited space stations. Captive scientists were snatched unsuspecting, stolen for their remarkable talents. One of the greatest of these kidnapped researchers was Qwi Xux, an Omwati female, ethereal and beautiful, who possessed a faint sheen of feathers instead of hair. She was the only survivor of a large group of students who had been put through rigorous tests by Tarkin himself.

The austere research station was run by a Twi'lek administrator named Tol Sivron and was guarded by four Imperial Star Destroyers. This small but powerful battle fleet was commanded by

Daala, one of Tarkin's greatest students and also his lover. Upon giving her this assignment, Tarkin had increased her rank to admiral, making her the highest-ranking female in the Imperial military. Daala remained isolated, never questioning her orders; her job was to ensure that the scientists in the research station continued to work without interruption.

For years, the intensive design process continued. Maw scientists proposed their ideas, and Tol Sivron demanded demonstrations and further reports. Concepts were rejected, others modified, until finally Grand Moff Tarkin returned to the Emperor with a blueprint and a recommendation. Weapons-systems developer Umak Leth and project engineer Bevel Lemelisk proposed a moon-sized battle station that boasted a gigantic superlaser powerful enough to break a planet into rubble.

The grand moff was eager to establish his Tarkin Doctrine in the Outer Rim territories. Its key precept was "Rule through fear of force rather than by force itself," which the Emperor adapted to mean

*Tarkin and Lemelisk —*
*architects of terror*

"Rule through fear instead of through idealistic government agencies." The battle station would crush any resistance, any question of the Emperor's supremacy. With the Death Star, unruly worlds could be simply erased.

Pleased, the Emperor approved the plans for a prototype to test the Death Star concept, since the monumental cost of a final station would never be undertaken without a proof-of-principle test. Inside Maw Installation, work crews of Wookiee slaves assembled a scaled-down version of the core superlaser and mounted it inside a stripped-down superstructure, an armillary sphere similar to the skeleton employed in the final design.

When the superlaser proved as effective as expected, the construction of the full-scale Death Star began under the guidance of Bevel Lemelisk as chief engineer and was supervised by Darth Vader himself. The station was built in orbit around the penitentiary planet Despayre in the Horuz system, using labor taken from the prison exiles as well as Wookiee slaves. Throughout the long construction, Tarkin's personal slave, the Mon Calamarian known as Ackbar—later to command the Rebel fleet—was forced to cooperate, though Ackbar knew how much bloodshed the Emperor would cause with such a terror weapon.

Despite the intense secrecy and security shrouding the project, delays, shortages, and sabotage plagued the huge construction site. When Tarkin and his engineer began to lose control of the schedule, however, a grim Darth Vader came to the site and executed several workers and supervisors. Soon thereafter, the Death Star was back on track.

The Rebel Alliance learned of the Death Star project through an informant on Ralltiir; the information was later confirmed by the Empire's own Lord Tion. Upon the station's completion, but before it could be tested, an assassination attempt nearly took Tarkin's life. He avoided death, but his Mon Calamarian slave Ackbar did escape and soon joined the Rebels.

Knowing that the Alliance's only chance lay in obtaining a copy of the station's blueprints and analyzing them for vulnerabilities, Bail Organa and Mon Mothma set up multiple plans for the capture

*Slavery on Despayre*

operation. Toprawan rebels, in a raid on a space convoy, stole most of the technical information before it could be transferred to the Imperial Information Center. On Danuta, an untested Alliance agent and former stormtrooper officer named Kyle Katarn broke into an Imperial facility and made off with another set of plans. When combined, the two readouts formed a complete schematic of the Death Star from pole to pole.

But Imperial Intelligence learned of the leak. Star Destroyers blockaded the Toprawa system while stormtroopers moved in to crush the Rebels and recover the plans. The Alliance's only hope was a risky in-system data transmission. Princess Leia Organa, adopted daughter of Bail Organa, arrived in the Toprawa system under cover of diplomatic immunity. Her consular ship *Tantive IV*

intercepted the Death Star plans and vanished into hyperspace. Tragically, the Rebels on Toprawa—led by Commander Bria Tharen and Red Hand Squadron—were all killed.

With the Empire's secret weapon exposed, Darth Vader pursued the fleeing princess in the Imperial Star Destroyer *Devastator*. He vowed to retrieve the stolen information, at any cost.

## Preparations for Battle
**0 B.B.Y.**

Just before the Rebel leaders authorized the Toprawan operations to capture the Death Star plans, Mon Mothma grew alarmed at the number of Imperial Intelligence agents who were digging for any Rebel activity. She wisely instructed Jan

Dodonna—the retired general in charge of the Dantooine headquarters base—to move his operations to an even more isolated facility—the Massassi ruins on the fourth moon of Yavin.

Dodonna himself was an experienced fighter, a brilliant tactician, and had been one of the first captains of a Republic Star Destroyer. Though loyal to his government, Dodonna had grown disturbed by the Emperor's harsh tactics. Rather than speak out and commit what he considered treason, however, Dodonna had simply offered his resignation, which was gladly accepted by younger Imperial military commanders. When the Empire determined they couldn't retrain or convert Dodonna, a secret order was issued for his prompt and quiet execution.

Learning of the termination instructions, Mon Mothma had sent a desperate message to inform him and to sway him to her cause. Dodonna initially refused; according to his rigid military standards, the Rebellion was a treasonous insurrection against the lawful government. But when Imperial assassination forces charged in unannounced and tried to kill him in cold blood, Dodonna fled in his nightshirt, fighting his way out. Spurred by that cowardly betrayal, Dodonna became a staunch member of the Alliance.

Mon Mothma's suspicions about the Dantooine headquarters proved correct when an Imperial tracking device was found in a cargo shipment. Efficiently and quickly, General Dodonna stripped and abandoned the base and moved all supplies to the jungle moon of Yavin. There, he and his growing number of troops waited for battle.

As an inevitable outgrowth of the Corellian Treaty, the document that had formally united the various anti-Empire resistance groups, Mon Mothma issued a strongly worded Declaration of Rebellion against Palpatine and his policies. In response to this widely disseminated Declaration, the Emperor formally disbanded the Imperial Senate, sweeping away the final vestiges of the Old Republic. Palpatine placed regional governors, ruthless grand moffs like Tarkin, in direct control over the sectors.

If it hadn't been apparent before, it was blindingly obvious now: The conflict between Rebel Alliance and Empire could never be settled by political means.

## The Capture of Princess Leia
0 B.B.Y.

Leia Organa, young and fresh and exuberant, disseminated much of the propaganda and delivered many important coded messages that helped to bind the Alliance together. Because of her outgoing nature, she traveled from world to world on well-publicized "mercy missions," which were often a cover for her Rebel activities. Darth Vader and the Emperor suspected Organa's involvement, but could never prove it.

Organa was the perfect agent to receive the Death Star plans from the Toprawan rebels, and having done so, she immediately set course back to Alderaan, where she planned to pass along the plans to her adopted father Bail Organa and to the other leaders of the Rebellion. Time was of the essence. If the Death Star became operational, the battle station could launch an unparalleled reign of terror across the entire galaxy.

Darth Vader was ruthless in the pursuit of his quarry. Vader's Star Destroyer *Devastator* easily caught up with Organa's much smaller *Tantive IV* at the Outer Rim world of Tatooine. The tiny vessel was boarded by Imperial stormtroopers, and in the ensuing firefight, Organa managed to plant the Death Star readouts inside a small astromech droid. This droid, R2-D2, was instructed to deliver the plans to a reclusive Jedi Knight and hero from the Clone Wars, General Obi-Wan Kenobi, who had gone into isolation on Tatooine. R2-D2, along with his counterpart, protocol droid C-3PO, escaped the battle in a tiny escape pod, but the princess was captured.

Organa was brought as a prisoner to Grand Moff Tarkin's newly completed battle station. There, she resisted Vader's rigorous interrogation methods and continued to conceal the location of the secret Rebel base. Tarkin, anxious to test his new Death Star and to reinforce the Emperor's iron grip, found another way to coerce her: he threatened to destroy Alderaan, Organa's peaceful homeworld, unless she divulged the information he requested.

Knowing full well the capabilities of the superweapon, and Tarkin's own record for ruthlessness, Organa understood he was not bluffing.

*The last hours of Alderaan*

Reluctantly, she gave the location of the Dantooine base, hoping that it had already been abandoned, as planned. Tarkin, though, decided to use Alderaan as a brutal example for the Rebels and the entire galaxy.

In one of the darkest acts committed by the Empire, the Death Star destroyed Alderaan and its billions of inhabitants, with no warning. Leia Organa was returned to the detention block and scheduled for execution.

## A New Hope
### 0 B.B.Y.

At the same time Princess Leia was being sentenced, events unfolding on the desert world of Tatooine would ultimately shape the Emperor's defeat. The two droids carrying the stolen Death Star plans were captured by Jawa traders and sold to an out-of-the-way moisture farm. There, a young farmer named Luke Skywalker accidentally discovered Organa's holomessage hidden inside R2-D2.

It was R2-D2 who led Skywalker to the reclusive Jedi Knight, Obi-Wan Kenobi. Seeking to complete his mission for Leia Organa, the R2 unit escaped into the desolate Tatooine wastes. Skywalker and C-3PO located him, only to be attacked by savage desert dwellers known as Tusken Raiders. Kenobi intervened and took the trio back to his desert dwelling, where Leia's recording was finally delivered to its intended recipient.

Reluctantly, Kenobi agreed to help take the Death Star plans to Senator Bail Organa on Alderaan—in part driven by another, unspoken incentive. Kenobi alone knew that Luke Skywalker was actually the son of Anakin Skywalker, the Jedi who had become Darth Vader. And Luke showed a great affinity for the Force.

Skywalker's home was destroyed by Imperials searching for the droids. His adopted aunt and uncle were killed, and he had no choice but to accompany Kenobi on his mission.

As the Imperial net tightened around Tatooine, Kenobi commissioned a pair of small-time smugglers—Han Solo and his copilot Chewbacca—to spirit them away. Solo's ship, the *Millennium Falcon*, barely escaped Imperial troops and TIE fighters as they blasted away from Tatooine.

En route to Alderaan, Kenobi began training Skywalker in the ways of the Force. When they arrived in the Alderaan system, however, they found that the entire planet had been destroyed, and their vessel was captured by the Death Star.

Attempting to escape from the battle station, Skywalker discovered that Leia Organa herself was being held prisoner there, and convinced Solo to help in her rescue. Kenobi, meanwhile, sabotaged the tractor beam that prevented their ship from fleeing. But before he could return to the ren-

*Obi-Wan Kenobi's sacrifice*

dezvous point, Kenobi encountered his nemesis and former student, Darth Vader. While Skywalker, Solo, Organa, and Chewbacca returned to the *Falcon*, ready to fight their way out, the great Jedi Obi-Wan Kenobi sacrificed his life to let them get away.

Bearing the precious Death Star plans, the *Falcon* raced into hyperspace and to the new Rebel base on Yavin 4, despite the fact that the Imperials had placed a tracer on their ship. On the jungle moon, General Dodonna and his team of experts frantically studied the battle station's design to find a flaw, even as the station itself arrived in the system to destroy the base.

The Rebels' only chance was to send a small ship, which would target a tiny thermal exhaust port on the surface of the Death Star. Proton torpedoes deposited into the shaft would reach the hypermatter core and trigger a chain reaction.

Thus, as the Death Star moved into a firing position from which it could destroy the jungle moon, swarms of small Rebel fighters attacked like stinging insects. Imperial TIE fighters, including one flown by Vader, swarmed out in response. Many Rebels died in the Battle of Yavin, but one pilot—Skywalker himself, using his newfound skills with the Force—scored a direct hit. This resulted in the destruction of the Death Star and the death of Tarkin.

It was an enormous victory for the Rebel Alliance.

## Impact and Consequences
### 0–0.5 A.B.Y.

In his own advanced TIE fighter, Darth Vader escaped the destruction of the Death Star.

During the battle, he had sensed that the pilot who destroyed the station showed unusual strength in the Force. Already suspecting the pilot's possible heritage, Vader chose not to report back to Palpatine in person. Instead, the Dark Lord spent the next month on a private mission, running down hints about the newest Rebel hero. The torture of a captured Rebel on Centares revealed the truth: the destroyer of the Death Star was Luke Skywalker, Vader's own son.

Back on Coruscant, the Emperor was greatly displeased with the design flaw that had allowed the Rebels to annihilate his Death Star. He summoned Bevel Lemelisk, the original designer of the superweapon, and executed him in the most horrific manner possible. Palpatine took great pleasure in watching the engineer scream and squirm.

But the genius and imagination of such a brilliant man as Lemelisk could not be wasted. Palpatine used his own experimental cloning apparatus to resurrect the weapons engineer. Restored to life and vividly remembering the agony of his execution, Lemelisk had no choice but to work even harder to modify the Death Star design.

Some have questioned the Emperor's wisdom in building a second Death Star—but to abandon the entire concept would have been utterly foolish. The superweapon *worked*, as the destruction of Alderaan had proved. Other than a carelessly uncovered thermal exhaust port, the Death Star achieved its design specifications. No one in the Empire could simply scrap such an expensive creation when the flaw could easily be rectified.

Whenever he perceived a slowness or lack of enthusiasm on the part of his pet engineer, the Emperor executed and resurrected another cloned Lemelisk. This occurred several times more, and with the clarity of hindsight, it seems obvious that Palpatine was testing the cloning process, driven by self-interest as the powers of the dark side continued to destroy his body.

Vader and the Emperor briefly turned their attentions away from the Rebels to the Bounty Hunters Guild instead. At the urging of Prince Xizor, the criminal godfather of the Black Sun syndicate, and over Vader's objections, Palpatine approved a plan to eliminate the Guild. The famous hunter Boba Fett was hired to be the agent of the Guild's destruction. In a bloody conflict known as the Bounty Hunter Wars, Fett succeeded in fragmenting the organization into innumerable splinter groups and free agents. Over the next few

*The* Executor *nears completion*

years, Vader frequently employed these rogue bounty hunters for his own purposes.

## Rebel Trap
### 0–0.5 A.B.Y.

Immediately after celebrating their victory, the Alliance prepared to abandon their exposed base on Yavin 4. The destruction of the Death Star had been a miracle, and the Rebels knew they wouldn't stand a chance against a full Imperial armada. Fortunately, much of the Rebel fleet, including the huge Mon Calamari cruisers commanded by Ackbar and the refugee vessels containing the government-in-exile, had not been present at Yavin and were already scattered across space.

General Dodonna orchestrated the Yavin base's evacuation. After the heavy equipment was success-

fully removed, but before the Yavin command and support staff could leave, a flotilla of Imperial Interdictor cruisers appeared in the system and cut off the hyperspace escape routes. Curiously, the warships did not move to attack; instead, they formed a loose blockade, preventing Dodonna, Organa, Skywalker, and other notable Rebels from escaping.

The blockade had been ordered by Darth Vader, who did not want the base ground into dust—at least not yet. At the starship yards of Fondor, the first Super Star Destroyer, christened *Executor*, was nearing completion. It was to be Vader's new flagship, carrying as much military might as an entire fleet of smaller ships. As payback for his humiliation at the Death Star, Vader wanted to use the *Executor* as his personal sword of vengeance against the Rebel insurgents.

Other high-ranking Imperials derided Vader's

*Dark Troopers*

choice of military strategy, viewing it as foolish grandstanding. Several admirals secretly plotted to sabotage the *Executor*. Admiral Griff, pretending to be one of their number, provided key information about the Super Star Destroyer's construction to the Rebel Alliance. Luke Skywalker ran the blockade and infiltrated the construction yards at Fondor, but Griff's "treachery" turned out to be a ruse, and Skywalker was nearly captured. He had done little damage, but managed to return to the Rebels with a great deal of information about the huge battleship.

Skywalker continued to elude the blockade. While returning from a different mission, he confounded Imperial pursuit by plunging his ship into the slipstream of a passing hypercomet. Following the comet's trajectory along an asteroid-filled orbit, Skywalker crashed in an isolated system on a forgotten, frozen planet named Hoth. There, he encountered an exiled Imperial governor who had built a primitive home in the ice fields. Skywalker killed the treacherous exile—actually a human replica droid—in self-defense and then reported to the Alliance, suggesting Hoth as a possible location for their next headquarters stronghold.

## Imperial Counterstrike
### 0.5–2 A.B.Y.

Skywalker and others proved adept at using small ships to slip through the Imperial blockade of Yavin 4, enraging local fleet commanders who impressed upon Vader the need for a quick and decisive strike. Consequently, the *Executor*'s construction was stepped up. General Dodonna was concerned: while small ships like the *Falcon* could run the blockade, larger vessels would surely be captured. Dodonna contacted Mon Mothma and Ackbar with the Alliance fleet and arranged for a diversionary assault.

The Empire's attack finally came, six months after the Battle of Yavin. While Ackbar staged a feint in the Vallusk Cluster to draw off most Imperial forces, the mighty *Executor* arrived to decimate the Yavin base. Dodonna scrambled all of the base's fighters and transports, but stubbornly refused to evacuate himself until the others were away. The old general set off a series of concussion charges that wiped out an entire squadron of attacking TIE bombers. Dodonna was believed killed in the explosion, but in reality he was taken, critically wounded, into Imperial custody. After a few months spent in a holding cell, he became one of the first inmates in the new Imperial prison known only as *Lusankya*.

The evacuating Rebels successfully rendezvoused with the main Alliance fleet, intending to establish a new base on icy Hoth. Instead, they were forced to put their plans on hold until they could replenish their equipment stores, medical supplies, and foodstuffs. In a dangerous gamble, the Alliance negotiated with Imperial Overlord Ghorin of the Greater Plooriod Cluster for several shipments of badly needed grain, then turned the tables on Ghorin when they discovered the grain was poisoned.

Alliance agent Kyle Katarn, who had helped capture the Death Star plans, was pressed into service when Mon Mothma learned of the Empire's Dark Trooper project slated to create mechanized super stormtroopers. Katarn scuttled the operation by destroying the Dark Troopers' spacegoing construction site, and also rescued Crix Madine from an Imperial prison. Madine was an elite Imperial who had decided to defect to the Rebels after being forced to release an incurable plague on a planet. En route to the Alliance, Madine was nearly recaptured by the Empire during a layover on Corellia, but was rescued by Rogue Squadron—an elite group of starfighter pilots cofounded by Luke Skywalker and Wedge Antilles. Mon Mothma welcomed Madine into the Rebel Alliance and made him a general. Madine would work closely with Rogue Squadron for several years.

Stress took its toll on Rebel leadership. Bail Organa had been killed with the destruction of Alderaan, leaving Mon Mothma and Garm Bel Iblis as the highest-ranking Alliance representatives. The two rarely saw eye-to-eye, and when Mon Mothma ordered an attack on Milvayne, Bel Iblis viewed it as suicidal. He took his loyal forces and seceded from the Rebellion. His private army would score many independent victories over the next nine years.

The loss of Bel Iblis was offset when the Bothan politician Borsk Fey'lya and his sizable faction joined the Alliance. Fey'lya had been impressed by the Rebel victory at Yavin and made the move not for ideological reasons, but to gain status and power.

The Rebellion staged many guerrilla-style strikes against the Empire over the next year, including the Ram's Head mission, which demolished four Star Destroyers in dry dock. But the Alliance fleet remained scattered and on the run as it searched for another central base. The jungle planet Thila was briefly used, but abandoned when it was suggested that the Empire would expect the Rebels to move to a jungle world like Yavin 4. Alliance engineering teams laid groundwork on a number of possible worlds, including Hoth, but Mon Mothma continued to keep her options open.

The Imperials, too, sent out fleets to search for their enemies, launching thousands of automated probe droids. But the tremendous number of uncharted settlements and smuggler encampments created hundreds of false alarms.

## Circarpous Joins the Resistance
### 2 A.B.Y.

As the business hub of the area known as the Expansion Region, Circarpous IV is home to many of the galaxy's top financial leaders. Disgusted by the astronomical tariffs and self-destructive spending so common in Palpatine's Empire, these ruling financiers agreed to covertly fund the Rebel Alliance, pending a face-to-face meeting with Leia Organa. Organa and her protocol droid traveled to a rendezvous on Circarpous IV, escorted by Luke Skywalker.

An engine malfunction caused the two Alliance ships to crash on Circarpous V—a drenched, strategically worthless swamp planet known locally as Mimban—where the Empire had secretly established an illegal dolovite mine. Organa and Skywalker were captured. Darth Vader headed for the system as soon as he was notified, but the two Rebels escaped into the swamp before he arrived.

Vader caught up with his quarry at the vine-

*Meeting the Dark Lord*

encrusted Temple of Pomojema. The temple held the fabled Kaiburr Crystal, a luminous shard capable of magnifying the Force a thousandfold. Skywalker took up his lightsaber and faced Vader in a one-on-one duel.

It is interesting to note that Skywalker, still an untrained Jedi, held his own against his much more experienced opponent. Possibly, the Kaiburr Crystal provided an edge, but Skywalker later admitted that the spirit of Obi-Wan Kenobi appeared to have inhabited his body, guiding his actions as a puppeteer directs a marionette. Kenobi's energy propelled Skywalker in a furious drive that severed the Dark Lord's sword arm, but the effort seemed to exhaust Skywalker's intangible benefactor. Vader shrugged off his grievous injury, and only a chance misstep plunged him into a crumbling well and allowed Skywalker to escape.

When they rejoined the Alliance fleet, Organa notified the Circarpousians of the Imperial dolovite mine on Mimban. Outraged by the subterfuge, the Circarpous business underground opened a covert supply line to the Rebels. The flow of credits proved a critical factor in strengthening the Alliance military, and they purchased a KDY Planet Defender ion cannon for installation at their next base.

The recovered Kaiburr Crystal did not perform to expectations, however. Skywalker discovered that the power of the Kaiburr Crystal decreased in direct proportion to its distance from Mimban and, more specifically, from the Temple of Pomojema itself.

Little more than a curiosity, the trinket remained in Skywalker's possession for years. Eventually he used it as a teaching aid and even experimented by using it as a focusing crystal in a lightsaber. He found the resulting blade to be remarkably strong and energy efficient.

## Home in the Ice
### 2–3 A.B.Y

Mon Mothma eventually agreed to establish the new Rebel command headquarters on the frozen world of Hoth. Alliance engineers completed the work that had been started months earlier, constructing a base that took advantage of the climate.

Echo Base was commanded by General Carlist Rieekan, one of the survivors of Alderaan who had watched as his own world was destroyed by the Death Star. Leia Organa also took up residence in the ice tunnels, choosing safety over physical comfort. However, one element of warmth began to enter her life, as the first hints of a tumultuous romance began to appear between herself and Han Solo.

The Rebels made every effort to keep their headquarters a secret and minimized the number of ship arrivals and departures. Han Solo had several run-ins with bounty hunters while off world on Ord Mantell, but none of the mercenaries learned the location of Echo Base.

Meanwhile, Mon Mothma continued to gather forces at the main Rebel fleet, preparing for another strike. Before she could take action, the Alliance suffered a defeat in the Battle of Derra IV. A badly needed supply convoy and its starfighter escort were blasted to bits in an attack orchestrated by Darth Vader himself. The death of the squadron's flight leader elevated Luke Skywalker to the rank of commander, but nothing could replace the loss of the critical munitions shipment.

It had been years since their major victory on Yavin, and the Empire continued to hound them. It was a dark time for the Rebellion.

# A LIGHT ECLIPSED

## The Battle of Hoth
### 3 A.B.Y.

One of the numerous probe droids dispersed by Imperial search parties picked up faint transmissions in the Hoth system. Upon inspecting the frozen planet, the probot discovered evidence of Echo Base and sent an immediate signal to Darth Vader's flagship. Vader deployed his personal Star Destroyer fleet, the Death Squadron, to attack the base.

Intercepting the probot's signal, General Rieekan realized the Hoth base was sure to be the target of an Imperial attack. He had witnessed firsthand the destruction of Alderaan, and he ordered an immediate evacuation of the base. Though the

Rebels had powerful defenses, Echo Base had depended upon secrecy rather than military strength. Leia Organa and Rieekan instructed all supply ships to be loaded and to depart. It would be a desperate race.

Vader's fleet arrived before the first transport could be launched, but a surprise blast from the Rebels' new ion cannon cleared an escape corridor for the big ships. While Imperial AT-AT walkers attacked the base from ground level, Rebel snowspeeders fought against them in a losing battle. Many defenders sacrificed themselves to buy time for the remaining forces to get away.

Echo Base fell after a great loss of life on both sides. Just as Vader strode into the ruined command center, Leia Organa escaped with Han Solo in the *Millennium Falcon*. Luke Skywalker escaped separately.

Vader launched his fleet into full pursuit. At this time, though he understood Luke Skywalker was his son, he did *not* suspect that Leia Organa was his daughter. Nevertheless, Organa was a powerful figure in the Rebellion—someone to be apprehended at all costs. Solo proved a remarkable pilot, eluding pursuit by flying directly through the dense heart of the Hoth asteroid field. Though they escaped, his ship's hyperdrive was severely damaged.

To assist in the hunt, Vader called in a rogue's gallery of bounty hunters, most of them independent agents since the destruction of the Bounty Hunters Guild. Among the hunters was Boba Fett, who had enjoyed a special relationship with Vader since before the Battle of Yavin, when Fett had recovered the severed head of an Icarii prophetess on the Dark Lord's behalf.

Believing they had escaped Imperial capture, Solo patched together a hyperdrive backup and limped across the Ison Corridor to reach the gas world of Bespin. On Cloud City he met up again with Lando Calrissian, former owner of the *Millennium Falcon* and now a respectable businessman. Though they had had their disagreements in the past, most notably over the Battle of Ylesia, Solo still considered Calrissian a friend and requested his assistance in getting repairs for his ship.

But Boba Fett had tracked Solo to Cloud City, and he betrayed their location to Vader. Vader coerced Calrissian into setting a trap for Solo and Organa, and the two Rebel fugitives were captured. He proceeded to torture Han Solo, to no apparent purpose. In reality, Darth Vader meant to lure his true prize to Cloud City: Luke Skywalker.

## *A New Jedi*
### 3 A.B.Y.

After fighting bravely during the Battle of Hoth, Skywalker left the ice planet to follow a vision he had received from Obi-Wan Kenobi. He flew to the uncharted swamp planet Dagobah in search of a mysterious Jedi teacher named Yoda. When Skywalker met the unassuming and gnomish crea-

ture, though, he couldn't believe Yoda to be a great warrior.

Yoda, former member of the Jedi Council and famed mediator of the *Chu'unthor* incident, reluctantly agreed to train the doubting youth in the ways of the Jedi. He warned his pupil that the path would be difficult, but that he must be strong. Skywalker spent many long and discouraging days testing himself in the Force, attempting to meet the strange and impossible challenges Yoda threw at him. He learned to face his fears and to trust his instincts.

As he opened his mind and explored his Jedi abilities, Skywalker experienced another vision, one in which his friends Han Solo and Leia Organa were held in brutal captivity on Bespin. Despite Yoda's dire warnings that it was a trap, Skywalker followed his heart to Cloud City, just as Vader had hoped.

*The collapse of Echo Base*

*Training of a Jedi*

Finished with Han Solo, Vader had the hapless smuggler frozen in a block of carbonite and delivered him to Boba Fett. Vader intended to use the same freezing process on Skywalker, and he prepared to capture the novice Jedi. Fett left Cloud City with the preserved Solo, heading for Tatooine, where he would collect the price Jabba the Hutt had placed on Solo's head.

When Vader's trap was sprung, Skywalker fought surprisingly well. He had an unlikely ally in Lando Calrissian, who knew the Imperials had placed him in a no-win situation. Calrissian called for an evacuation of Cloud City, and in the resulting chaos he took the *Falcon* and escaped with Leia Organa and Chewbacca. Meanwhile, Vader and Skywalker fought each other over the wind core of Cloud City, resulting in the loss of Skywalker's right hand.

Darth Vader then revealed to his opponent the terrible truth—that *he* was Luke Skywalker's father. He beseeched his son to join him in overthrowing the Emperor. Refusing, Skywalker allowed himself to fall into the seemingly bottomless core shaft of Cloud City. Utilizing his Jedi powers, he managed to fall through an airshaft, and as he desperately clung to a weather vane underneath the floating metropolis, he was retrieved by the *Falcon*. The escapees fled the system to rendezvous with the remainder of the Alliance fleet.

This was a devastating defeat for the Rebellion. The base on Hoth had been destroyed, Han Solo had been lost, Luke Skywalker had discovered his dark heritage, and the ragtag fleet seemed to have no chance for victory.

Nevertheless, the Alliance pressed on. Rumors began to surface of a second, even larger Death Star currently under construction above the sanctuary moon of Endor. Concrete information became the top priority. Rebel agents managed to infiltrate and destroy the Empire's experimental superlaser test bed, the *Tarkin*, but this was a limited victory. If a second Death Star were completed, it could spell certain doom for the Rebel Alliance.

*Prince Xizor*

## Prince Xizor and Black Sun
### 3.5 A.B.Y.

The unstable political situation fostered by the Rebellion caused certain parties to cast their eyes toward the Imperial throne.

Xizor, a reptilian prince from Falleen, was the head of Black Sun, the Empire's largest criminal syndicate. He had masterminded the Bounty Hunter Wars a few years earlier and was said to be the third most powerful person in the galaxy, behind Palpatine and Vader. Xizor decided to increase his rank by eliminating Vader, his long-time rival. Prince Xizor was one of the few who knew of the blood ties between Darth Vader and Luke Skywalker.

Palpatine wanted to turn Skywalker to the dark side of the Force, and he entrusted Vader with the task of capturing the boy unharmed. To make Vader look incompetent in the eyes of the Emperor, Xizor decided he wanted Skywalker dead.

Black Sun criminal operatives began hatching assassination plots against Skywalker, who was busy tracking down Boba Fett and the carbon-frozen body of Han Solo. Distressed by the attempts on Skywalker's life, Leia Organa ironically turned to Black Sun, hoping the syndicate's underground spy network could uncover the identity of the assassins.

Skywalker returned to Tatooine, where he constructed a new lightsaber to replace the weapon he had lost on Cloud City. When he received a message from Bothawui, Skywalker and smuggler Dash Rendar went to the Bothan homeworld to help capture an Imperial freighter that was carrying plans for the Empire's second Death Star.

Skywalker and a squadron of Bothan pilots intercepted the Imperial freighter and disabled it, though the cost in Bothan lives was high. They brought the freighter's computer core to the nearby planet Kothlis, where a crack team of data slicers decrypted the blueprints and construction schedules. Though the Rebels congratulated themselves on their victory, it was later learned that Palpatine had allowed the freighter to be captured in order to lure the Alliance fleet into a trap at Endor.

On Kothlis, Skywalker was captured by bounty hunters; fortunately, the Imperial computer core was spirited away by Bothan technicians and eventually made its way into the hands of Mon Mothma. As Vader rushed to Kothlis to collect his son, Skywalker managed to escape.

On Coruscant, Organa and Chewbacca disguised themselves as bounty hunters to gain access to Prince Xizor's opulent fortress. At first, the Falleen crime lord was polite and gracious—even seductive—toward his guests, but then he imprisoned Organa. Chewbacca escaped, as part of Xizor's master plan: the Wookiee would notify Skywalker, and when Skywalker arrived, he would die.

Skywalker and his companions came to Organa's rescue. They broke into Xizor's castle, found the princess, then set off a time-delayed thermal detonator to cover their escape. When Xizor realized he had less than five minutes before the thermal detonator destroyed his fortress, he fled to his orbiting skyhook *Falleen's Fist*. The resulting implosion of Xizor's castle left a gaping hole in the Coruscant cityscape.

Aboard the *Falleen's Fist*, Xizor ordered his personal navy to destroy the escaping *Falcon*. Solo's ship fought valiantly, but was quickly over-

*The capture of the second Death Star plans*

whelmed, and was soon overtaken by a vast flotilla of Imperial warships led by the Super Star Destroyer *Executor*. The *Executor* and her TIE squadrons, however, ignored the *Falcon* and opened fire on Xizor's vessels instead.

Darth Vader, never a subtle or patient man, had been driven over the edge by Xizor's brazen attempt to eliminate Skywalker. The Dark Lord delivered an ultimatum: if Xizor did not immediately recall his navy and surrender himself into Imperial custody, the *Executor* would destroy his skyhook. Xizor refused to respond, and Vader's gunners blasted the *Falleen's Fist* into flaming debris.

Xizor's death created a power vacuum within Black Sun. His second in command, the human replica droid known as Guri, dropped out of sight, and Xizor's various lieutenants began squabbling. The body count climbed as the struggles escalated into open warfare.

While Vader was preoccupied with Black Sun, one of the Emperor's grand admirals finalized his plans for a daring, but ultimately doomed, coup d'état. Immediately after Xizor's death, Grand Admiral Zaarin attacked Vader's fleet in the Ottega system and captured the Emperor's private shuttle-craft at Coruscant. Zaarin's plot was defeated by loyal Imperial forces, but the traitor managed to escape to the Outer Rim. Soon afterward, Zaarin was eliminated by Grand Admiral Thrawn.

# ALLIANCE TRIUMPHANT

## The Rebellion Regroups
### 4 A.B.Y.

Finally, a complex and daring plan freed Han Solo from the clutches of Jabba the Hutt, resulting in the death of the sluglike gangster and the collapse of the Desilijic crime family. Leia Organa, Lando Calrissian, and Solo rejoined the Rebel fleet in preparation for a major strike against the Empire.

Luke Skywalker, though, returned to Dagobah to continue his training under Yoda. When he arrived, however, he found the nine-hundred-year-old Jedi Master near death. Yoda confirmed that Darth Vader was indeed Skywalker's father. Then he faded away, to become one with the Force. Another startling realization came when Skywalker realized Leia Organa was his own sister! They were twins, separated and hidden from each other at birth. Even Vader didn't know Organa's true heritage. Reeling from the revelation and the death of Yoda, Skywalker returned to the fleet.

On the Rebel flagship out in open space, Alliance leader Mon Mothma addressed the troop leaders and explained the Rebellion's plan. Bothan spies had delivered the decrypted computer core from Kothlis, containing the details of the second Death Star's construction site. Many Bothans had died to make this data available. As Mon Mothma and Admiral Ackbar planned their attack, another piece of information galvanized them: Emperor Palpatine himself would be at the station on an inspection tour. If they could strike and succeed in destroying the new battle station, they would eradicate the evil despot himself.

## The Battle of Endor
### 4 A.B.Y.

After gathering in the Sullust system and executing a feint attack, Rebel commandos slipped through the Imperial security net around Endor. A team led by Leia Organa, Luke Skywalker, and Han Solo—newly promoted to general—crept through the dense forest to destroy a shield generator that protected the Death Star's orbital construction site.

*Admiral Ackbar*

Unfortunately, the team encountered numerous difficulties, and Skywalker allowed himself to be taken captive. As the main Rebel attack fleet swept from hyperspace to strike the Death Star, the shield generator continued to protect the target.

Vader took the captive Jedi to the Death Star and presented him to Emperor Palpatine. When the Rebel fleet attacked, Skywalker realized that the entire situation had been a web of deceit spun by Palpatine himself: it was all a trap. An enormous Imperial battlefleet emerged at the far side of Endor and began hammering the Alliance armada.

Skywalker appealed to his father, trying to touch his heart and turn him back to the light side of the Force; but Vader remained unswayed.

*Death of the* Devastator

While Rebel forces continued to be decimated, the Emperor manipulated father and son to battle each other with lightsabers. During the struggle, Vader's resolve began to falter as he saw the goodness and earnestness in his son. He learned of his own daughter, Skywalker's sister—Leia Organa. Frantic that he had betrayed his sister, Skywalker unleashed his pent-up rage, which gave him the strength to severely wound Darth Vader. Seeing Skywalker's anger, the Emperor applauded, pleased to see him take the first steps toward the dark side.

But Skywalker surprised him by surrendering, refusing to continue the fight that would have resulted in his father's death. The furious Emperor then used his own dark Force powers to attack, trying to destroy Skywalker with blasts of blue lightning. As he watched the agony of his son and the

Emperor's glee, Vader finally broke the hold of evil that had suffocated him for so long, and he fought back. Vader grabbed the energy-seething Palpatine and hurled him into a Death Star shaft, where the evil leader was disintegrated. The shock waves of dark power, though, had mortally wounded Vader, and Skywalker could do nothing for his dying father, the terrible enemy who had saved him in the end.

He dragged his father to a shuttle bay, but Anakin Skywalker died before they could escape, and so became a part of the Force. Luke took the black body armor with him as he flew away.

The shield generator was finally destroyed, and Rebel starfighters led by Lando Calrissian and Wedge Antilles raced into the superstructure of the Death Star, toward the reactor core. Outside,

*Heroism on Endor*

Admiral Ackbar's overall fleet continued their battle against the Imperial Star Destroyers and the flagship *Executor*. After A-wing pilot Arvel Crynyd's suicidal sacrifice destroyed the bridge of the Super Star Destroyer, the out-of-control *Executor* crashed through the hull of the Death Star. Calrissian and Antilles dropped a warhead into the reactor core and raced back out to space, barely one step ahead of the intense detonation wave.

All around the galaxy, freedom-loving citizens celebrated the end of the New Order and the death of Emperor Palpatine. Though many difficulties remained, and the Empire was far from vanquished, the Battle of Endor succeeded where so many other struggles had failed.

At last, a New Republic could be born.

## The Truce at Bakura
### 4 A.B.Y.

Though the Imperial fleet retreated from Endor, the Rebel Alliance had no time to savor their victory. The day after the Emperor's death, an Imperial drone ship arrived at the Death Star's cooling wreckage with a message addressed to Emperor Palpatine. "Bakura is under attack by an alien invasion force from outside your domain. We have lost half our defense force and all outer-system outposts. Urgent, repeat urgent, send stormtroopers."

Bakura was a distant Imperial world in the Outer Rim, and no Imperial troops could possibly arrive to rescue the Bakurans. Ironically, the Rebel victory at Endor had doomed an innocent planet. Mon Mothma refused to allow this and gathered a small task force to go to the remote planet's defense. Commander Skywalker, still suffering from his injuries at the hands of the Emperor, received a visit from the disembodied spirit of Obi-Wan Kenobi. Kenobi urged his former protégé to attend to the Bakura matter personally, and Skywalker became the task force's commander.

Skywalker led five Corellian gunships, one corvette, and the *Millennium Falcon* toward the edge of known space and the border of the Unknown Regions. When they arrived at Bakura, they learned the nature of the alien invasion threat.

The Ssi-ruuk, a species of warm-blooded saurians, had embarked on a campaign of conquest, centered around entechment, a process that transferred a human prisoner's life energy into the control circuits of a battle droid, giving the Ssi-ruuk a cheap and expendable fighting force. If they succeeded in enteching the population of Bakura, the Ssi-ruuk would have enough mechanical warriors to pose a significant threat to the greater galaxy.

The beleaguered Imperials of Bakura welcomed the small Alliance fleet, despite the two sides' long history of mutual animosity. Eager to discuss a formal truce, Leia Organa met with Imperial Governor Wilek Nereus in the capital city of Salis D'aar. Governor Nereus, along with Prime Minister Yeorg Captison and his beautiful niece Gaeriel Captison, listened to the Alliance's offer. Nereus was mistrustful, but when he received confirmation of the Emperor's death, he realized this was Bakura's only hope for survival. The governor accepted Organa's help and agreed to a cease-fire. With a handshake, the first truce between Rebel and Imperial forces took effect.

Later that first evening, Leia Organa received a visitation by an unwelcome presence—the spirit form of Anakin Skywalker, her true father. The man who had been Darth Vader begged his daughter for her forgiveness.

Organa had learned of her parentage only days earlier and was unable to ignore the fact that Vader had tortured her aboard the Death Star, had turned Han Solo over to Boba Fett, and had blasted her homeworld of Alderaan into cinders. The apparition vanished and never appeared to his daughter again.

The Ssi-ruuk invasion fleet prepared for their next strike against Bakura. On board the mighty flagship *Shriwirr*, the Ssi-ruuk admiral Ivpikkis readied his battle droids for a single, overwhelming assault. One of Ivpikkis's subordinates owned a brainwashed human "pet" who had been raised by the Ssi-ruuk since he was a young boy. This human collaborator, Dev Sibwarra, was Force-sensitive and detected Luke Skywalker. He alerted his masters. The Ssi-ruuk hoped this powerful Jedi would bring them the capability of enteching victims across

*A historic armistice*

great distances, sucking their life energies from afar. So Sibwarra secretly contacted Governor Nereus with an offer. If the governor would turn over Skywalker, the Ssi-ruuk fleet would leave Bakura in peace.

Nereus was far too shrewd to take the aliens at their word, but he saw a devious way to eliminate *both* threats—Skywalker and the Ssi-ruuk—with a single thrust. He placed three Olabrian trichoid egg pods into Skywalker's food. The bloodsucking, highly contagious larvae would hatch in Skywalker's body once he was safely aboard the Ssi-ruuk flagship, killing him in gruesome fashion and infecting the aliens with a lethal parasite to which they had no natural immunity.

Confident of victory, Nereus arrested Leia Organa on charges of sedition. Many of Bakura's citizens considered the action a clear abuse of authority, and rioting broke out in Salis D'aar. Amid the confusion, Han Solo rescued Organa from prison, and the two boarded the *Falcon* to help defend against the imminent alien attack.

Skywalker was captured by the Ssi-ruuk in the Salis D'aar spaceport. Brought aboard the *Shriwirr*, he was hooked into an entechment rig. Dev Sibwarra, impressed by the Jedi's heroism, was

finally able to shrug off his masters' brainwashing and think for himself. Sibwarra helped Skywalker escape, and the two humans fought their way through the corridors of the *Shriwirr*, causing tremendous damage. Afraid they would be killed far from their consecrated homeworlds—a terrible fate, according to their religious beliefs—Ivpikkis and the Ssi-ruuk crew escaped the vessel in life pods and were recovered by other warships.

Meanwhile, in orbit above Bakura, the Rebel and Imperial fleets formed a united front against the invaders. The Ssi-ruuk armada was mercilessly bombarded. In order to live and fight on, the saurians began a full retreat. Every Ssi-ruuk vessel, except for the abandoned flagship *Shriwirr*, vanished into hyperspace toward the Unknown Regions.

But Nereus turned traitor yet again. With the Ssi-ruuk gone, he ordered his fleet to open fire on their ostensible allies. The Rebel flagship and many other ships were destroyed. The surviving Rebel fighters were caught in a bottleneck with no hope of escape. Their only chance lay in destroying the Imperial command ship *Dominant*. General Solo grimly lined up a "carom shot" in which the *Falcon* would ram a small Imperial patrol craft, ricocheting the patrol craft into the *Dominant*'s main generator. Success meant escape for the Rebel fleet, but death for everyone aboard the *Falcon*. Leia Organa transmitted her farewell to the other Alliance ships. "Scatter the fire of Rebellion," she said, firmly believing these to be her last words. "It will flare up everywhere the tinder is dry."

The *Dominant*, however, broke formation to strike at the *Shriwirr*. The *Falcon* aborted its carom shot and instead rescued Luke Skywalker and Dev Sibwarra from the damaged *Shriwirr*. Skywalker had already sensed the presence of the Olabrian trichoid larval parasites in his bronchial tubes and eliminated the threat with help from the Force.

The Rebel fleet rallied from near disaster and forced its enemies to the brink of defeat. Commander Pter Thanas, leader of the Imperial defense force, surrendered. On Bakura, Governor Nereus was captured by resistance fighters and killed in a mishap not long afterward.

It was a welcome victory. Prime Minister Captison assumed control of Bakura and joined the Rebels' fledgling Alliance of Free Planets. Commander Thanas oversaw the Imperial withdrawal from Bakura and then defected, agreeing to lead the Bakuran home defense force. Senator Gaeriel Captison had grown quite close to Luke Skywalker over the course of the incident, but she loved her homeworld even more. She married Commander Thanas and was eventually elected prime minister of Bakura. One of her first actions was to commission new, powerful defensive warships in case the Ssi-ruuk should ever return.

Despite all the medical attention Luke

*Admiral Ivpikkis of the Ssi-ruuk*

Skywalker could provide, Dev Sibwarra succumbed to injuries sustained during the battle aboard the *Shriwirr*. But Skywalker now realized that other people existed with the capacity for using the Force. He vowed to find more candidates and eventually restore the order of Jedi Knights.

## Onward to Ssi-ruuvi Space
### 4–5 A.B.Y.

The Ssi-ruuk incident placed the Alliance in a bind. Mon Mothma knew that they had a long and exhausting fight ahead of them to reclaim the galaxy from the Empire. At the same time, they couldn't allow the Ssi-ruuvi Imperium time to regroup and strike other helpless worlds; with sufficient entched prisoners to power their war machines, the reptilian invaders might prove unstoppable.

The New Republic formed an invasion task force that would journey to the enemy homeworld, with a dozen Nebulon-B frigates and smaller vessels at their disposal. The spearhead of the operation was the repaired and refitted Ssi-ruuvi flagship. The Alliance renamed the vessel the *Sibwarra*, but her crew commonly called her the *Flutie*—a derisive nickname for the Ssi-ruuk, due to their musical speech patterns.

Life aboard the *Sibwarra* was exceedingly odd. Throughout their tour of duty, the crew struggled with the ship's baffling onboard equipment. The original bridge controls were replaced with a standardized rig, and Skywalker's protocol droid C-3PO provided a translation glossary of the Ssi-ruuvi written language. Nevertheless, several crew members were injured or killed by misunderstood alien devices.

Mon Mothma provided the Empire with all the Rebel intelligence data on the Ssi-ruuk, hoping to generate a two-pronged attack. The Imperials, however, were preoccupied with their own problems.

It was quite a surprise, then, when the *Sibwarra* arrived at the Ssi-ruuvi star cluster and found a half-beaten foe. Another force from deep in the Unknown Regions had already attacked the Ssi-ruuvi Imperium on the opposite front, leaving devastation in their wake. Recent interpretations of the data have suggested that the attackers were the Chiss, the blue-skinned humanoid race of which Imperial Grand Admiral Thrawn was a member.

The *Sibwarra* and her escorts engaged Ivpikkis and the alien fleet as they battled their way to the Ssi-ruuvi homeworld. Eventually the two sides reached a standstill. The Rebels attempted negotiations, which proved inconclusive. Apparently satisfied that the Ssi-ruuk could not mount another invasion, Mon Mothma turned her attention to the numerous other crises facing her new government. She ordered the vessels to fall back and assist in the liberation of Clak'dor VII, which was currently struggling for freedom.

## PART V

# BIRTH OF THE NEW REPUBLIC

While Leia Organa, Han Solo, and Luke Skywalker defended Bakura from the Ssiruuk, Mon Mothma was making preparations to establish a new galactic government. Clearly, it could take years, even decades, to fully eradicate the Empire, but the victory at Endor would be a symbolic starting point to mark a new era.

Within days of that victory, the Rebel Alliance officially became the Alliance of Free Planets, established as an interim organization until the details of the government could be worked out. One month after Endor, Mon Mothma formally issued the Declaration of a New Republic.

Though the Battle of Endor is viewed as the beginning of the New Republic era, Mon Mothma's declaration marked the "official" establishment of the government. The document was signed by Mon Mothma, Leia Organa, Borsk Fey'lya, and Admiral Ackbar, as well as officials from Corellia, Kashyyyk, Sullust, and Elom. Under the New Republic's first charter, these eight individuals composed the New Republic Provisional Council. Mon Mothma was elected chief councilor.

For several months, the New Republic made no large-scale military incursions into Imperial territory. Instead, they consolidated their holdings and won over hundreds of planets through diplomacy. News of the Emperor's death caused countless worlds to enter the New Republic's fold, most of them in the Rim territories. Captain Wedge Antilles and the X-wing pilots of Rogue Squadron acted as scouts, escorts, and negotiators during this period.

## Imperial Fragmentation
### 4–4.5 A.B.Y.

The New Republic saw no need for an immediate strike at the Empire, since the Empire was doing a fine job of tearing itself apart. Without Palpatine's commanding presence, the Imperial war machine proved unfocused. After the destruction of the second Death Star, the Imperial fleet continued to fight the Rebels, but were systematically beaten back by their numerically inferior foe. Captain Gilad Pellaeon of the Star Destroyer *Chimaera* ordered the fleet to retreat and regroup at Annaj, where the first signs of stress began to show.

Admiral Harrsk, commander of one task force within the Endor fleet, viewed the death of the Emperor as a great opportunity. Unwilling to take orders from Pellaeon, a mere captain, Harrsk took his segment of the fleet to the restricted Deep Core at the very center of the galaxy. There, among the secure Imperial safe worlds, Harrsk began building up his own pocket empire.

Though Harrsk was the Empire's first breakaway warlord, he wouldn't be the last. The Empire had long rewarded ambition over cooperation; only intimidating leaders like Palpatine and Vader had kept their subordinates in line. Suddenly, post-Endor, everyone wanted to rule the Empire, or at least create their own kingdoms. More than any other factor, warlordism was responsible for the decline of the Empire.

Many other warlords broke away in the first few months. Admiral Teradoc followed Harrsk's lead and established a miniature empire on the outskirts of the Deep Core, just days after the Imperial debacle at Endor. Admiral Gaen Drommel used the Super Star Destroyer *Guardian* to subdue his home sector. Grand Moff Ardus Kaine, Tarkin's successor, walled off a large chunk of the Outer Rim Territories and dubbed it the Pentastar Alignment. Admiral Zsinj, ruler of the Quelii sector, would later prove to be one of the New Republic's most formidable foes.

*Sate Pestage*

### Black Nebula
### 4–4.5 A.B.Y.

In the meantime, behind the scenes, the Black Sun criminal syndicate had never recovered from the death of its leader, Prince Xizor. Various lieutenants, or vigos, began to fight one another for what remained of the syndicate. One of Black Sun's lesser operatives, a Jeodu named Dequc, tried to revive the organization under the name Black Nebula, with himself as its head. The Emperor had ordered Dequc eliminated, and mere days before Endor, Mara Jade, one of the Emperor's Hands, executed him on Svivren.

Jade later learned, however, that the victim on Svivren had been a decoy. Dequc continued to expand Black Nebula in the post-Palpatine Empire, until Mara Jade tracked him down and killed him several months later.

At the same time, Savan, Prince Xizor's niece, attempted to piece together the remaining factions of Black Sun. The key to Savan's plot was the human replica droid known as Guri, who had been Xizor's second-in-command and knew all the syndicate's secrets. Savan located Guri on Hurd's Moon, where she was undergoing synaptic rewiring to erase her memory and her assassin-droid programming.

Councilor Leia Organa and Generals Han Solo and Lando Calrissian also journeyed to Hurd's Moon, attempting to prevent the rise of another destructive criminal empire. After a shootout, they took Savan into custody. Guri, her criminal programming purged, was allowed to go free.

Black Nebula crumbled without Dequc, and Xizor's vigos murdered each other in an internecine bloodbath. Black Sun was dead, and it would remain defunct until the New Republic inadvertently resurrected the syndicate during the liberation of Coruscant three years later.

### Isard's Ascension
### 4.5–5 A.B.Y.

Ysanne Isard's conspiracy began to bear fruit when the New Republic threatened Brentaal, a wealthy and influential Core World not far from Mon Mothma's home planet of Chandrila. As the New

And unbeknownst to all, the threat of Palpatine did not disappear. As with Obi-Wan Kenobi, the Emperor's spirit form survived when his body died. Palpatine's life essence made a tortuous journey to his hidden Deep Core throneworld of Byss, where it inhabited a fresh young body cloned using his own genetic source materials. Palpatine's clone began to reconsolidate his own forces, though it would be years before he made his presence known to the galaxy.

Sate Pestage, the Emperor's former grand vizier and the man responsible for keeping the Empire intact, had been cunning enough to assume the Imperial throne upon learning of his master's death. But the grand vizier lacked the charisma and influence to lead the Empire, and he had a host of enemies within the Imperial Palace. His chief rivals were Palpatine's former advisory staff, who formed a tribunal known as the Ruling Circle. As they schemed to overthrow the new Emperor, Pestage plotted to keep the Ruling Circle in check. Ysanne Isard, head of Imperial Intelligence, acted as a neutral intermediary between the two parties.

Neither faction realized Isard's true goal until it was too late. Isard was secretly pitting each side against the other so she could rise from their ashes and rule as empress.

Republic military geared up for an all-out assault, Sate Pestage vowed that Brentaal would not fall.

Acting on Isard's advice, Pestage allowed the incompetent Admiral Isoto to defend Brentaal. There, despite the efforts of the Empire's best fighter pilot, Baron Soontir Fel, and the skills of the legendary 181st Imperial fighter group, Isoto's bumblings allowed the New Republic to capture the world. During the final battle, Baron Fel was taken prisoner by the New Republic, and he would later

*The capture of Brentaal*

fly with the X-wing pilots of Rogue Squadron.

To all appearances, Pestage was responsible for the loss of Brentaal, and the Ruling Circle screamed for his head. Knowing that Isard had sold him out, Pestage made preparations to defect. On Axxila, he held a secret meeting with Councilor Leia Organa to discuss terms. In exchange for leaving Coruscant undefended against a New Republic assault, he asked for twenty-five planets he could rule as he pleased. Realizing that Coruscant was the key to the war effort, Organa agreed to Pestage's offer, despite her own misgivings.

Isard learned of the Axxila talks and immediately informed the Ruling Circle of Pestage's treachery. An order was issued for his arrest, and the Ruling Circle set itself up as the new governing body in the Empire.

Sate Pestage fled to Ciutric, but was apprehended by the local Imperial governor. Though the Axxila deal was obviously dead, the New Republic had to take action. If Pestage were rescued by the New Republic, it would serve as an example to other high-ranking Imperials and encourage more defections. Rogue Squadron and a commando team were sent to Ciutric to retrieve Pestage.

The rescue operation was unsuccessful. Pestage was murdered by Imperial Admiral Krennel, who then seized Pestage's personal territory and set himself up as the Empire's latest breakaway warlord. On Coruscant, Ysanne Isard ruthlessly exterminated the Ruling Circle and assumed the throne. Isard would succeed where the others had failed, and hold the crumbling Empire together for more than two years.

Eight months after the Battle of Endor, Ackbar and the New Republic fleet made another aggressive push into Imperial territory. Concerned that the campaign might presage a siege of Coruscant, Isard recalled hundreds of Star Destroyers to defend the capital planet and other key Core Worlds.

One of the Imperial armadas that received the order was the Black Sword Command in the Koornacht Cluster, a little-known patch of territory at the fringes of the Deep Core. As the Black Fleet prepared to depart the central shipbuilding planet of N'zoth, the shipyards' Yevethan dockworkers erupted in a shocking uprising. Led by underground commando Nil Spaar, the Yevetha murdered thousands of Imperials, captured hundreds more, and seized every Star Destroyer in the Black Fleet armada—including the Super Star Destroyer *Intimidator*.

The Yevetha covered up the incident. The New Republic never heard a word about it, and Isard—operating on inaccurate intelligence data—believed that the Black Fleet had perished in a debacle at Cal-Seti, several sectors away from N'zoth. The Koornacht Cluster would remain a closed-border curiosity until the frantic events of the Black Fleet Crisis, twelve years in the future.

One year after the Emperor's death, the Central Committee of Grand Moffs decided to increase

*Ysanne Isard*

their own power base by moving against Isard. They proclaimed their own candidate—Trioculus, a former Kessel slavelord—as Imperial leader and attempted to rally the fleet behind him. Some followed their lead, but the bulk of the fleet, including Captain Pellaeon of the Star Destroyer *Chimaera*, remained loyal to Isard.

The New Republic moved against the grand moffs under the auspices of the Senate Planetary Intelligence Network (SPIN), a short-lived analysis and infiltration task force formed by Mon Mothma. Isard, meanwhile, freed Jabba the Hutt's father, Zorba, from prison and sent him into the fray as her unwitting agent. Zorba seized Cloud City from Lando Calrissian, who had only recently rescued the city from the clutches of the Empire. In the end, no fleet battle occurred. Trioculus, Zorba, and a shadowy group of mystics called the Prophets of the Dark Side wiped each other out in an internal struggle. Those grand moffs who had been involved in the conspiracy were executed, and Isard's position at the head of the Empire became more secure than ever.

A few months later, Ysanne Isard was instrumental in foiling a New Republic espionage mission to Coruscant. Pilot Tycho Celchu, a member of Rogue Squadron, took a TIE fighter captured during the truce at Bakura and infiltrated the Imperial capital. Isard, however, uncovered the spy and imprisoned him in a hellish prison known only as *Lusankya*. Celchu eventually escaped to the New Republic, but was viewed with suspicion by many, who suspected he had been brainwashed into becoming a sleeper agent.

## General Skywalker
### 5–5.5 A.B.Y.

Throughout the Trioculus affair, the New Republic was engaged in a protracted military campaign for possession of Milagro, a world located at a key hyperspace junction. The Empire was prepared to lay waste to Milagro rather than allow the Rebels access to its manufacturing facilities. Following three months of exhausting clashes between AT-AT walkers and the New Republic army, the defeated Imperials slagged the planet's surface with a with-

ering orbital bombardment, then fled.

The New Republic remained in the system, using the Dreadnaught *New Hope* as an orbital headquarters. When a damaged Imperial Star Destroyer leapt into the Milagro system, hoping to effect repairs, it stumbled into a brawl with the *New Hope*. General Han Solo led the fighter attack against the Star Destroyer, while Mon Mothma coordinated the battle from the bridge of the *New Hope*. Finally, Luke Skywalker's superior X-wing tactics forced the Imperials to surrender. The captured Star Destroyer was renamed the *Crynyd* in honor of A-wing pilot Arvel Crynyd, whose self-sacrifice at the Battle of Endor took down the Super Star Destroyer *Executor*. For his heroism at Milagro, Commander Skywalker was at last promoted to the rank of general.

General Skywalker was quickly saddled with the responsibilities of command, a burden he loathed. Ever since his experience at Bakura, Skywalker had grown less interested in military conquest and more interested in the spiritual understanding of the Force. His encounter with Dev Sibwarra had convinced him that great deeds could be accomplished by restoring the order of Jedi Knights. Skywalker's views were reinforced when he witnessed the heroic deeds of Kyle Katarn—a Force-sensitive individual who, five years earlier, had helped recover the Death Star plans and sabotaged the Empire's Dark Trooper program. Now Katarn was realizing his own potential as a Jedi.

Several of the Emperor's dark-side adepts, led by the Dark Jedi Jerec, had attracted corporate backers and formed a warlord cabal. Their influence was limited, but Jerec had discovered the Valley of the Jedi on Ruusan, where the spirits of the Brotherhood of Darkness and the Army of Light had been trapped in limbo for a thousand years. Jerec planned to use the Valley's power to topple Isard and rule a vast new empire.

Katarn single-handedly defeated Jerec and his minions before the Dark Jedi's grandiose plans could come to fruition. Skywalker, impressed, offered to train Katarn as a Jedi apprentice, but the other man declined. Soon afterward, the New Republic became bogged down in a brutal military campaign in the Inner Rim. Skywalker led his troops onto the battlefields of Mindor, digging out

entrenched pockets of Imperial resistance. Stormtroopers under Lord Shadowspawn fought to the last man, and Skywalker was dismayed at the bloodshed and unnecessary loss of life.

Less than six months after receiving his general's commission, Luke Skywalker resigned from the New Republic military.

## The Last Grand Admiral?
### 6 A.B.Y.

Emperor Palpatine frequently rewarded his most capable servants with grandiose titles, further encouraging the notorious Imperial culture of greed and ambition. The best stormtroopers were molded into Royal Guards, and there were rumors that the best Royal Guards became Imperial Sovereign Protectors on Byss. Initially, the highest possible rank in the Imperial Navy was admiral, until Palpatine created the elite rank of grand admiral; there could never be more than twelve at one time.

The twelve grand admirals, easily recognizable by their stark white uniforms and braided gold epaulets, were the best of the best—unparalleled geniuses at military strategy. In the aftermath of Endor, had the surviving grand admirals united against their common enemy, the New Republic might have been wiped out while still in its infancy.

Fortunately that threat never materialized. The first grand admiral to fall was Zaarin, when he attempted a coup d'état against the Emperor—just before Endor—and failed. Many other grand admirals perished with the second Death Star—thanks to Palpatine's decision to keep them aboard the battle station rather than send them out to direct the fleet. The remainder of the original twelve met their fates in the ensuing months.

Grand Admiral Syn was outfought by Ackbar during the liberation of Kashyyyk, his flagship vaporized. Grand Admirals Grunger and Pitta turned warlord and annihilated each other in a bitter but futile fight for control of the Corellian sector. Grand Admiral Takel was executed by Trioculus, while the fanatical Grand Admiral Il-Raz committed suicide by plunging his flagship into the heart of the Denarii Nova. Grand Admiral

Batch was assassinated by his second in command, who then took the ships in Batch's task force and joined Warlord Harrsk in the Deep Core.

Grand Admiral Grant, the so-called last grand admiral, defected to the New Republic on the condition that he be granted immunity from prosecution for war crimes and allowed to retire to Rathalay. The defection took place two years after Endor. The New Republic closed the books on the Emperor's grand admirals, thinking they had finally accounted for all of them.

No one realized that one grand admiral remained at large, and he was possibly the most dangerous of all. Blue-skinned Thrawn had officially been promoted to grand admiral by Palpatine in a secret ceremony following the treason of Grand Admiral Zaarin. Soon afterward, Thrawn had been sent to the Unknown Regions, accounting for the New Republic's oversight. Years would pass before Thrawn's return, but the New Republic would once again learn to fear the title of grand admiral.

## The Battle for Coruscant
### 6.5–7 A.B.Y.

Two and a half years after the birth of the New Republic, the Empire was still the galaxy's dominant government. Despite the rise of rogue warlords, Imperials held a majority of settled planets and had a stranglehold on the important Core Worlds. Without an aggressive military push, the New Republic would never bring about an end to the Galactic Civil War.

The most effective way to eliminate the Empire would be to capture Coruscant, the universal symbol of governmental power and authority. The New Republic began seizing planets in Imperial territory as "stepping-stones" to strike at Coruscant. As part of the mobilization, Wedge Antilles was recalled from a propaganda tour and restored to active duty. Antilles's legendary X-wing unit, Rogue Squadron, was reformed with a roster of new pilots.

After two costly attacks, the New Republic captured Borleias, in the Colonies region. Borleias was perfectly situated as a forward base for a Coruscant assault. Admiral Ackbar, however, knew that the

*Coruscant falls to the New Republic*

capital planet's defensive energy shield would negate any orbital bombardment. Before the attack could begin, Coruscant's shield would have to fall.

Antilles and Rogue Squadron were sent undercover into Imperial City to sabotage the planet's shield generator. Also, sixteen of the galaxy's worst criminals were freed from the spice mines of Kessel and loosed on Coruscant, in the hopes that they would foster chaos. The latter decision was unusual for the New Republic and was opposed by many members of the ruling council, who were proven correct in the end. The freed criminals, led by Y'ull Acib, resurrected the defunct Black Sun criminal cartel, which would plague the New Republic in later years.

Rogue Squadron's operatives gambled that if they could condense a large amount of water vapor and create a monster storm, they could knock out Coruscant's shields with lightning strikes. The Rogues commandeered a forty-story construction

droid to take them to a command building, then took remote control of one of the planet's orbiting solar mirrors. The tightly focused light beam from the mirror flash-boiled one of Imperial City's artificial reservoirs. The steam cloud coalesced into an angry cloudburst, and soon the shields collapsed.

With Coruscant vulnerable, Ackbar leapt into the system with a full armada. The battle was intense, but surprisingly easy; Ysanne Isard had kept only a handful of Star Destroyers to defend the capital. Ackbar wiped out all resistance, and at last Coruscant was in the hands of the New Republic.

## The Krytos Virus
### 7–7.5 A.B.Y.

When the New Republic secured the Imperial Palace, they discovered that Isard had vanished. Worse, she had left behind a sick and dying world, for Isard's chief scientist, Evir Derricote, had

*The* Lusankya *escapes its tomb*

engineered an artificial plague—the Krytos virus.

Within days of transmission, the Krytos virus turned healthy flesh into a bloody soup. Isard had seeded Coruscant's water reservoirs with the plague before the Rebel arrival, and millions of citizens had already contracted the disease. However, Derricote had carefully tailored the Krytos virus to affect only specific nonhuman species—Sullustans, Gamorreans, and others. The fact that Coruscant's human population was immune drove a wedge between the New Republic's member species.

The Krytos plague spoiled the New Republic's triumph and made it appear ineffectual and weak. Thus, governing the civilian population of Coruscant proved nearly impossible. Furthermore, Mon Mothma was forced to spend millions of credits on voluminous amounts of bacta to treat the infected and research a vaccine—credits that the near-bankrupt government didn't have.

Another event diverted the public's attention during this difficult time: the trial of Tycho Celchu. Immediately following the liberation of Coruscant, Celchu, a member of Rogue Squadron, had been arrested for treason and the murder of his fellow pilot Corran Horn. Prosecuting attorneys at his trial claimed Celchu had been operating as a brainwashed Imperial agent ever since his incarceration in the Empire's *Lusankya* prison.

The truth was shocking: not only was Celchu innocent, but Corran Horn was alive. Horn had been secretly captured by Isard and himself imprisoned in *Lusankya*, where he was forced to endure regular torture and indoctrination sessions. His only relief came in conversation with his fellow prisoners, one of whom was the famed Alliance leader Jan Dodonna, who had been captured during the evacuation of Yavin 4 seven years earlier.

Horn escaped, forcing Isard to abandon her hiding place. As the members of Rogue Squadron flew a mission above Imperial City, a panicked call suddenly came from the Manarai Mountains district. Antilles and his squadron watched as a massive object rose from the subterranean depths, obliterating vast tracts of homes and businesses as it came to the surface—a Super Star Destroyer that answered to the name *Lusankya*. Despite the efforts of Rogue Squadron to stop it, the *Lusankya* tore a gaping hole out of Imperial City's heart, killing mil-

lions. It then vanished into hyperspace, taking with it Ysanne Isard, her forces, and many prisoners.

The presence of Corran Horn, alive, cleared Celchu of the murder charge. Luke Skywalker investigated Horn's background and discovered that the pilot was actually the grandson of the great Jedi Nejaa Halcyon, who had eliminated a Dark Jedi enclave decades earlier. Horn refused Skywalker's offer to train him as a Jedi, though he reconsidered his decision years later.

New Republic scientists developed a cure for the Krytos virus by mixing bacta with *kor*, a rare grade of the spice ryll. The resulting vaccine, rylca, was administered to Coruscant's alien population and prevented further loss of life. However, though the immediate threat had been averted, interracial suspicions remained volatile for some time.

## The Bacta War
### 7.5 A.B.Y.

Ysanne Isard fled Coruscant aboard the *Lusankya* and quickly acted to hold her power base. At Thyferra, the bacta-manufacturing planet, she supported a coup and was elected head of state by the victorious faction. The New Republic was unhappy with the development, but it was against their principles to depose a duly-elected planetary leader. Since the Thyferran government refused to move against Isard, Wedge Antilles and Rogue Squadron resigned from the New Republic fleet. As civilians, they answered to no one and were free to move against Isard on their own.

But the bacta planet was defended by four capital ships: the *Lusankya*, two Imperial Star Destroyers, and a Victory Star Destroyer. A direct, frontal assault would be a quick and expensive way to commit suicide. Instead, Antilles flitted around like a Sacorrian grain fly—stinging Isard, then retreating to a safe distance before she could swat back. The Rogues occupied an abandoned space station near Yag'Dhul and hired smuggler Booster Terrik to manage the station. Terrik obtained weapons from the smuggling kingpin Talon Karrde, and Rogue Squadron began harassing Isard's bacta convoys.

Rogue Squadron destroyed one capital ship in a fight near the rubble of the Alderaan Graveyard and convinced the captain of another to defect with his ship. With half of her defensive force suddenly gone, Isard ordered the *Lusankya* and her remaining Star Destroyer to blast the Yag'Dhul space station to atoms.

Antilles and the other Rogues seized the opportunity and jumped into hyperspace to attack the now-undefended Thyferra. At Yag'Dhul, the *Lusankya* closed to firing range, but the space station suddenly locked on to the Super Star Destroyer with over three hundred proton torpedoes. Knowing that no vessel's shields could withstand such a volley, the *Lusankya* fled to Thyferra, and the remaining outgunned Star Destroyer surrendered.

It was all a bluff perpetuated by Antilles. The Yag'Dhul space station didn't have *any* torpedoes, just three hundred targeting locks. The torpedoes were aboard the small armada of freighters and X-wings heading for Thyferra.

At the bacta planet, the Rogues and the *Lusankya* both emerged from hyperspace and fell upon one another with a vengeance. More than eighty proton torpedoes impacted against the Super Star Destroyer, collapsing its shields and ripping its guts open. When Booster Terrik arrived, commanding the newly captured Star Destroyer, and joined the fight, the ailing *Lusankya* surrendered. The damaged *Lusankya* was towed to a secret shipyard for extensive repairs.

Sadly, Jan Dodonna and the rest of the Imperial prisoners had been transferred off the ship weeks earlier. Their rescue would have to wait for another day.

Ysanne Isard was smart enough to know when she was beaten and attempted to escape Thyferra. Her shuttle was destroyed while trying to make the jump to hyperspace, and Isard was believed killed. Isard, however, had engineered the incident to cover her tracks. She spent the following years putting herself back together mentally, and would plague the New Republic again in the wake of the Thrawn incident.

Antilles and Rogue Squadron were welcomed back as heroes. After much wrangling with New Republic Intelligence, Booster Terrik was allowed to keep his captured Star Destroyer, which he renamed the *Errant Venture*. The ship became a movable trading bazaar, famous for eclectic merchandise.

In the aftermath of the Bacta War, the New Republic captured another Star Destroyer, the *Tyrant*, from an underdefended Imperial fueling outpost. This ship had been a part of Darth Vader's Death Squadron and had assisted in the decimation of Echo Base on Hoth. Impressed by the symbolism, Councilor Leia Organa renamed the vessel *Rebel Dream* and made it her personal flagship.

## The Hunt for Zsinj
### 7.5–8 A.B.Y.

The New Republic had been right about one thing: controlling Coruscant was the key to the Galactic Civil War. As soon as Isard lost control of the capital world, the fragmentation within the Empire grew more severe as officers lost faith in their leaders. A coalition of moffs and Imperial advisers replaced Isard, but their power quickly slipped away in favor of warlords like Zsinj.

Warlord Zsinj became the most powerful Imperial warlord, having gained many new officers, ships, and planets during the post-Isard defections. He was arrogant enough to fight his war on two fronts, against the New Republic and against his former comrades in the Empire, whom he viewed as weak-willed and ineffectual. Furthermore, he possessed the mighty Super Star Destroyer *Iron Fist*, which could take on an entire armada by itself. The New Republic made the liberation of Zsinj's dominion a top priority and put together a task force under the command of General Han Solo to hunt down the warlord. The task force departed on its mission just prior to the events of the Bacta War.

Aboard the Mon Calamari flagship *Mon Remonda*, Solo probed the borders of Zsinj-controlled territory and witnessed firsthand the horrors the warlord perpetuated on worlds that resisted his will. Solo was supplemented by the best military units the New Republic had to offer, including the legendary Rogue Squadron, but another group of X-wing pilots would provide the key to toppling Warlord Zsinj.

Commander Antilles, following his reinstatement in the New Republic military, chose not to join the *Mon Remonda* mission. Instead, Antilles assembled a new group of pilots—Wraith

Squadron, composed of commandos, snipers, spies, and infiltrators. Soon after their formation, the Wraiths captured a Corellian corvette belonging to Zsinj and decided to pose as the corvette's standard crew. The ruse allowed them to infiltrate Zsinj's fleet, where they learned of an ambush planned against the New Republic on Ession in the Corporate Sector. The Battle of Ession was a victory for the New Republic, which demolished one of Zsinj's Star Destroyers and bombed a key manufacturing plant into oblivion.

The subterfuge with the captured corvette would not work a second time, so the commandos of Wraith Squadron changed tactics. They posed as a pirate band in order to work their way into Zsinj's loose organization of freelance raiders. The warlord hired the disguised Wraiths as mercenaries for his strike on the vast shipbuilding facilities in the Kuat system. Kuat Drive Yards, still allied with the Empire, had nearly completed a new Super Star Destroyer. Zsinj planned to steal the colossal vessel and pair it with the *Iron Fist* to deliver a double hammer blow to his enemies. New Republic saboteurs foiled Zsinj's plans by destroying both of the new vessel's topside shield generator domes, and the unprotected warship was blasted into scrap by Solo and the *Mon Remonda*, though the *Iron Fist* escaped into hyperspace.

After a brief layover to repair damage to the *Mon Remonda*, Solo headed back out to hunt down Zsinj. The warlord, however, had a more devious plot afoot. Several of Zsinj's pet scientists had developed a method of rapid, forced brainwashing that could turn even the most placid citizen into a raving murderer, and the technique was tailored to work with specific species—Twi'leks, Gotals, Sullustans, and others. Much as Ysanne Isard had attempted to do with the "aliens only" Krytos virus, Zsinj preyed on the suspicions and resentment that many species felt toward humans.

Project Minefield, as it was known in Zsinj's organization, resulted in hundreds of deaths, including several high-profile assassination attempts. A brainwashed Twi'lek tried to kill Ackbar, while Mon Mothma's loyal Gotal bodyguard suddenly turned on her, but was killed before he could injure the chief councilor. Aboard the *Mon Remonda*, a Twi'lek A-wing pilot shot out

*Warlord Zsinj*

the bridge viewport and nearly killed Solo through explosive decompression. Fortunately, New Republic Intelligence cracked the pattern behind the attacks and shut down Project Minefield before it could cause further havoc.

In an unprecedented move, the New Republic formed a loose alliance with the Empire to wipe out Zsinj. The Imperial fleet had their own anti-Zsinj task force, led by Admiral Rogriss. A New Republic representative held a secret meeting with Rogriss aboard his flagship, and the two sides hammered out an uneasy agreement. Each side would exchange all intelligence data it had gathered on Zsinj's organization, no strings attached. The Empire and the New Republic now viewed Zsinj as their common foe.

Growing frustrated at the length of the campaign and the paucity of his victories, Solo authorized a number of lures to draw out Zsinj and force a confrontation. Since the warlord increasingly regarded the conflict as a personal showdown between himself and Solo, a fake mockup of the *Millennium Falcon* was constructed and flown to worlds deep in Zsinj's territory. This vessel was later fitted with a bomb and used to destroy an enemy Dreadnaught.

Zsinj, however, did not take the bait. He realized the Imperial–New Republic collaboration was

crippling his ability to hold his kingdom together, and devised a secret stratagem of survival. Since his enemies seemed fixated on the destruction of the *Iron Fist*, Zsinj resolved to give them the illusion of what they craved. His agents gathered up all the wreckage of the Super Star Destroyer ruined at Kuat and pieced it back together in a hodgepodge of structural beams and hull plates. On the bow of the makeshift vessel they printed the words IRON FIST, then waited for the warlord's orders.

Solo and Rogriss collaborated on an assault in the Vahaba asteroid belt that severely damaged the real *Iron Fist*. The wounded Super Star Destroyer jumped to the nearby system of Selaggis, but Solo followed with his full fleet, intent on blasting Zsinj into vapor. As the *Mon Remonda* closed to firing range, the crippled *Iron Fist* disappeared into a black cube of nothingness.

Warlord Zsinj had obtained an orbital night-cloak—a string of satellites that would absorb all visible light. By deploying the nightcloak in a cube pattern, he created a small hideaway that his enemy's sensors couldn't penetrate. The decoy Star Destroyer was already in position inside the night-cloak, and Zsinj triggered its destruction. Then the *Iron Fist* jumped to hyperspace.

When the nightcloak collapsed, Solo saw the wreckage of a Super Star Destroyer that clearly bore the markings of the *Iron Fist*. Confident that Zsinj's fleet had been crippled beyond recovery, Solo ordered a triumphant return to Coruscant.

## The Hapans and the Dathomir Nightsisters
### 8 A.B.Y.

General Han Solo and the *Mon Remonda* returned to Coruscant. The arduous, five-month campaign had exhausted everyone in the task force, and Solo planned to put his crew in for some much-needed

*The Hapan envoy to Coruscant*

downtime. When he arrived at the capital world, however, he was startled to find dozens of saucer-shaped Battle Dragons in orbit. The mysterious Hapans were making a social call.

Any description of the Hapes Consortium requires superlatives; it is the most powerful, most wealthy, most cultured, and most standoffish political federation in its region of space. Three thousand years earlier the Hapan queen mother had sealed the borders of the star cluster, and as Hapes developed in isolation behind the Transitory Mists, legends of its fantastic riches continued to grow.

Several months earlier, Councilor Leia Organa's diplomatic visit to the Hapan worlds had convinced Queen Mother Ta'a Chume to consider the possibility of a union with the New Republic. The Hapan honor fleet circling Coruscant was a remarkable sight, for this was the first time in millennia that the reclusive society had made significant outside contact.

In Coruscant's Grand Reception Hall the Hapan delegation presented Councilor Organa with many extravagant gifts, including several Imperial Star Destroyers captured by the Hapans during recent border skirmishes. But the final gift was the biggest surprise of all. Prince Isolder, the queen mother's son and heir, presented himself to Organa as a marriage suitor.

Organa was shocked, but though she had for years been romantically entangled with Han Solo, she was politically savvy enough to realize the benefits of an arranged marriage between two political factions. Her own royal upbringing on Alderaan had previously exposed her to such maneuverings. Mon Mothma, knowing that the Hapan navy and treasury could help greatly in ending the Galactic Civil War, urged her friend to accept Isolder's offer.

General Solo, however, grew deeply jealous of the attention showered on her. Hoping to reclaim Organa's affection, he won a habitable planet, Dathomir, worth 2.4 billion credits, in an outrageously high-stakes sabacc game. Solo hoped the planet could house the homeless refugees of Alderaan. Unfortunately, Dathomir was deep in the heart of Zsinj's territory. Disappointed that his gamble had failed, and desperate to get Leia Organa's attention, Solo impulsively resigned his general's commission and kidnapped her, accom-

*Isolder, the Chume'da of Hapes*

panied by the faithful Chewbacca and a flustered C-3PO.

The *Millennium Falcon* emerged from hyperspace near the blue-green world of Dathomir. There, Solo discovered that Zsinj had built an impressive orbital stardock above the planet, where the Super Star Destroyer *Iron Fist* was undergoing reconstruction. The *Falcon* fell under attack and barely managed to touch down on Dathomir's forested surface.

The group headed off on foot through the woods, but were soon intercepted by a patrol of female warriors belonging to the Singing Mountain Clan. The women rode tamed rancors, similar to the one that Jabba the Hutt had kept as a pet beneath the floor of his palace. These women, the Witches of Dathomir, could cast "magic spells" by tapping into the Force; they were the descendants of Allya, a fallen Jedi Knight who had been exiled to the planet more than six centuries in the past.

Luke Skywalker, meanwhile, had been scouring the galaxy for lost secrets of the once-great Jedi order. On Toola he discovered data cards telling the story of the crashed Jedi training ship *Chu'unthor*, and Master Yoda's efforts to recover the vessel from Dathomir. Skywalker returned to Coruscant and learned of his sister's kidnapping; before long he had agreed to team up with Prince Isolder of Hapes on a rescue mission to Dathomir.

Skywalker discovered that the planet's overwhelming life energy had a peculiar magnifying effect on his Force abilities, allowing him to accomplish feats that had previously been beyond him. He and Isolder discovered the rusting wreck of the *Chu'unthor* and met Teneniel Djo, a beautiful witch of the Singing Mountain Clan. She reunited them with Solo and Organa.

But an outcast clan of witches, the Nightsisters, made an attack on the Singing Mountain Clan in an attempt to steal the *Falcon*. The Nightsisters possessed dark-side powers and had an army of Imperial slaves at their disposal, remnants of a group abandoned by the Emperor eight years earlier. There had been an Imperial prison on Dathomir, but when the Emperor had learned of the Nightsisters, he had destroyed all the prison's starships from orbit; better to lose a prison than to allow rival Force users loose on the galaxy.

The Nightsisters were desperate to escape their planet, and directed their prison army in a fierce but ultimately futile attack on the Singing Mountain stronghold.

## The Death of Zsinj
### 8 A.B.Y.

Warlord Zsinj was well aware of the existence of the Nightsisters and the extent of their power. He opened negotiations with Gethzerion, leader of the Nightsisters, and delivered an ultimatum. Gethzerion would give him Han Solo, or he would activate his orbital nightcloak—the light-absorbing device that had been used at the Battle of Selaggis. A full array of nightcloak satellites in position around Dathomir would turn the planet into a frozen ice ball within days.

When he learned that the Nightsisters' attack on the Singing Mountain Clan had failed, Zsinj activated the nightcloak to encourage Gethzerion's immediate compliance. The skies grew dark and the temperature plunged, as the shrewd witch made her counteroffer. Gethzerion agreed to provide Solo, but also asked for a ship to provide a means of escape from her dying planet. The

Nightsisters promised to fly the vessel deep into New Republic territory and carve out a path of destruction that would help satisfy Zsinj's thirst for revenge. Impressed, Zsinj agreed to send two transports—an armed craft for transporting Solo, and a defenseless, stripped-down model for the Nightsisters to use as they pleased.

Han Solo was brought to the Imperial prison, where Zsinj's twin shuttles were just landing. Gethzerion turned traitor, killing all the Imperial guards—including Zsinj's longtime aide, General Melvar—with a crushing blow of Force energy. Solo was saved from certain death by the timely arrival of the *Falcon*, but Gethzerion and her followers escaped on the armed shuttle. The Nightsisters were intercepted just outside the atmosphere by two of the warlord's Star Destroyers. After a brief but withering crossfire, all that remained of the shuttle was glowing metal.

The Nightsisters were gone, but Zsinj's fleet still barricaded Dathomir. The *Millennium Falcon* knocked out the orbital nightcloak, and the full battle fleet of the Hapes Consortium arrived to take on the *Iron Fist* and dozens of Zsinj's smaller warships. During the chaos, Solo flew the *Falcon* straight at the bridge of the *Iron Fist* and released a pair of concussion missiles at point-blank range. Warlord Zsinj was vaporized in an instant. The Battle of Dathomir was over.

In the aftermath, Singing Mountain Clan Mother Augwynne united the witch clans of Dathomir and petitioned for planetary membership in the New Republic. Luke Skywalker was given a box filled with log recorder discs from the *Chu'unthor* wreckage, which would prove invaluable when he established the Jedi academy.

Prince Isolder of Hapes had fallen madly in love with Teneniel Djo of the Singing Mountain Clan, a development that outraged Queen Mother Ta'a Chume. Nevertheless, Isolder soon married Djo, making her the heir apparent to the throne of the Hapes Consortium. Isolder and Djo soon had a daughter, Tenel Ka, who proved very strong in the Force.

The adventure on Dathomir had caused Han Solo and Leia Organa to grow even closer to one another, and they agreed to be married upon their return to Coruscant. The New Republic citizenry

*The wedding of Han Solo and Leia Organa*

were more than willing to forgive Solo for his kidnapping escapade, in large part because it had provided such entertaining fodder for the daily newsnets. Since Organa wasn't willing to press charges, the New Republic Inner Council made no move to censure Solo and tried to cover up the incident, as well as the embarrassing security breach that it highlighted.

The wedding was held in the Alderaanian consulate building on Coruscant, attended by hundreds of friends and dignitaries and watched on holovid by billions across the galaxy. For weeks afterward the event was endlessly replayed, and the coverage was universally positive.

## Picking up the Pieces
### 8.5 A.B.Y.

Prince Isolder vowed to join the New Republic after the Dathomir incident, but his pledge did not sit well with the Hapan Royal Court and the individual planetary potentates. Queen Mother Ta'a Chume was only too willing to bend to their will in the interest of preserving internal stability. Hapes promised to commit their full Battle Dragon armada "in due time." Mon Mothma's hoped-for strategic alliance never materialized.

The sudden implosion of Warlord Zsinj's domain emboldened the Imperial fleet. The coalition of advisers that had supplanted Isard worked furiously. Now that the goal had been achieved, Admiral Rogriss and other fleet commanders moved to seize the newly liberated territory. All pretense of former partnership with the New Republic was abandoned.

One benefit of the Hapan incident was the New Republic's acquisition of several new Star Destroyers, which were presented to Leia Organa as gifts during the Coruscant reception. Though the Hapans did not directly participate in any of the

battles, these warships, added to the Star Destroyers the New Republic had already captured, gave the fleet some formidable muscle when Admiral Ackbar led the New Republic to the Outer Rim to fight over the scraps of Zsinj's empire.

Ackbar and Rogriss ran directly into a *third* fleet—that of Warlord Teradoc, the self-appointed high admiral. The New Republic Star Destroyers were thrown into the worst of the fighting and consequently took the brunt of the punishment. Most of the Hapan ships, as well as the Star Destroyer *Crynyd*, were destroyed. The *Emancipator* and *Liberator* suffered severe damage and were recalled to undergo extensive repairs at the Hast shipyards. At the Battle of Storinal, Princess Leia's flagship *Rebel Dream* was mercilessly shelled by the Imperial Star Destroyer *Peremptory* and recaptured by the Empire, its crew of thirty-seven thousand taken prisoner. Organa Solo was on Coruscant at the time of the incident.

But for every hit the New Republic took, they gave it back to the Empire threefold. Admiral Rogriss lost the majority of the engagements. The New Republic at last captured Kuat, giving them access to the system's unparalleled shipbuilding docks, though damage to the yards was so extensive that new construction was delayed indefinitely. Unfortunately, the Kuat Drive Yards design team escaped to the Deep Core aboard the half-completed warship *Eclipse*. Bloodied, Rogriss ordered a retreat. Warlord Teradoc, whose hit-and-run strikes had made him an exasperating gadfly, scurried back to his own territory. Admiral Ackbar fortified his newest gains. The New Republic now controlled three-quarters of the settled galaxy. And during the relentless battles, the Republic and Empire suffered grave fleet losses. The construction and acquisition of new warships became a top priority for both sides.

## PART VI

# EMPIRE RESURGENT

**T**hough the New Republic kept busy with rogue warlords such as Zsinj, the Imperial dominion had been reduced to a mere quarter of what Palpatine had once called his own, most of it in outlying sectors along the Rim. The surviving moffs were forced to fight the Republic on one front, while simultaneously keeping their beloved Empire from splitting into ideological factions under squabbling warlords.

Since Imperial forces had suffered decisive defeats at Endor and Coruscant, overconfident New Republic prognosticators predicted the imminent end to all Imperial resistance. But the wheels of the Empire continued to turn, even in secret. The next two years very nearly saw the death of the New Republic.

## THE DEPREDATIONS OF GRAND ADMIRAL THRAWN

**9 A.B.Y.**

The ailing Empire needed a miracle, and they got one when a brilliant military commander emerged from the Unknown Regions—Thrawn, the last of the Emperor's grand admirals, who had been isolated since before the Battle of Endor. Upon his return Grand Admiral Thrawn picked the Imperial Star Destroyer *Chimaera* as his flagship, making Captain Pellaeon—who had ordered the Imperial retreat after the disaster at Endor—his de facto second in command. This further elevated Pellaeon in the eyes of the moffs.

For six months, Thrawn reorganized the fleet and executed strategic raids along the New Republic–Imperial border. While these incursions weren't sufficient to panic the New Republic, they deeply impressed the moffs, governors, and other political leaders. Thrawn was effectively handed the reins of the Empire.

At the time, the moffs felt their action was quite shrewd. Thrawn was a political outsider, and an alien no less—a prime candidate to become a puppet figurehead. Their decision backfired, however, when Thrawn proved to be incredibly popular, not just among the fleet, but with the Imperial citizenry at large. The moffs had unwittingly set a precedent that would repeat itself throughout the remaining history of the Empire—rule by the most distinguished military commander, instead of by the craftiest politician.

*Grand Admiral Thrawn*

Thrawn consolidated loyal Imperial forces, then isolated and marginalized warlord fiefdoms such as Admiral Krennel's domain and Grand Moff Kaine's Pentastar Alignment. Before long, he made his first overt strike against the New Republic, capturing key information from the library world of Obroa-skai. Analysis of the data led him to Wayland, site of the Emperor's secret Mount Tantiss storehouse. On Wayland, Thrawn collected three items.

The first was a functional cloaking device, an offshoot of the Project Vorknkx research conducted before the Emperor's demise. The second was an array of Spaarti cloning cylinders stored deep in the bowels of Mount Tantiss—technology that the Emperor had adapted for his own uses in the Deep Core. The third "item" was the mad Jedi Joruus C'baoth, apparently a clone of the original Jedi Master Jorus C'baoth. Joruus C'baoth had been stranded on Wayland for years and was completely insane.

Thrawn was protected from C'baoth's abilities by the Force-blocking influence of ysalamiri creatures. He secured C'baoth's cooperation by promising him he could deliver Luke Skywalker and Leia Organa Solo, as well as Organa Solo's unborn twins. The lunatic Jedi Master wanted to mold this group into his evil, twisted apprentices.

Joruus C'baoth linked the ships of Thrawn's fleet together via the Force, to form a supernatural fighting team. Grand Admiral Thrawn was determined to hold up his end of the bargain. Twice, he dispatched teams of Noghri death commandos to kidnap Luke Skywalker and Leia Organa Solo, but both attempts failed.

Thrawn activated the cloning complex and began producing thousands of clone soldiers; he also sent a Spaarti cylinder to his secret base in the Unknown Regions for a special project: *producing a clone of himself*. As Thrawn knew well, previous experiments had failed disastrously when clones were grown too quickly, largely due to interference generated by life forces and to the subtle pull of the Force. However, he employed Force-blocking ysalamiri that would allow him to grow clones in mere days, instead of months or years. However, though he gained an endless supply of loyal vat-grown troopers, he did not have the military infra-

structure needed to outfit and transport them to the battlefield. Even Thrawn was desperate for starships.

The grand admiral developed a novel way to restock his fleet and simultaneously rob the New Republic of much of its own. Mole miners, compact burrowing vehicles, also were capable of drilling through a starship's hull. Thrawn planned to steal dozens of mole miners, then use them to deliver armed boarding parties to every New Republic warship stationed at the Sluis Van shipyards.

Unfortunately for the galaxy's unluckiest entrepreneur, Thrawn chose the planet Nkllon for his mole miner raid. Lando Calrissian had invested millions of credits into the construction of Nomad City, an ambitious mobile mining complex that remained on the cool shadow side of the planet throughout Nkllon's ninety-day rotation. Nomad City had just begun to turn a profit when one of Thrawn's Star Destroyers arrived, stealing fifty-one of the expensive mole miners.

## Talon Karrde and the Smugglers
### 9 A.B.Y.

Following the theft, Calrissian accompanied Han Solo to Myrkr, the base of operations for smuggling kingpin Talon Karrde. Solo intended to convince Karrde to ship cargo for the New Republic, and Calrissian hoped his underworld contacts might help them to set up a meeting. Neither man realized, however, that Talon Karrde had a very familiar figure locked up in a storage silo.

Several days prior, Luke Skywalker's X-wing had been yanked out of hyperspace by an Interdictor cruiser and severely damaged by Thrawn's flagship. Stranded without power in the middle of the interstellar void, Skywalker was picked up by Karrde's personal freighter. The smuggling chief remembered the sizable Imperial bounty that had been placed on his captive's head, and imprisoned Skywalker at his base.

Karrde hadn't counted on his prisoner's resourcefulness. Shortly after the arrival of Solo and Calrissian, Skywalker escaped and stole a Skipray blastboat, but Mara Jade, Karrde's second in command, followed in a second blastboat. The

*The battle of Sluis Van*

derers, but Karrde's men sprang an ambush and rescued them. Karrde's actions placed him squarely on the side of the New Republic, and he evacuated his Myrkr base just ahead of Thrawn's reprisal force.

Calrissian sustained a minor wound during the fighting, so Skywalker, Calrissian, and Solo departed and headed for the medcenter at Sluis Van. They arrived just as Grand Admiral Thrawn unleashed his fleet on the Sluis Van shipyards, using the new cloaking device to increase his element of surprise.

Commander Wedge Antilles and Rogue Squadron—coincidentally at Sluis Van on escort duty—fought against the enemy starfighters, but Calrissian soon realized Thrawn's swarms of TIE fighters were merely a distraction. As dogfights raged above the orbital dry docks, the Nkllon mole miners jetted to the docked vessels and drilled through the bulkheads of the New Republic ships. Commando teams leapt out and seized control of the bridges. Within minutes, dozens of hijacked capital ships pulled out of their berths and headed toward a hyperspace jump point on the fringe of the system.

Calrissian's presence made all the difference. The administrator of the Nkllon mines transmitted the master control code that reactivated all the mole miners simultaneously. Obediently, the machines began to drill again, and they kept drilling—straight through the sensitive navigation and propulsion controls. Thrawn was forced to retreat without his prize.

However, more than forty New Republic warships were grievously damaged, and removed from military service until their bridges could be rebuilt—a lengthy process that would take many months. Though he did prevent the grand admiral from capturing the vital ships, Calrissian's last-ditch solution made him persona non grata in the New Republic Fleet Command office.

## The Noghri Switch Sides
### 9 A.B.Y.

During the Battle of Sluis Van, Chewbacca had placed Leia Organa Solo under his personal protection on the Wookiee homeworld. But even the guardianship of a Wookiee city was unable to

high-speed chase ended when both ships collided and crashed.

Skywalker and Jade were forced to hike through Myrkr's dense forest for three days. The trees were infested with thousands of ysalamiri, meaning that Skywalker could not connect with the Force; it was as if he had suddenly gone blind, like the legendary Jedi Ulic Qel-Droma.

During their trek, Jade informed Skywalker that she had once been an elite Emperor's Hand, in the service of Palpatine. Since Luke Skywalker was indirectly responsible for the Emperor's death, she had vowed to kill him and avenge her former master. But Mara Jade put aside her homicidal impulses until they reached Hyllyard City at the edge of the forest.

An Imperial scout patrol picked up the two wan-

prevent a third attack by the Noghri. They failed again, but this time Organa Solo captured one of the creatures alive, a Noghri commando named Khabarakh.

The history of the Noghri was laid bare in the Kashyyyk interrogation chamber. Khabarakh, like all members of his species, revered Darth Vader as an avenging savior. Vader had come to the Noghri homeworld, Honoghr, decades before and had seen the devastation that had been wreaked on the planet's ecosystem by a crashed starship. The Empire promised to restore Honoghr, and the grateful Noghri vowed to serve Vader as his private death commandos. In truth, the Imperial restoration teams deliberately kept Honoghr poisoned, thus holding the Noghri in the Empire's thrall.

The extent of the Empire's deception was unknown to either Khabarakh or Organa Solo, but she suspected she might bring the aliens around through diplomacy. After all, she was the daughter and heir of Darth Vader, and the Noghri would grant their savior's offspring an audience. Organa Solo, Chewbacca, and the droid C-3PO boarded the Noghri's ship for the journey to his homeworld.

Honoghr was a blasted wasteland, covered with endless, scorched plains. The Noghri were continually on the verge of catastrophic famine. Organa Solo and her companions met with the clan and discussed how the New Republic might help. Many Noghri were suspicious of her motives, but accorded Organa Solo the respect she was due as a blood relative of Vader.

Before long, she uncovered the truth concerning the Empire's trickery. Instead of purifying Honoghr's parched soil, Imperial decontamination droids had been prolonging the devastating famine for decades. Filled with justifiable rage, Organa Solo revealed this to the Noghri, winning them over to her side.

Immediately, word went out to all Noghri death commandos currently on missions for the Empire. Secretly, they abandoned their assignments and returned to Honoghr, or attempted to sabotage various Imperial efforts. News of the Empire's treachery even reached the Star Destroyer *Chimaera*, where the Noghri warrior Rukh was employed as Grand Admiral Thrawn's personal bodyguard. Rukh chose to bide his time, waiting for the appropriate moment.

## The Katana *Fleet and the Clone Troopers*
### 9 A.B.Y.

Thrawn's machinations extended beyond military maneuvers; he manipulated financial records and banking transactions to make it appear as if Admiral Ackbar, the commander of the New Republic fleet, was guilty of treason. At the urging of the Bothan councilor, Borsk Fey'lya, Ackbar was placed under house arrest until the matter could be resolved.

Han Solo and Lando Calrissian decided to investigate the matter on their own. They went to the jungle planet New Cov, where their vessel was threatened by an Imperial Star Destroyer. Three vintage Clone Wars–era Dreadnaughts mysteriously arrived to provide cover fire, then escorted them to the Dreadnaughts' hidden staging area, a prefabricated military command center run by General Garm Bel Iblis. In the nine years since he had quit the Rebel Alliance, the legendary Corellian senator had built up an impressive private army. His hit-and-run strikes against the Empire had been successful, but limited in scope. His stubborn pride, and simmering anger toward Mon Mothma, had prevented him from rejoining the New Republic.

Bel Iblis's Dreadnaughts came from the *Katana* fleet. The two hundred *Katana* Dreadnaughts had been the object of countless "lost treasure" hunts for generations, but now, with both sides in the Galactic Civil War desperately in need of warships, the acquisition of the lost armada could easily tip the scales. While Bel Iblis did not know the location of the fleet, he had a contact who did, a Captain Hoffner; unfortunately, before Solo and Calrissian could meet with him, Grand Admiral Thrawn apprehended the man.

The smuggling chief Talon Karrde had also discovered the location of the *Katana* fleet and had just been rescued by Luke Skywalker and Mara Jade from a prison cell aboard the *Chimaera*. This evened the scales; both the Empire and the New Republic had a route to the lost fleet. The New Republic hastily threw together a strike team and arrived at the barren point in space where the forgotten Dreadnaughts had been drifting for decades. Thrawn's forces arrived moments later, and a raging space battle broke out while Skywalker and Solo boarded the flagship *Katana*. Unexpected reinforcements—General Garm Bel Iblis and his Dreadnaughts, along with members of Talon Karrde's smuggling organization—briefly bolstered the New Republic, but the Imperials called in their own reserves.

Aboard the *Katana*, Skywalker and Solo fought off a boarding party of stormtroopers. It was Solo who remembered that the *Katana* fleet had been primarily slave-rigged. The slave controls in the *Katana*'s bridge allowed Solo to reactivate one of the idle Dreadnaughts and remote-steer it straight into the nose of the Star Destroyer *Peremptory*. Both ships exploded in a spectacular fireball. Suddenly outnumbered, the Imperials fled.

The New Republic's victory celebration was dampened by two pieces of sobering news. Out of the original two hundred Dreadnaughts, only fifteen remained; the remainder were already in Imperial hands. And when the bodies of the dead stormtroopers aboard the *Katana* were examined, a chilling fact came to light. Each corpse shared the same face.

News that the grand admiral had resurrected the forbidden science of cloning terrified the New Republic and proved to be a very potent weapon in Thrawn's psychological war to undermine his enemy's morale. Mon Mothma and the others pictured a new round of Clone Wars, and finding Thrawn's cloning complex became their top priority.

Fortunately, Admiral Ackbar was reinstated as fleet commander, the financial scandal having been revealed as an Imperial setup. Calrissian returned to Nkllon and his Nomad City mining operation, but Thrawn attacked the planet again and left the operation in tatters.

On Coruscant, Leia Organa Solo gave birth to twins—a girl and a boy, Jaina and Jacen—who were to join the new generation of Jedi Knights.

Mara Jade again found herself acting in service of the New Republic, but because she had been an Emperor's Hand, she did so under a shadow of suspicion. Leia Organa Solo knew not to judge Jade by her past. As Emperor's Hand, Jade had been privy to many of Palpatine's secrets—including the location of the Mount Tantiss cloning facility on

*The new generation*

Wayland. Jade, Skywalker, Solo, Chewbacca, Calrissian, and their droids headed for Wayland to destroy Thrawn's ready-made soldier factory.

Upon reaching Mount Tantiss, the others investigated the cloning chamber, while Skywalker and Jade headed for the Emperor's auxiliary throne room to look for a master self-destruct switch. Waiting for them in the throne, like a spider at the center of its web, was Joruus C'baoth.

The demented Jedi Master easily overcame both Skywalker and Jade. While he cruelly toyed with them, he unleashed a shocking surprise: secretly, C'baoth had grown a special clone from Skywalker's own genetic material—from the hand he had lost at Cloud City. The mindless drone, Luuke Skywalker, was his exact duplicate.

The clone wielded its own lightsaber—the blue-bladed saber that had once belonged to Anakin Skywalker. Given to Luke by Obi-Wan Kenobi, it had been considered lost since the tragic events on Cloud City. The doubles squared off in a frenzied duel. Though she had often expressed her desire to murder the man who had brought about the Emperor's death, Mara Jade ended the combat by killing the Luuke clone. C'baoth, in a fit of rage, collapsed the chamber's ceiling, but Jade skewered him cleanly through the torso.

Deep in the lower levels, Calrissian and Chewbacca sabotaged the central equipment column of the cloning complex, triggering an irreversible overload spiral. The entire infiltration team escaped just as Mount Tantiss exploded.

The laboratory's destruction also meant the loss of priceless artworks and historical artifacts, trophies stored in the Emperor's private vaults. It seemed to bury forever all evidence of a long-standing scandal—Bothan involvement in the devastation of Caamas—much to Councilor Borsk Fey'lya's relief. More than a decade would pass before a data card plucked from the rubble would stir up old animosities and touch off a galaxywide search for the Caamas Document.

## Thrawn's Fall
### 9 A.B.Y.

Grand Admiral Thrawn seemed infallible in his military strategy. While the Emperor had used cloaking devices for the straightforward purpose of disguising warcraft, as in the experimental "Phantom TIE" project, Thrawn relished devising ingenious, nonstandard uses for the invisibility screen. One ruse was to cloak a number of cruisers and slip them beneath a planet's energy shield. When an attacking Star Destroyer fired at the shield, its lasers dissipated harmlessly, but the cloaked cruisers waiting beneath the shield at precise, predetermined locations fired their lasers simultaneously, creating a fascinating illusion that the Star Destroyer's lasers could punch through energy barriers. This trick worked so well that dozens of planets, thinking their security hopelessly compromised, surrendered to the Empire without a fight.

Thrawn also used cloaking technology to create an innovative siege weapon. After fitting twenty-two asteroids with cloaking devices, Thrawn's Star Destroyers carried them to Coruscant. The Imperial armada was outnumbered and outgunned by Coruscant's formidable defenses, but Thrawn dumped the invisible asteroids into close planetary orbit, then retreated into hyperspace, basically creating an unseen hazard field around the capital world. The New Republic couldn't risk dropping Coruscant's energy shield lest one of the asteroids

impact the heavily populated surface. Neither could they allow space traffic too close to the planet for fear of a collision. Until the New Republic could find a way to detect and eliminate the invisible obstacles, Coruscant was thoroughly blockaded.

Ackbar and the other fleet commanders planned a retaliatory raid that would severely damage Thrawn's Imperial shipbuilding capability and simultaneously net them a sophisticated gravfield detector that could pinpoint the elusive asteroids' mass shadows. Thrawn learned of the raid, though, and was waiting for the New Republic armada when it emerged from hyperspace at Bilbringi.

Commander Wedge Antilles and Rogue Squadron led the fighter attack against the Empire, while Admiral Ackbar launched withering cannonades from his capital ships. Talon Karrde's smuggling associates executed quick hit-and-fade strikes against the Imperial defense platforms, forcing Thrawn to split his forces. Nevertheless, the grand admiral's tactical expertise was superior to that of

*A twisted genius dies*

anyone else on the battlefield, and it seemed only a matter of time before he won the day.

The New Republic was handed a victory through a chance occurrence for which no one had planned. Thrawn's Noghri bodyguard Rukh was present on the bridge of the Star Destroyer *Chimaera*, and thanks to Leia Organa Solo's diplomatic visit to Honoghr, he had already determined to betray his master. As Rukh witnessed the unfolding battle, he put thought to action: the bodyguard fatally stabbed Thrawn through the heart. Rukh fled the scene and tried to reach a shuttlecraft, but was intercepted and executed by a stormtrooper squad under the command of Major Grodin Tierce.

Captain Pellaeon immediately took command of the beleaguered Imperial fleet, but was smart enough to realize he had no hope of winning the battle. Pellaeon ordered a full retreat, to live and fight again another day.

The Imperial fleet regrouped near the Unknown Regions while Pellaeon assessed the situation. Thrawn had captured an astonishing amount of territory, nearly doubling the size of the Empire, but it had been held together by his authority alone. Without a similarly charismatic leader the union would splinter yet again. Pellaeon, while respected, was not such a leader. The Empire reverted again into warlordism, and the New Republic began recapturing its lost territory, planet by planet.

## THE RETURN OF ISARD

**9–10 A.B.Y.**

While the New Republic reveled in the victory, ominous developments bubbled just beneath the surface. On Byss in the Deep Core, Emperor Palpatine's spirit finally recuperated from its difficult transition into a new clone body. Palpatine knew the New Republic had little interest in the Deep Core, since hyperspace lanes into the star-choked region were practically nonexistent. Protected from prying eyes, the resurrected Emperor secretly began contacting fleet commanders, warlords, and moffs. Those who pledged fealty to their former master were rewarded; those who resisted were slaughtered. The Imperial war fleet swelled in size as new ships arrived daily.

One of those contacted was Ysanne Isard, Palpatine's would-be successor who had held the fragmenting Empire together for nearly three years. Isard was insane with fear of being executed for her eventual failure, and devised a strategy to win a place of honor for herself in Palpatine's new Empire. Her peace offering would be the Super Star Destroyer *Lusankya*, undergoing reconstruction in a New Republic dry dock.

Meanwhile, New Republic forces were amazed at the ease with which they swept up small pieces of the Empire, as if the Imperial fleet had gone into hiding. The New Republic Provisional Council made their next goal the liberation of the Ciutric Hegemony, a region dominated by Imperial Admiral Krennel. According to New Republic Intelligence, the prisoners who had once suffered aboard the *Lusankya* were likely to be found within the borders of the Ciutric Hegemony. The New Republic leadership placed a high priority on recovering the *Lusankya* inmates, particularly General Jan Dodonna, Rebel hero of the Battle of Yavin.

A raid by Rogue Squadron ended in failure, but surprisingly the Rogues were rescued by TIE Defender pilots in the service of Ysanne Isard. The crafty Imperial leader had escaped from certain death at the end of the Thyferran Bacta War and had been lying low for over two years, plotting her return to power. Isard met with her old enemies and explained that she had as much stake in bringing down Krennel as they did: the warlord had betrayed her years before and had stolen the *Lusankya* prisoners from under her nose. Worse, Krennel was in league with a clone of Isard, grown through unknown means years before Grand Admiral Thrawn had activated the Mount Tantiss cloning facility. In exchange for the destruction of her clone and the humiliation of Krennel, Isard agreed to assist Rogue Squadron in their mission.

The Rogues posed as TIE pilots hoping to defect to Krennel's empire, while a New Republic commando team prepared to spring Dodonna and the other prisoners. Admiral Ackbar commanded a substantial force of New Republic capital ships and support craft, drawn from the defenses around the Bilbringi system shipyards. All three groups coordinated their actions in a single, unified assault on Krennel's heavily defended throneworld of Ciutric.

Isard did not participate in the mission; instead, she treacherously struck the weakened defenses of the Bilbringi shipyards containing the *Lusankya*. Isard's handpicked infiltration team quickly seized the Super Star Destroyer's bridge and prepared to steer the monstrous vessel toward the nearest hyperspace jump point. Isard's treachery had not taken New Republic Intelligence entirely by surprise, though. Agent Iella Wessiri had prepared for a possible hijack and already had a team in place to prevent the theft. In a confrontation inside Isard's former quarters, Wessiri shot and killed the deranged Isard. The *Lusankya* was recovered.

The attack on Krennel's base was a success. Admiral Krennel and the Isard clone were killed.

The *Lusankya* prisoners were rescued and brought back to the New Republic for medical treatment and psychological evaluations. General Dodonna, however, adamantly refused and insisted on an immediate meeting with Mon Mothma to discuss the current state of the Galactic Civil War. Dodonna formed a body of aged advisers called the "gray cadre," including such luminaries as Adar Tallon and Vanden Willard, and reassumed the role of senior military adviser as if he had never left it.

Krennel's dominion crumbled, and the New Republic navy pushed forward still farther. In only a short time since the death of Thrawn, the Empire had lost nearly all of its recently won territory. Tasting victory, the New Republic fleet advanced outward into the Imperially held sections of the Rim, leaving Coruscant and the Core Worlds relatively unprotected.

Which was exactly how Emperor Palpatine wanted it.

# THE RESURRECTION OF EMPEROR PALPATINE

**10 A.B.Y.**

In the six years following the Emperor's death at Endor, the New Republic had established itself as a governing force and as a military power. But without the thousands of Jedi Knights who had formed the backbone of the Old Republic, the political confederation remained a precarious one. At no point was that deficiency more obvious than during Palpatine's ghastly return—a nightmarish year of horror, calamity, and ruin.

Immediately after the defeat of Admiral Krennel, the Imperial fleet commanders joined with surviving members of the Emperor's ruling council, a development no one had predicted. The unified Imperial force launched from the Deep Core with stunning violence, surprising the New Republic, whose own fleet was hopelessly out of position in the Rim. Within days, the Imperials conquered several key systems, forcing Mon Mothma to consider a last-ditch plan for the defense of Coruscant itself. She didn't get the chance.

An Imperial armada began a merciless bombardment of Coruscant's energy shield, waiting for the shield to buckle and break. Rather than see the civilian population decimated, Mon Mothma evacuated the capital world. Ralltiir, Chandrila, Esseles, and other key Core Worlds soon fell to the Imperials, and the leaders of the beleaguered New Republic returned to guerrilla fighting to defeat their old enemy.

The resurrected Palpatine had done a better job of reuniting the Imperial factions than anyone before him, including Thrawn. Only the Emperor could rule the Empire. Surviving warlords such as Harrsk, Delvardus, and Teradoc swore obedience to the same master and fought under the same banner, as did the loyal Imperial forces under Pellaeon. The New Republic remained unaware of the true reason for this sudden unification.

Immediately, everything appeared to fall apart. Once Coruscant was theirs, the factions of the Empire fell upon each other like nek battle dogs. The brief but bloody civil war, known as the Imperial Mutiny, involved the ruling council, the moffs, the fleet, the Inquisitorius, COMPNOR, and the Imperial Security Bureau, each trying to claim the whole sabacc pot at the expense of the others.

The New Republic seized this chance to create confusion among the feuding Imperials, using two captured Star Destroyers to conduct hit-and-run sorties into the war zones. Longtime Alliance hero Wedge Antilles commanded vast forces in his new role as general, while others, including Han Solo and Lando Calrissian, reactivated their commissions and returned to the military.

In one such raid over the battleground that had devastated Coruscant, the Alliance Star Destroyer *Liberator*, commanded by Luke Skywalker, Wedge Antilles, and Lando Calrissian, crashed into the planet's city-covered surface. After losing all contact with them, Leia Organa Solo and her husband, together with Chewbacca and the protocol droid C-3PO, led a mission to rescue their fallen comrades. The young Solo twins, Jacen and Jaina, had been sent away to the safety of an isolated base, code-named New Alderaan.

Taking the *Millennium Falcon* into the heart of the battle zone, they found Antilles and Calrissian barricaded and fighting for their lives. Then, with a swirl of the Force, Jedi Luke Skywalker strode into the fray and single-handedly defeated an AT-AT walker.

He instructed his comrades to leave while they had the chance, vowing to remain behind on devastated Coruscant. He sensed a dark force growing, an evil power reaching out to him, and coming to the Imperial capital world. The others wanted to stay behind with Skywalker, but he commanded them to leave. Retreating, they watched as a gigantic hole opened in space, a barely controlled Force storm that sucked the battlefield debris through a rift in the universe—dragging Luke Skywalker and his astromech droid R2-D2 with it.

Skywalker was taken to an Imperial dungeon ship at Byss, in the heart of the Deep Core. He waited, a prisoner, eager to learn of this new threat. When guards took him to meet his captor, Skywalker strode boldly into the shadowy citadel—only to learn that the mysterious dark-side nexus was none other than the cloned reincarnation of Emperor Palpatine.

Skywalker learned that, using the same technology he had tested on his weapons engineer,

***Emperor Palpatine***

Bevel Lemelisk, the Emperor had set up a laboratory and stronghold on Byss where dozens of fresh, identical bodies waited to host his energy force. Restored to physical life by ancient Sith secrets, the Emperor had allowed the petty squabbling among his warlords to rage on while he quietly rebuilt his forces, preparing a massive blow against all who would deny him everlasting dominion.

In the prison on Byss, the Emperor tempted Skywalker, trying to use the same tactics that had drawn his father, Anakin Skywalker, to evil. No longer the impulsive youth at war with his own anger, Luke Skywalker faced a moment of great decision. He believed he had to use the Emperor's own knowledge of the dark side against him. Thinking he could be stronger, believing he could trick Palpatine and destroy the dark side from within, Skywalker agreed to join him.

While this drama unfolded, the New Republic government-in-exile established a secret new Pinnacle Base on the isolated fifth moon of Da Soocha, at the heart of Hutt Space. The resurrected Emperor, having waited until the Imperial Mutiny had culled out the weak among his followers, launched a strike on the ocean world of Mon Calamari. Palpatine's weapons of choice were huge

*World Devastators attack Mon Calamari*

destructive machines—World Devastators—that had been built at the shipyards of Byss. Designed by Umak Leth, one of the original masterminds behind the Death Star, these World Devastators consumed everything in their path, destroying ships and structures to provide huge amounts of raw materials. Inside, automated manufacturing plants recycled the raw materials and spewed out vast numbers of war machines, which continued to ravage the peaceful world.

The combined military might of the ragtag New Republic rushed out to fight the World Devastators and suffered significant losses. The terrible machines seemed unstoppable. The Alliance Star Destroyer *Emancipator* crashed into the resource-hungry mouth and was turned into scrap.

As the battle continued on Mon Calamari, the captive Luke Skywalker sent a vision to his sister, Leia Organa Solo. At first she saw a terrible echo of Darth Vader, then realized it was her own brother. Skywalker told her that his destiny had led him to the dark side, which he felt was the only path to save the galaxy. He told her to stay away—but she didn't listen.

Knowing that the Force would lead her to him, Organa Solo intended to rescue her brother. Though she was pregnant with her third child, she gathered Han Solo to make a run to the Deep Core. First, they journeyed to Nar Shaddaa, where they planned to get information and resources they needed by linking up with Solo's former girlfriend, Salla Zend, and a smuggling buddy, Shug Ninx. Han Solo hoped that these allies would help them infiltrate the Emperor's stronghold.

On the smugglers' moon, Organa Solo came across a decrepit crone, Vima-Da-Boda, a fallen Jedi overlooked in the great purge. Vima-Da-Boda gave Organa Solo a mysterious gift—an ancient lightsaber. Through the Force, Organa Solo also saw her brother under the control of the Emperor, commanding the Imperial forces continuing to destroy Mon Calamari.

They departed from Nar Shaddaa aboard Salla Zend's freighter, which was licensed to haul military cargo to the Deep Core. Once in port at Byss, Organa Solo used her fledgling Jedi powers to guide them to the citadel. They were captured and brought before Skywalker, who was now the Emperor's protégé in command of the new Imperial forces, including even the World Devastators laying waste to Mon Calamari.

In secret, though, Skywalker transmitted faulty commands to the World Devastators, so that they crashed. Several of the gigantic war machines were taken down by New Republic reinforcements.

Like a puppet of the dark side, Skywalker presented the captives to the Emperor. Sensing total victory, Palpatine tried to tempt Organa Solo into fighting against her own brother, to get her to join the dark side. But she refused. The resurrected Emperor showed them his storehouse of clones, proving that he could never be defeated. When he attacked her with a blast of the Force, Skywalker made no move to intercede, and General Solo was helpless. Though Skywalker insisted he was trying to save the galaxy, Han Solo judged him by his actions, not his promises.

The Emperor came to Leia Organa Solo in her cell, revealing that he knew of Skywalker's plans to trick him, but he was confident he would win in the end. Palpatine showed her an ancient artifact, the Jedi Holocron, a teaching device used by ancient Jedi Masters. Playing on her emotions, he also claimed that his aging body would soon be burned out by the dark forces he wielded—and he wanted to shift his consciousness into the new baby Organa Solo carried within her. She fought the ailing Emperor, stole the precious Holocron, and escaped.

When Salla Zend showed up to rescue them, Luke Skywalker helped divert the guards so that Han Solo, his wife, and the others could escape. But Skywalker refused to go with them; he had more work to do on Byss. Using the secrets of the dark side, Skywalker tricked them by creating an illusionary double of himself that vanished as soon as the *Millennium Falcon* left the system. He also loaded the override codes for the remaining World Devastators into R2-D2's memory circuits, so that Alliance forces were able to complete their victory at Mon Calamari.

Before the decrepit Palpatine could use his sorcery to switch into one of his new clones, a grim Luke Skywalker marched into the laboratory chamber and smashed tank after tank, destroying almost all of the Emperor's bodies. But before he could finish his dreadful task, the weakening

Palpatine succeeded in transferring his consciousness to one of the last remaining clones, a strong and agile fifteen-year-old. Filled with dark-side power, the reborn Emperor engaged Skywalker in a ferocious lightsaber duel, and he forced the Jedi Knight into submission.

Broken and lost, Skywalker accompanied the victorious Emperor in his enormous flagship *Eclipse* to the hidden New Republic stronghold on Pinnacle Base, just as the *Millennium Falcon* arrived. There, the Emperor issued a bold ultimatum: he would destroy all the Rebels, unless the pregnant Leia Organa Solo agreed to come to his ship. He meant to crush her will and bring her over to the dark side to stand beside her brother, and he wanted the child she carried so it would one day act as a repository for his consciousness.

Seeing no other choice, Organa Solo went to the Emperor's ship—but she defied him and still tried to bring Skywalker back to the light side. The Emperor forced the two of them to duel, but Organa Solo managed to break the hold of evil. Instead, Skywalker finally turned on Palpatine.

As they battled with lightsabers, the desperate Emperor sensed defeat. He summoned up a huge Force storm, far more powerful than the one that had swept Coruscant. But this time, when Skywalker and his sister turned their combined resistance against him, Palpatine could no longer control what he had unleashed. As brother and sister fled, the Force storm consumed the gigantic black ship and, presumably, all that remained of the Emperor.

## Operation Shadow Hand
### 10 A.B.Y.

Again the Rebel triumph was to be short-lived. Palpatine had anticipated even this worst-case scenario and had hidden one of the clones in a secret location on Byss, though it would take time for him to reach it. His loyal forces already had a plan to execute—Operation Shadow Hand, designed to subjugate the galaxy in a series of unstoppable wave assaults. Palpatine's military executor, Sedriss, led the operation, assisted by seven of the Emperor's most skilled dark-side adepts, a group he called his Dark Jedi.

*The resurrected Emperor*

Executor Sedriss consolidated the forces remaining in the newly subjugated Core and Colonies regions. First, he targeted the weapons factories on Balmorra, which had turned against Imperial domination. But when Sedriss attacked the weapons world, his forces were rebuffed by massive new combat droids. Declaring an uneasy truce, Sedriss offered to buy the new weapons and established a time and place for delivery. It was a forced bargain the weapons sellers never intended to keep.

Upon returning to Byss, Sedriss found that two of the Emperor's dark-side adepts had turned traitor and completed destroying the clone laboratory, so they could control the Empire themselves without worrying about Palpatine's return. Fiercely loyal even in his master's absence, Sedriss killed the saboteurs and turned at last to see the Emperor reborn, in his only remaining clone body. Rewarded for his faith, Sedriss received the mission to track down Luke Skywalker and bring him back to the Emperor—alive.

Palpatine's traitorous adepts had not been working alone. Carnor Jax, one of the Emperor's crimson-armored Royal Guardsmen, had paid the Byss clonemaster to damage the genetic structure of all the clones, knowing it would trigger a premature aging cycle and a quick death for a resurrected Palpatine. Jax escaped Sedriss's notice and quietly waited for his own chance to ascend the throne.

Meanwhile, Skywalker studied the Holocron his sister had captured. Learning of another surviving Jedi, Skywalker traveled to the abandoned space city of Nespis VIII and found Kam Solusar, a hard-bitten survivor of Darth Vader's Jedi Purge. Initially angry and reclusive, Solusar faced Skywalker in an ancient and risky Jedi game called *lightsider*. After Skywalker bested him, Solusar finally agreed to join the other Jedi.

Knowing the fledgling New Republic needed Jedi Knights, and armed with further clues from the Holocron, Skywalker and Solusar proceeded to the ruined library world of Ossus, which had been obliterated by the Cron cluster explosion four millennia earlier during the Sith War. There among the blasted rubble, they found a group of primitive shamans, the Ysanna, who exhibited a weak and untrained ability to use the Force. The Ysanna worshipped an enormous, twisted tree that grew among the ruins.

Before Skywalker and Solusar could complete their search for precious information, Executor Sedriss tracked them down. When his Imperial shock troops attacked, the Jedi and Ysanna warriors managed to drive them back. Desperate, Sedriss took as hostage a young Ysanna woman, Jem. Then, surprisingly, the twisted tree's branches and roots began to move and grappled with the executor. The tree was none other than the ancient Jedi Master Ood Bnar, who had clung to life and remained dormant since the conflagration swept Ossus millennia ago. Master Ood had stirred again to fight the dark-side warrior, and destroyed both himself and Sedriss in a final confrontation.

Beneath the ruins of the dead tree Jedi, Skywalker uncovered a precious stockpile of ancient lightsabers, protected all these centuries. Taking this discovery as an omen, Skywalker and Solusar allowed two of the young Ysanna—Jem and her brother Rayf—to accompany them for further training in the ways of the Force.

Also intent on finding other Jedi Knights, Leia Organa Solo went to the underworld of Nar Shaddaa, where she tracked down the fallen and homeless Jedi Vima-Da-Boda. She and Han Solo

retrieved Vima and took her through many adventures back to Pinnacle Base. Along the way they also found another Jedi warrior, Empatojayos Brand, who had lost much of his body during an earlier battle with Darth Vader; Brand was more prosthetic than human, but he could still use the Force in the battle against the dark Empire.

Meanwhile, Palpatine's weapons designer Umak Leth had completed a terrible new armament, the Galaxy Gun. In orbit around Byss, this weapon could fire hyperspace projectiles to any part of the galaxy and destroy any target, completely without warning. Palpatine launched the first projectile toward Pinnacle Base, hoping to destroy the Rebels with a single blow.

The projectile annihilated the hidden moon just as Skywalker returned from Ossus with Kam Solusar and his two new Jedi trainees. They watched in horror as the Rebel base exploded before their eyes, and they feared that Mon Mothma and all the leaders of the New Republic had been wiped out. However, the core of the resistance had discovered that spies had transmitted the coordinates of Pinnacle Base to Byss; recalling General Rieekan's wise decision to evacuate Echo Base on Hoth, Mon Mothma ordered immediate flight from the hidden moon. The resistance departed in a fleet of transport carriers just as the projectile annihilated the base.

Realizing the seriousness of this new threat, New Republic commando and sabotage teams attacked the Galaxy Gun, but were unable to destroy it. The Emperor continued to launch his deadly projectiles, destroying unruly worlds and bringing the resistance to its knees. Within a short time, Palpatine regained key territories in the Inner and Outer Rim. The future of the New Republic looked bleak.

Skywalker and his companions went to the secret world where the Solo twins, Jacen and Jaina, had been taken for protection following the loss of Coruscant. But the Emperor's commando forces struck there, too, poisoning Skywalker—who was healed thanks to the skills of old Vima-Da-Boda—and killing Jem Ysanna. The survivors fled to the derelict space city of Nespis VIII, far from any other planet, where Skywalker had met Solusar not long before. There, Leia Organa Solo gave birth to her third child, who was named after her father, Anakin.

Mon Mothma and the leaders of the New

*The final death of Palpatine*

Republic regrouped on the derelict floating city following the evacuation of Pinnacle Base. When he discovered the location of the latest Rebel hideout, the Emperor launched yet another projectile from the Galaxy Gun. The surviving New Republic forces barely escaped before the ancient space city was destroyed. The ragged remnants of the cowed Alliance scattered across the galaxy, fleeing in separate small groups.

## *Palpatine Vanquished*
## 11 A.B.Y.

Though Palpatine seemed to be winning his war of conquest, his final cloned body began to fail him, aging at a rapid rate and eaten from the inside by his dark powers and the cellular sabotage of Carnor Jax. He tried to clone other bodies so he could resur-

rect himself again, but Jax's manipulations had tainted even the genetic source material. Palpatine's scientists and physicians could offer no solutions.

Attempting to find an answer, Palpatine journeyed to the Sith funeral world of Korriban, and the spirits of fallen Dark Lords informed him only that he needed to find another body, a Jedi body. They told him where to find the baby Anakin Solo, a child strong in the Force.

The Emperor brought his giant new flagship, *Eclipse II*, to Onderon, where the Solos had moved their three children for safety. While New Republic defenders attacked the Imperial juggernaut in orbit, Luke Skywalker and his Jedi companions sought out Palpatine himself. They did not find the Emperor aboard the flagship, though; as a ruse, he had left a decoy while he slipped down to where Leia Organa Solo was hiding.

During the space battle, Lando Calrissian infiltrated the enormous flagship and, using R2-D2's computer specialization, sabotaged the automated hyperdrive engines. *Eclipse II* took off into hyperspace, despite the best efforts of the Imperial commanders to regain control of their vessel.

R2-D2 had set the coordinates to match the location of Umak Leth's Galaxy Gun, which had just prepared to launch another planet-destroying missile. But the out-of-control Imperial flagship crashed into the huge weapon, destroying both in a titanic collision. The final armed projectile tumbled without guidance, pulled by the gravity of Byss itself, and detonated, turning the central world of the Deep Core into space debris.

The final battle, however, was fought on the surface of Onderon. Barely able to walk in his festering body, Palpatine still used Sith powers to trick his way past the guards. Summoning his remaining energies despite the damage it caused him, he faced Organa Solo, demanding her baby as the new repository of his spirit. She fought back, but was no match for the Emperor's dark powers.

Before Palpatine could take infant Anakin, though, Luke Skywalker and the other Jedi arrived and joined the battle. Young Rayf Ysanna and the cyborg Jedi Empatojayos Brand were both mortally wounded in the confrontation. Refusing to surrender to his inner anger, Skywalker tried to take Palpatine alive. But Han Solo shot the old man with his blaster.

As the Emperor fell toward death yet again, he attempted to send his spirit into the baby Anakin, but he was intercepted by the dying Empatojayos Brand. Clasping himself to the light, Brand held the Emperor's dark presence within his own body as they both succumbed.

With all of his clones destroyed, Emperor Palpatine was finally and truly defeated. Without orders, the confused Imperial fleet went into retreat, abandoning Coruscant and other Core planets. Mon Mothma spread the news that the New Republic had once again regained control. To cement the victory, the leaders reestablished their capital on devastated Coruscant. It was an important symbolic gesture, to add continuity to the galactic government.

This fresh start allowed them to establish a new system of government. The Provisional Council and position of chief councilor had worked effectively in the past, but that government had lost Coruscant to Palpatine. A new, more powerful single leader was needed, as was a more clearly defined governmental hierarchy. Mon Mothma was elected chief of state and president of the senate. Leia Organa Solo was elected her second in command, the minister of state.

## Jax, Kanos, and the Interim Council
### 11 A.B.Y.

The Empire finally collapsed, its death presided over by a former Royal Guardsman named Carnor Jax. Palpatine's scarlet-robed bodyguards had been trained on the harsh planet Yinchorr to show unswerving loyalty, but Jax's dreams of power had overcome his devotion. Jax had arranged for the insidious sabotage of Palpatine's clones, a shortsighted and selfish move. When the last clone finally succumbed on Onderon, Jax was left to rule over a dying Empire.

The speed with which the Empire crumbled was amazing, surpassing the mass confusion that had occurred following the Battle of Endor. Jax ordered the massacre of the remaining Royal Guards on Yinchorr and manipulated the creation of a thirteen-member Interim Council to succeed Palpatine, placing himself as senior member. Powerful alien leaders, including a Devaronian, a Whiphid, a Givin, and a Defel, were granted membership in the Interim Council, a remarkable move for the historically antialien Empire. Carnor Jax felt that alien strength might give new life to the dying Imperial military. Unfortunately, it was too little, too late.

Many fleets refused to follow the dictates of the council. Admiral Harrsk returned to his power base in the Deep Core, and other warlords followed suit, realizing that the protected region offered an opportunity for them to regroup and plan their next course of action.

Carnor Jax and the Interim Council held the Empire proper, a narrow band stretching from the Outer Rim to the Colonies. But even this would not remain intact. The last of the Emperor's Royal

Guardsmen, Kir Kanos, had learned of Jax's culpability in Palpatine's death and had survived the massacre on Yinchorr. Kir Kanos vowed to track down his former comrade-in-arms and execute him as a traitor.

On Phaeda, an Imperial holding in the Outer Rim, Jax's Star Destroyers attempted to capture Kanos, but he escaped back to Yinchorr. Jax followed, leaving one of his ships at Phaeda, where it was surprised by General Wedge Antilles and the New Republic Super Star Destroyer *Lusankya*.

After years of time-consuming repairs, the *Lusankya* had finally been relaunched in the wake of Operation Shadow Hand, and it was still such a secret that many Imperials were unaware of its existence. Antilles, aided by Rogue Squadron—in B-wings and E-wings that better suited the mission profile—captured the Star Destroyer and liberated Phaeda.

At Yinchorr, Kir Kanos used a booby-trapped assault bomber to annihilate Jax's flagship. On the surface of the barren world, Kanos and Jax faced off inside the abandoned training compound for Royal Guards, a place of dark memories for both of them. On an elevated platform suspended above a bottomless pit, Kanos killed his rival, then vowed to avenge his master further by destroying every member of the sham council.

While Kanos began moving against his enemies, another group was also trying to sabotage the council—the criminal organization Black Sun. The syndicate arranged to have several of the council members replaced with clones. After several assassinations had already thinned out the ranks of the council, the ranking member, Xandel Carivus, decided to disband the organization and rule alone as the new emperor. Carivus was operating on the instructions of Nom Anor, a shadowy figure whose motivations and true allegiances remain a mystery.

His actions angered Baron D'Asta, a pro-Imperial business leader who controlled the largest privately owned fleet in the galaxy. Baron D'Asta's fleet attacked the council headquarters on Ord Cantrell, forcing "Emperor" Carivus to sue for peace. In a confrontation on the planet's surface, Kir Kanos executed the spurious emperor.

With the Interim Council gone and most of the Imperial fleet disappearing into the Deep Core to form warlord allegiances, die-hard Imperial planets like the academy world Carida were left with no significant defensive forces. Carida and many other worlds throughout the former Imperial jurisdiction drew in upon themselves, fortifying their planetary defenses against any New Republic invasion. The New Republic chose to leave most of these "fortress worlds" alone, hoping that a lack of trade would eventually force them to open up their borders.

Pellaeon, now a vice admiral, reluctantly joined the Deep Core warlords. His Star Destroyer *Chimaera* had been severely damaged and abandoned during the capture of Duro amidst Operation Shadow Hand; many of Pellaeon's most loyal and skilled officers had been killed. Lacking his power base and his flagship, Pellaeon cast his lot with High Admiral Teradoc, who possessed the largest intact military. Pellaeon felt that this would provide a safe haven for his surviving fleet until the post-Palpatine confusion could be sorted out. Teradoc placed Pellaeon in charge of a huge flotilla of *Victory*-class Star Destroyers.

In response to the resurrected Emperor's brutal assaults, the New Republic ordered a sweeping new warship development program, and the New Class warships were built. During the days of the Rebellion, most of the Rebel warships had been secondhand Corellian models, captured Imperial craft, or heavily modified noncombat vessels, such as Mon Calamari cruisers, originally built as pleasure liners. The ease with which Palpatine's clone had been able to rout the New Republic fleet highlighted the need to replace these aging and outdated craft.

The New Class consisted of eight basic designs: the *Agave*-class picket ship, the *Warrior*-class gunship, the *Sacheen*-class light escort, the *Hajen*-class fleet tender, the *Majestic*-class heavy cruiser, the *Defender*-class assault carrier, the *Endurance*-class fleet carrier, and the *Nebula*-class New Republic Star Destroyer. The first finished New Class ship was the *Sacheen*, but it would be years before all eight designs were engineered and manufactured.

## PART VII

# THE RETURN OF THE JEDI KNIGHTS

## SKYWALKER'S JEDI ACADEMY

**11 A.B.Y.**

After the fall of Grand Admiral Thrawn and the final defeat of the resurrected Emperor, the New Republic understood the need to consolidate their political hold on the worlds that had joined the Rebel Alliance. Recognizing this need for a unifying force, Luke Skywalker spoke before Mon Mothma and the senate on the oratory floor of the former Imperial Palace. He voiced his dream to re-create the Jedi Knights, a beacon of hope that had been nearly extinguished by Palpatine's slaughters.

Though his own training had not been completed by Obi-Wan Kenobi or Yoda, Skywalker asked permission from the chief of state to train others in the use of the Force. Old Vima-Da-Boda had vanished shortly after the defeat of the resurrected Emperor, too broken and guilt-ridden to return to a normal life. But Skywalker knew that his sister Leia Organa Solo, her three children, Kam Solusar, the Witches of Dathomir, Kyle Katarn, and even Mara Jade had all exhibited an aptitude for the Force. Surely, there must be others across the galaxy who showed similar latent abilities. Since he had not known about his own affinity before meeting Kenobi in the Jundland Wastes on Tatooine, Skywalker surmised that others might be unaware of their powers. Mon Mothma agreed to sponsor a search for Force-talented candidates.

Skywalker traveled far and wide across the New Republic. He went to the volcanically active planet Eol Sha, where he found a fiery-tempered leader named Gantoris, who proved to be powerful in the Force. Next, he tracked down the cloud prospector

Streen, living as a hermit in an abandoned floating city on Bespin.

He found Tionne, a woman with only a minor talent in the Force, but who showed a great interest in the history of the Jedi. Skywalker discovered her in the ruins of Exis Station, site of the Jedi convocation called by Nomi Sunrider four thousand years earlier. The unstable star had entered a flarestorm phase, and Skywalker barely managed to move the

*The Jedi praxeum*

station to safety in time for Tionne to salvage important historical records. In subsequent years, Tionne became a scholar and assistant instructor at the Jedi academy.

He found other candidates, including the clone Dorsk 81, the warrior woman Kirana Ti from Dathomir, and Corran Horn from Rogue Squadron. New Republic Commander Kyle Katarn, who had spent the previous year battling Palpatine's Imperials and investigating a Sith temple with Mara Jade, also joined the first batch of students. Achieving such success, Skywalker was optimistic about bringing back the Jedi. But to do so, he needed a formal training center.

After consultations with his sister, Skywalker chose the abandoned Rebel base on Yavin 4 for his *praxeum*, a place for the learning of action. He gathered his candidates in the temple ruins left by the ancient Massassi and began to instruct them in the ways of the Force.

## Maw Installation
### 11 A.B.Y.

Luke Skywalker wasn't the only one whose plate was full. In an attempt to open a diplomatic dialogue with miners of the economically important glitterstim spice, General Han Solo and Chewbacca flew the *Millennium Falcon* to Kessel. Since the fall of the Empire, freed inmates from the Imperial correctional facility there had been running the operations; Solo hoped to convince Kessel to join the New Republic.

However, reactionary defensive forces from Kessel's garrison moon shot down the *Falcon* without identifying the ship or its occupants. Solo and his Wookiee copilot were taken prisoner by Moruth Doole, an old rival of Solo's who had set himself up as Kessel's planetary governor. Seeing his grave error in firing upon such important representatives, Doole attempted to cover up the incident; he disguised the damaged ship and sent his two captives to work in the spice mines, while publicly denying that Solo had ever arrived.

While working in the horrendous mines, however, Solo and Chewbacca befriended a fellow prisoner, Kyp Durron, a streetwise young man who, they discovered later, had a strong affinity for the

*Admiral Daala*

Force, having been trained by Vima-Da-Boda years before. Durron helped the two break out of the mines, and they escaped from Kessel, under hot pursuit by Doole's space navy.

In desperation, their vessel plunged into the navigational nightmare of the Maw black hole cluster, where enormous gravity wells made a maze of hyperspace paths. In his smuggling days, Solo had flown the Kessel Run, but never this close to the black holes. Most paths were either dead ends or went down the gullet of a singularity. Only Durron's intuitive use of the Force allowed them to reach the gravitational stability at the center of the cluster.

Unfortunately, this was the location of Grand Moff Tarkin's secret weapons research center, Maw Installation, where the Death Star and other superweapons had been developed. The first prototype Death Star—constructed to prove the feasibility of the planet-destroying superlaser—still remained there. Four Imperial Star Destroyers, led by Tarkin's former lover Admiral Daala, had remained to guard the research station.

Solo and his companions found themselves captured again, this time by an Imperial commander who had no inkling that the war was over and the Emperor killed. The isolated Star Destroyer fleet had never received orders to move, never learned of the Imperial defeat. Admiral Daala refused to believe what her new captives told her. She chose to believe, instead, that these were spies.

In captivity, Solo met Qwi Xux, the brilliant female scientist who along with Bevel Lemelisk and Umak Leth had developed the Death Star concept. Since Tarkin and Bevel Lemelisk had left the research station, Qwi Xux had worked alone to develop a small, but even deadlier, weapon—the Sun Crusher—which could set up a chain reaction at the core of a sun, causing it to go supernova.

Duped and brainwashed, Qwi Xux remained unaware of what her weapon designs were used for. During his captivity, Solo told her about the Rebellion, the fall of the Empire, and the errors of Palpatine's policy. Xux broke through the brainwashing and remembered how she had been commandeered to come to this station, how she had watched her fellow test students executed, her own village burned from orbit by Tarkin's turbolasers.

Eventually, Solo convinced her to turn against the Imperials and help them escape. Together, they stole the Sun Crusher and headed out of the black hole cluster, destroying one Star Destroyer by ramming its bridge. Daala's remaining Star Destroyers fired at them, but the Sun Crusher's powerful quantum armor provided complete protection.

Daala could not allow the Rebellion to have the new superweapon, nor could she let Han Solo reveal the secret location of Maw Installation. She had to act. Finally breaking her orders to remain in place, she threw everything into pursuit, back to the open space around Kessel.

Meanwhile, a concerned Leia Organa Solo had tried to track down her missing husband at his original destination. Moruth Doole denied that the Millennium Falcon had ever arrived on Kessel. Suspicious of his answer, though, she discreetly asked her brother, Luke Skywalker, to retrace Han Solo's route even as he continued his search for Jedi candidates; Solo's old partner Lando Calrissian accompanied him.

Arriving on Kessel in disguise, the two discovered the Falcon hidden on Kessel's garrison moon; they confiscated the ship and attempted to escape. Caught at his deception, Moruth Doole launched his space navy after them.

As the Falcon headed toward the black hole cluster and their only hope of escape, the Kessel forces became more desperate, firing wildly. Just before they could plunge into the Maw, though, another ship streaked out—the Sun Crusher, with Admiral Daala's Imperial fleet right on its heels.

The Kessel fleet and Daala's three remaining Star Destroyers collided in a titanic and unexpected space battle, which destroyed most of the unruly Kessel warships. The Sun Crusher and the Millennium Falcon escaped into hyperspace and made their way back to Coruscant.

Now unleashed from her confinement and knowing the truth about the fall of the Empire, Daala vowed to make up for her absence, even if the war was already over. She still had three powerful Star Destroyers under her command, and she would fight alone against the Rebels. She engaged in her own guerrilla war, hit-and-run strikes designed to do as much damage as possible to her enemies. There was no way to resurrect the Empire, but she wanted to inflict pain on the New Republic, possibly even to fragment it into civil war.

## Political Troubles
### 11 A.B.Y.

During a seemingly minor spat at a Coruscant diplomatic reception, an angry Ambassador Furgan from the Imperial fortress world of Carida hurled his drink in Mon Mothma's face, then stormed off. It was not realized until much later that Furgan had staged this action to contaminate Mon Mothma with a slow-acting, specially tailored toxin that, over time, debilitated the chief of state. As Mon Mothma grew gravely ill from the poison, medical droids could find nothing wrong with her, and rumors spread that she was dying. The New Republic was thus weakened and became unstable in a time of crisis.

Around this time, on a diplomatic mission to Vortex, a world plagued by hurricane winds,

Admiral Ackbar made a piloting error and crash-landed, killing hundreds of people. In disgrace, Ackbar resigned from his duties and retired to his watery homeworld of Mon Calamari, much as General Obi-Wan Kenobi had gone to ground in the deserts of Tatooine. In search of strength and solidarity for the government, Leia Organa Solo went to Mon Calamari herself to talk to Ackbar, hoping to convince him to return, to fill the New Republic's need for leadership. She was joined on her mission by the female Mon Calamarian ambassador Cilghal.

Admiral Daala's renegade Imperial fleet struck Mon Calamari during Organa Solo's search for Ackbar. Three Star Destroyers appeared over the oceans and began to attack the floating cities. While the minister of state transmitted a frantic call for assistance, Ackbar was forced to take charge to defend his people, destroying one of the attacking warships. During the battles, Organa Solo also recognized that Ambassador Cilghal showed undeveloped Jedi potential.

After devastating the planet, Daala's remaining forces fled into hyperspace. The ordeal gave a reticent Ackbar his catharsis, and he made his decision that he was willing to fight again—but when Organa Solo asked him to return with her to Coruscant during Mon Mothma's decline, he refused. His main duty was to his homeworld, helping his people rebuild. He could not take the place of the chief of state, though she grew weaker day by day.

## Exar Kun's Revenge
### 11 A.B.Y.

The continuing threats to the New Republic reinforced Luke Skywalker's urgent need to reestablish the Jedi Knights. The training of candidates on Yavin 4, however, involved trial and error. He always reminded himself of Obi-Wan Kenobi's failure in training Anakin Skywalker, which unwittingly led to the creation of the evil Darth Vader.

Fiery-tempered Gantoris, the first candidate Skywalker had found in his Jedi search, began to receive secret guidance from a grim spirit that haunted his dreams. Before he was ready, Gantoris built his own lightsaber and challenged Skywalker to a duel. The Jedi Master was astonished at his student's skill, but deeply disturbed by the risks he took. That night, Gantoris was found burned to a crisp, consumed by a black fire from within. It was a terrible thing to behold, and Skywalker forced the students to remember that the dark side always remained with them.

Han Solo's experience on Kessel and inside the Maw cluster had also convinced Skywalker of Kyp Durron's Force abilities, and so he accepted the young man into the Jedi academy, though he detected a disturbing psychological shadow in Durron's personality.

Durron proved to be a phenomenal student. With his rough upbringing in the Empire, he had instinctively used the Force all his life, though without guidance, and he rapidly surpassed the other students. He was anxious to learn more, and faster, but Skywalker advised caution; these were words Durron didn't want to hear.

In the privacy of his quarters, the young man encountered a hooded figure, the same presence that had corrupted Gantoris: the ancient spirit of Exar Kun, the long-dead Dark Lord of the Sith who had used Massassi slaves to build the temples on Yavin 4 and had spearheaded the legendary Sith War. The spirit of Exar Kun, trapped for four thousand years, had been awakened by the Jedi trainees and their explorations of the Force. Restricted in his ethereal form, Kun convinced young Durron to seek greater pathways of power; the Sith Lord's plan was to achieve his own freedom.

Secretly believing he would be able to control the Force—and not be controlled by it—Kyp Durron dabbled in the dark side. Finding a weak point in his student's personality, Exar Kun increased the young man's hatred of the Empire, feeding it, brainwashing Durron to believe that he was the best hope for the New Republic. Admiral Daala, who had tortured him during his imprisonment in Maw Installation, continued to prey on helpless star systems, taking her toll in innocent blood. Perhaps, Exar Kun suggested, Durron could stop her himself.

When Luke Skywalker disagreed with him about using extreme force against the Imperials, Durron convinced himself to undertake a mission. His goal: to wipe out the renegade fleet and save thousands, if not millions, of lives. After such a success, Durron could then proceed to punish those star systems that still refused to join the New Republic.

Manipulated by Exar Kun, Durron stole a ship from the academy and flew off alone.

At the same time, on Coruscant, the exiled Maw scientist Qwi Xux urged the New Republic to get rid of the Sun Crusher. The Emperor might have used such a doomsday device, but not the New Republic. Grudgingly, the senators agreed to deposit the virtually indestructible weapon in the heart of the gas giant Yavin. Traveling with Xux, Wedge Antilles sent the Sun Crusher into the swirling maelstrom, where it would be out of everyone's reach. Thus Xux was the only person alive who carried the dangerous knowledge of the superweapon's workings.

However, Kyp Durron—driven by Exar Kun's spirit to destroy the Emperor's legacy—tracked down the Maw scientist on the lush jungle planet Ithor. When Qwi Xux entered her quarters, Durron used his newfound dark-side powers to attack her and wipe clean all the deadly weapons knowledge from her memory. Then he departed to continue his one-man war.

Utterly determined in his course of action, Durron returned to Yavin 4. Standing alone atop the academy's Great Temple, he used his now enormous powers to summon the Sun Crusher back out of the mists of Yavin. With the superweapon under his control, he could wreak total havoc among the remnants of the Empire.

Luke Skywalker confronted him there in a titanic duel of Jedi powers. But the spirit of Exar Kun finally revealed himself in order to assist Durron, using all the powers of a Dark Lord of the Sith. Even a Jedi Master could not withstand such an onslaught, and the two of them overwhelmed Skywalker, leaving him for dead. The Jedi students found their Master's motionless body, showing no signs of life—no breathing, no heartbeat.

Fleeing the scene, Kyp Durron piloted the Sun Crusher to where Admiral Daala's fleet had hidden inside the Cauldron Nebula, an ocean of coalescing gas. Aware of the superweapon's incredible power, Daala rallied her ships to flee into hyperspace, but Durron set off the weapon inside the nebula, causing a cluster of giant stars to go supernova. The shock waves turned the nebula into an inferno that to all appearances obliterated Daala and the last of her renegade Imperial fleet.

Leaving the galactic firestorm behind him, Kyp Durron vowed to take care of those remaining worlds that maintained Imperial sympathies. Durron reached Carida, a stormtrooper training center and home of the devious Ambassador Furgan, who had secretly poisoned Mon Mothma. When the planetary defenses mobilized instead of capitulating, Durron fired at Carida's sun, starting a chain reaction. The Caridans, including the ambassador, fled in their ships as the sun exploded, wiping out every living thing in the system. Furgan escaped, but was later killed in an abortive attempt to kidnap the youngest Solo child, Anakin.

At the Jedi academy, Luke Skywalker remained trapped in stasis for a month, neither dead nor alive. His sister, Leia Organa Solo, arrived with her twin children; with her own small grasp on the Force, she sensed that he was alive. In fact, Skywalker's spirit had been freed from his paralyzed body and was aware of his surroundings, though no one else could see him. He was trapped on the spirit plane, where he could directly fight the ancient Sith Lord Exar Kun, who vowed to kill him.

Kun's malevolent spirit possessed other Jedi students and used them as tools to destroy Skywalker's helpless physical body, but each time the plan was foiled. In one instance, Skywalker even directed the actions of young Jacen Solo to defend him with a lightsaber.

Once the true nature of the Dark Lord's threat became known to the trainees, Skywalker's students pooled their newfound powers. In a final battle, fighting alongside the spirit forms of Luke Skywalker and even the long-dead Jedi Master Vodo-Siosk Baas—whom Kun had slain on the Republic Senate floor four thousand years earlier—they vanquished Exar Kun for all time. Skywalker was restored to health.

## The Recapture of Maw Installation
### 11 A.B.Y.

Continuing his raids in Imperial territory, the vigilante Kyp Durron caused as much damage as an Imperial battle force. Han Solo and Lando Calrissian tracked Durron down and begged him to cease his depredations. Instead, Durron attempted to destroy the *Millennium Falcon*—but at the peak of his fury, the anger suddenly faded from him. The manipulative spirit of Exar Kun had been destroyed.

Realizing the magnitude of what he had done, Durron surrendered and agreed to return to Coruscant. After a hearing in which many voices were raised in opposition, an ailing Mon Mothma wielded her veto power. "You have the blood of billions on your hands, Jedi Knight, but I am not the one to judge you. Go to Yavin 4. Let the Jedi Master decide your punishment."

A devastated and repentant Kyp Durron arrived as the trainees tried to put their lives back together. He asked Master Skywalker how he could find forgiveness for the impetuous actions that had driven him to the dark side. Skywalker realized this was a crux point for a young man who had the potential to be a great Jedi; he needed to know if Durron had been irreparably damaged by Exar Kun.

Skywalker came to a decision. He announced that the Sun Crusher must be obliterated for all time, and that Kyp Durron would do it himself as an act of contrition. Together, they would go to the Maw cluster and plunge the superweapon into one of the universe's bottomless pits. They set off toward Kessel and the Maw.

Once Admiral Daala's Star Destroyers had been driven off, the New Republic had put together an occupying force that returned to the Maw Installation. Joining the troops were Chewbacca—who wished to free the remaining Wookiee slaves at the research facility—and Qwi Xux, though she had never regained her lost memories. The occupation force picked its way through the black hole cluster. Upon their arrival, the flustered research administrator Tol Sivron commandeered the Death Star prototype and escaped.

New Republic soldiers scoured through unfin-

ished works that had been under development by installation scientists, taking what could be adapted to defend the new government. Qwi Xux could recall no details as she revisited the place where she had spent most of her life. She read her own notes with growing horror, realizing how misled she had been.

Before the New Republic forces could consolidate the classified information, though, a battered old Star Destroyer appeared inside the Maw—the sole remaining ship from Daala's guardian fleet. While the other Imperial battleship had been destroyed in the Cauldron Nebula, Admiral Daala herself had survived, and she intended to take back Maw Installation, or die in the attempt.

Unlike Grand Admiral Thrawn, throughout her reign of terror Daala had never claimed to be a great military leader or strategist. She had no interest in ruling the Empire or governing conquered worlds; in short, she knew she couldn't win. Realizing her forces were vastly outnumbered, though, Daala intended to cause as much damage as possible, as revenge for what the Rebels had done to her way of life.

Thus, when she found her enemies stripping away the weapons discoveries in the very research installation Grand Moff Tarkin had charged her to protect, Daala was willing to obliterate herself and the occupation forces in a final flash of glory. With all her remaining weapons, she fired upon the installation as the occupation force scrambled to protect themselves.

Simultaneously, the administrator Tol Sivron took his commandeered Death Star prototype out of the black hole cluster to the nearby Kessel system. He used the superlaser to wipe out some of the massed New Republic battleships and to destroy Kessel's garrison moon. Upon encountering a coordinated resistance, however, and since the prototype had no TIE fighters or strategic defenses, Sivron changed course and rushed back into the Maw to hide.

Unaware of this chaos, Durron and Skywalker arrived at the Maw cluster on their own mission to destroy the Sun Crusher. There they saw the scrambled New Republic forces and the rubble of Kessel's destroyed moon. Racing inside to the Maw Installation, the two Jedi watched as the Death Star

*Locked in combat*

prototype appeared in space to join forces with Daala's lone Star Destroyer.

Unbeknownst to Tol Sivron, Han Solo had managed to hide the *Millennium Falcon* inside the tangled superstructure of the prototype as it fled from the Kessel system. With his companions Calrissian and their sometime-ally, Mara Jade, who had begun to hone her own Force skills, Solo worked to sabotage the Death Star's core superlaser before Sivron could fire on Maw Installation. The *Falcon* escaped from the prototype's superstructure as Sivron's teams desperately worked to repair the damage.

Impulsive, wanting to make up for the destruction he had caused, Kyp Durron raced back to the Sun Crusher. He used it to engage the prototype, while Chewbacca led a major offensive against Daala's remaining Star Destroyer. As the occupation force evacuated the installation, Daala came in on a suicide run, firing on the facility's main power

reactor, which exploded in a blinding flash, presumably destroying the Imperial ship. But the explosion blinded the sensors and Daala again escaped—this time to the remnants of the Empire in the Deep Core.

Flying alone, Kyp Durron led Tol Sivron's Death Star prototype in a cat-and-mouse game through the gravitational quicksand of the cluster. In a final gambit he lured the prototype too close to a black hole—and was trapped himself. As the Sun Crusher and the prototype both spiraled into the bottomless singularity, only a small message pod escaped from the Sun Crusher.

When the pod was recovered by Han Solo, he was astonished to find that Durron had managed to cram himself into the pod, breaking many bones in the process. He had placed himself into a Jedi trance, which kept him alive. Durron would recover and go on to perform great deeds of his own as a Jedi Knight, along with other Skywalker trainees, most notably in defeating a murderous leviathan on the mining world of Corbos.

On Coruscant, Mon Mothma clearly had not much longer to live. Leia Organa Solo discovered the secret of Ambassador Furgan's slow poison, but there was no known antidote. Concerned about the fate of the fledgling New Republic, Mon Mothma designated Organa Solo as her immediate successor.

In an unlikely gambit, the Jedi-talented Mon Calamarian Cilghal—one of Skywalker's trainees who had a special talent for healing—worked for hours at Mon Mothma's deathbed. Focusing her powers, Cilghal was able to remove the insidious poison one molecule at a time, leaving the retired chief of state weak and debilitated, but at last able to heal herself.

During a battle to save the third Solo child, Anakin, from an attack by Ambassador Furgan— which resulted in the ambassador's death—Ackbar regained his confidence as a military leader and finally offered his assistance to the new chief of state, as did Han Solo and many other heroes of the Rebellion. General Carlist Rieekan assumed Leia Organa Solo's former post as minister of state. After much turmoil, the New Republic looked forward to a time of peace and recovery.

Kyp Durron and Luke Skywalker returned to the Jedi academy, where the students welcomed them. Durron had been through his trial by fire and would be able to learn the ways of the Force, while avoiding the temptations of the dark side. New candidates were being found every day, and Skywalker had no doubts that the Jedi Knights would once again become the guardians of the New Republic.

## The Emperor's Hand and the Senex Lords
### 12 A.B.Y.

Following Admiral Daala's defeat and the destruction of the Sun Crusher, nearly a full year elapsed with few overt conflicts.

Corran Horn, one of the Jedi trainees who had helped defeat the spirit of Exar Kun, had left the academy in the middle of the Daala conflict to rescue his wife from Leonia Tavira, a pirate leader and former Imperial who coordinated her destructive raids from her flagship Star Destroyer *Invidious*. Over several months, Horn infiltrated the "Invid" pirates, where he fell afoul of Tavira's Jedi advisers.

The presence of new Jedi intrigued Master Luke Skywalker, and once the threat of Daala was removed, he teamed up with Horn on a successful rescue mission to Tavira's headquarters. The strange, reclusive Jedi sect called themselves the *Jensaarai*, and they traced their origin back several decades to the tutelage of Nikkos Tyris, an Anzati Dark Jedi. Despite their Sith influence, the *Jensaarai* were not sinister, and Skywalker resolved to continue studying their unique approach to the Force.

While Skywalker was on his quest, centralized Imperial authority collapsed utterly without the presence of a unifying military leader. The warlords in the Deep Core engaged in open warfare among one another, whole battle fleets clashing amid the dense backdrop of stars. The New Republic adopted a wait-and-see attitude, hoping that the Imperials would burn themselves out.

One warlord, Admiral Harrsk, began shuttling troops out of the Deep Core and amassing a force in the Atravis sector in the Outer Rim, where he was supported by several Imperial fortress worlds. While New Republic Intelligence kept a close eye on this development, they completely missed the ominous stirrings in the Senex and Juvex sectors of the Mid Rim.

Both the Senex and Juvex sectors are ancient aristocracies ruled by a multitude of houses, and both are generally left to their own devices. In his time, Emperor Palpatine kept only a token military force in the region, and the New Republic has had no success in persuading the Senex Lords to take a more active role in galactic affairs. Their arrogance and sense of noblesse oblige prompted them to forge an alliance with Roganda Ismaren. The woman did not have a blue-blooded pedigree or a personal war fleet, but she answered to the title by which Palpatine had called her—Emperor's Hand.

Palpatine had employed many Hands. The most famous, and possibly most respected, was Mara Jade; others included Maarek Stele, Arden Lyn, Shira Brie, and Roganda Ismaren. Following her master's death, Ismaren had gone to ground on the

*A harbinger of the Ismaren plot disrupts the Great Meet on Ithor*

sleepy world of Belsavis. As the years passed, she trained her son Irek in the ways of the Force. Irek Ismaren, who was rumored to be the offspring of Palpatine himself, had been implanted with a sub-electronic converter that allowed him to control any machine with a mere thought.

Roganda Ismaren located a long-dormant Imperial battlemoon—the *Eye of Palpatine*—and ordered her son to "call" the distant ship to Belsavis. The *Eye* was her bargaining chip with the Senex and Juvex Lords, and when she claimed she could retrieve it, they had no choice but to listen.

Chief of State Leia Organa Solo, meanwhile, attended to affairs of state, including a goodwill visit to the semiannual Ceremony of the Great Meet on the tropical planet Ithor. The elaborate festivities of the Ithorians are among the galaxy's most elegant events, but that year the good cheer was shattered by the arrival of a wild-eyed psychotic.

Once the raving lunatic was subdued, Han Solo recognized him as one of his former smuggling associates. The man mumbled about "the children of the Jedi." The chief of state's research into the subject revealed that many Force-strong children had once been sheltered on Belsavis. Under cover of a diplomatic visit, Organa Solo, her husband, Chewbacca, and R2-D2 headed to the frozen planet to investigate.

Belsavis's Plawal rift is a lush, steam-filled geothermal vent gouged into the planetary ice and capped by a transparisteel dome. Eighteen years prior to the Battle of Yavin, dozens of children had been sheltered there by Plett, a Ho'Din Jedi Master. The Emperor had sent the battlemoon *Eye of Palpatine* to destroy them, but it had miraculously failed to arrive and carry out its assigned massacre, and Plett and the children had fled to parts unknown.

Organa Solo hunted down clues in the Plawal rift and soon ran across Roganda Ismaren, whom she recognized from Palpatine's court. She also noted the presence of the aristocratic Senex Lords and Dr. Ohran Keldor, one of the Death Star's many early architects. Her curiosity, however, nearly got her killed. Ismaren stunned Organa Solo and took her prisoner, locking her in a room near the lip of the rift dome.

The chief of state gradually discovered that

*Roganda and Irek Ismaren*

Ismaren planned to acquire the *Eye of Palpatine* and had obtained Senex and Juvex financial backers, and she learned of Irek's ability to scramble electronics—an ability he planned to use on attacking New Republic fighter craft. But when the *Eye of Palpatine* finally emerged from hyperspace in the Belsavis system, Irek Ismaren found he could not control it after all. Without guidance, the ship reverted to its original mission—one of complete planetary annihilation.

The *Eye* prepared to bombard Plawal, but when it failed to fire, the people realized that even Irek could not command the devastating weapon. As soon as they became aware that the rogue death engine was out of control, bedlam ensued. Organa Solo broke away but chose a risky route for her escape—swinging from vine-coffee beds that dangled beneath the transparisteel dome. Hopping from one bed to the next, she stayed one jump ahead of the lightsaber-wielding Irek. Dr. Ohran Keldor was killed during the chase.

By the time things settled down, the Ismarens had vanished to seek asylum within the Senex sector. No charges were brought against the Senex or Juvex Lords for their part in the plot, since technically they had done nothing wrong; they had merely listened to Ismaren's proposal.

That left the *Eye* to be dealt with.

## *The* Eye of Palpatine
**12 A.B.Y.**

The colossal, asteroid-shaped *Eye of Palpatine* had been constructed in an era when Palpatine had needed to hide the extent of his power. His abominable action of wiping out every inhabitant in the Plawal rift—most of them children—would have caused untold outrage in the senate had it become known. So when Palpatine had sent the *Eye* on its deadly mission, he had ordered the ship's contingent of stormtroopers to await pickup on scattered worlds throughout the Outer Rim.

Luckily, Palpatine's plan never came to fruition. Thanks to sabotage by two Jedi Knights, Geith and Callista, the *Eye of Palpatine* had remained dormant in the Moonflower Nebula. The inhabitants of Belsavis had escaped, and the waiting stormtroopers grew old and died. The *Eye* slept for thirty years—until Roganda Ismaren found it.

Coincidentally, while Irek Ismaren was using his subelectronic converter to call the ship through the Force, Jedi Master Luke Skywalker had already encountered the *Eye* in the Moonflower Nebula.

There, the *Eye*'s automated lander followed its long-delayed programming and picked up Skywalker and two students, thinking they were waiting stormtroopers, and inadvertently carried them along for the ride.

The students, Cray Mingla and Nichos Marr, had recently joined the Yavin 4 praxeum. Mingla was a brilliant computer programmer and showed much promise as a Jedi, but her lover Nichos Marr had been diagnosed with fatal Quannot's syndrome. In order to preserve Marr's life, Mingla had transferred his consciousness into the body of an amazingly lifelike droid. She had hoped to parallel the Ssi-ruuk entenchment method of harnessing life energy, but instead it appears she accomplished little more than programming a droid with Marr's memories.

Trapped aboard the *Eye*, Skywalker and Mingla were forcibly brainwashed by the ship's automated indoctrination equipment. Skywalker had the strength of mind to overcome the imprinting, but the other fresh prisoners did not. The *Eye of Palpatine* had attempted to fulfill its programming by picking up its stormtrooper contingent—but after three decades, the troopers were just a distant

*Combat aboard the* Eye of Palpatine

memory. Undaunted, the *Eye* had apparently settled for whatever warm bodies it found in the appropriate places. As it continued along its path, the destructive vessel grabbed groups of hapless prisoners of various species from a swath of worlds.

Two tribes of Gamorreans were aboard, embroiled in a full-scale clan war. Each side had been brainwashed into believing *they* were loyal Imperial stormtroopers and their enemies were mutineers. Skywalker's left leg was severely mangled by a vibro-ax during a Gamorrean attack in their clan war, and he was forced to hobble about with a cane.

Talz, Kitonaks, Tusken Raiders, Affytechans, and other aliens aimlessly roamed the halls of the automated vessel, waiting for orders. Jawas began ripping out wires left and right, and a tribe of Sand People nearly killed Skywalker in a furious assault. To Skywalker, there appeared only one solution to the insane situation: get the aliens off the *Eye of Palpatine* and destroy the vessel before it could fulfill its original program and wipe out all life in the Plawal rift. But the person who destroyed it would have to remain on board to hit the switch. While the Jedi pondered, one of the Jawas gave him a long cylindrical object they had found on board: a lightsaber.

In the quartermaster's office, Skywalker discovered the saber's owner, Callista, who had once served the Republic as a Jedi Knight. And Callista was, for lack of a better term, a ghost. Much as Exar Kun had merged his spirit with the temples of Yavin 4, Callista had transferred her life essence into the *Eye's* central computer during her sabotage mission thirty years prior. For decades her consciousness had remained in the circuitry, manning turbolasers to prevent anyone from arriving and manually reactivating the deadly battlemoon.

Though they could communicate only through a computer screen, Skywalker came to feel that Callista—someone whose strength in the Force was as great as his own—was a woman with whom he could spend the rest of his life. The decision to destroy the *Eye* became an agonizing dilemma, for it meant he would destroy Callista, as well.

As time ran out, Skywalker and the others managed to get the aliens loaded aboard escape shuttles. He steeled himself to trigger the *Eye's* self-destruct, but Cray Mingla unexpectedly dropped her Master to the floor with a stun blast. Skywalker woke up on one of the fleeing lifeboats just in time to watch the *Eye of Palpatine* explode with a soundless roar.

During the New Republic's salvage recovery operations above Belsavis, a team of workers discovered a life pod containing Cray Mingla's hibernating body, held in stasis. Skywalker was puzzled that Mingla had chosen to live. But when he opened the pod's hatch, the woman who opened Cray's eyes, who lifted Cray's head, and who extended Cray's arms was not Cray Mingla. In the *Eye's* final moments, Mingla had voluntarily left her body and allowed Callista to step inside, the same form of Jedi spirit transference that had allowed Emperor Palpatine to inhabit a regular supply of fresh new clones. Nichos Marr had remained behind to trigger the destruction so that a reborn Callista could escape.

An unexpected side effect of the transfer was that Callista lost her ability to touch the Force or use any of her Jedi powers. For the moment, though, it seemed an acceptable price to pay. Skywalker and Callista were together, this time in body, as well as spirit.

# THE DARKSABER THREAT

**12 A.B.Y.**

With his beloved Callista suffering from her loss of Jedi powers, Luke Skywalker went to great lengths to understand her condition. At the praxeum, the historian Tionne uncovered tantalizing legends of Ulic Qel-Droma and his blindness to the Force during the Sith War, but even this story provided no suggestions for a solution. Skywalker concluded that he needed to go away with Callista and spend intense, isolated time where they could focus on salvaging her Jedi abilities. With permission from the chief of state, Skywalker departed on his quest.

By this time, several of the new Jedi trainees had built their own lightsabers and had become Knights of the Republic, including Cilghal, the Mon Calamarian ambassador who had healed Mon Mothma's illness. The cloned Jedi Dorsk 81 was accompanied by Kyp Durron on a journey to the clone's homeworld. Durron, still nursing his grudge against the Empire, wanted to proceed into the Deep Core, where the remnants of Imperial forces had hidden; there he would investigate what the enemy was planning.

Inside the Deep Core, Admiral Daala had been at work trying to unify the squabbling warlords into a full-fledged attack force. It wasn't until she allied herself with Vice Admiral Pellaeon—Thrawn's former second in command—that she made any headway. Prepared to do anything in the name of the Empire, Daala murdered thirteen of the strongest Imperial warlords, including Harrsk, Teradoc, and Delvardus, and gathered their forces under her own banner, vowing to fight the real enemy rather than each other. Pellaeon added his experience and wisdom to hers, and together they formed a formidable team.

Before his death, Superior General Delvardus had constructed a Super Star Destroyer, the *Night Hammer*, which Daala took as her own flagship. Aware of the battles she would have to fight against the Jedi Knights, she renamed it the *Knight Hammer*. Finally, having learned from mistakes during her first depredations, Daala coordinated her massive space fleet with Pellaeon and prepared to launch the combined forces at the New Republic. She intended to win this time.

## *The Hutt Plan*
### 12 A.B.Y.

While Daala amassed her forces, the reborn Black Sun criminal syndicate had implemented schemes of their own. Y'ull Acib had been overthrown and their new leader, Durga the Hutt, had established a secret construction base in the inhospitable asteroid belt famed for shielding the *Millennium Falcon* following the Battle of Hoth. Durga, now head of the Besadii clan, had also succeeded in dominating the other clans in his ambitious grab for power. Though

the asteroid field posed serious navigational hazards, the Hutts viewed it as a vast collection of mineral resources, ripe for exploitation.

Teamed with Imperial General Sulamar—whose rank actually was never recognized by the Imperial hierarchy—and the oft-executed and resurrected weapons engineer Bevel Lemelisk—who had worked at Maw Installation and supervised the construction of the first two Death Stars—Durga intended to build his own superweapon. A huge investment of Hutt family wealth went into this project, though frequent disasters and setbacks plagued every step of the scheme.

Durga and his partners had the resources and facilities in place. In order to obtain the weapons plans he needed, however, Durga and his entourage journeyed to Imperial City on an overblown diplomatic visit. Though Chief of State Leia Organa Solo despised all Hutts, largely due to her unpleasant experience with Jabba, their vast organized crime network was too powerful for the fledgling New Republic to ignore.

Making sweet-sounding promises, Durga suggested an alliance with the government. He pointed out that the Hutts controlled interests on a great number of worlds that had not yet sworn allegiance to the New Republic. Perhaps after an understanding had been reached with the Hutts, Durga suggested, he could recommend that these planets sign the articles of the New Republic. Though it was clear the chief of state did not believe him, Durga claimed the Hutts wanted to change their ways, to become respectable and have a genuine say in the large-scale government.

Durga's real reason in coming to Coruscant was to infiltrate the Imperial Information Center. During a staged disturbance, several small intelligent creatures—Durga's "pets"—slipped away and broke into the vast computers, where they copied the coded files of the original Death Star blueprints, the same files Princess Leia had at one time hidden inside her astromech droid, R2-D2. At the end of his diplomatic visit, with the stolen plans safely secured among his entourage, Durga departed. As he did so, he extended an invitation for Organa Solo to visit him on Nal Hutta, the central Hutt world.

Once he arrived back at the Hoth asteroid field,

*The Darksaber lies in wait*

Durga and General Sulamar set their teams to work in constructing their great weapon, code-named Darksaber. The structure was a bare-bones modification of the Death Star's planet-destroying superlaser, stripped down without the surrounding battle station, similar in principle to the Empire's experimental *Tarkin* superlaser. Once he possessed such an invincible weapon, Durga planned to extort protection money, taxes, and fees wherever he went. The Hutts could become the "crimelords of the galaxy."

Before long, however, the New Republic discovered that Durga had copied the plans. Chief of State Leia Organa Solo decided to determine exactly what the Hutts were up to. Mounting her own "diplomatic visit," she brought a New Republic show of force—ostensibly engaged in war-gaming exercises—to Nal Hutta.

General Wedge Antilles and Admiral Ackbar commanded the two-pronged military fleet. They were accompanied by General Crix Madine, the New Republic's chief of covert operations. Madine, who had assisted greatly in the Battle of Endor, was to use his espionage skills to uncover the Hutt plans.

When Organa Solo arrived on Nal Hutta, Durga pretended to be a gracious host. Though Madine managed to plant a tracer beacon on the Hutt ship, Durga succeeded in diverting the chief of state's attention. He revealed that Admiral Daala intended to launch a devastating military strike. Organa Solo reeled in shock; the New Republic had believed Daala dead, and her reappearance took them completely by surprise.

## Admiral Daala Returns
### 12 A.B.Y.

In the Deep Core, Admiral Daala served as the charismatic spokesperson amidst the reunited Imperial forces. She caused a dramatic attitude shift in the Imperial military when she allowed aliens and women to participate in active military service. Previously, with the exception of Carnor Jax's Interim Council, these groups had largely been excluded, thanks to Palpatine's prejudices. Daala hated administrative details and had no designs on running the Empire once she had accomplished her

vengeful aim. After the battle was won, she planned to let Pellaeon or another officer rule; she didn't care who, so long as the new leader brought back the Imperial way of life.

In closed command consultations, Daala and Pellaeon chose their all-important first strike. They would attack the Jedi academy on Yavin 4, wipe out the new Jedi Knights, and spread despair among their enemies. This was a battle they could certainly win, and it would cost them few casualties and little damage. The fleet had been gathered and supplied, all weapons systems were functional, and it was time to launch their attack.

During these preparations, though, Kyp Durron and Dorsk 81 infiltrated the Deep Core. Upon learning of Daala's plans, the two Jedi spies fled, beginning a race against time. Durron and Dorsk 81 rushed back to the New Republic, sounding the alarm.

## Durga's Folly
### 12 A.B.Y.

On their own private odyssey, Luke Skywalker and Callista remained unaware of the turmoil across the Deep Core and the New Republic. They continued their quest to restore Callista's Jedi powers. At her request, Skywalker took her to places that had been milestones in his own instruction, including Dagobah, where Skywalker had studied under Yoda, and Hoth, where he had first seen the apparition of Obi-Wan Kenobi. Skywalker and Callista suffered a disastrous attack by wampa ice creatures on Hoth and barely escaped in a damaged ship.

With their life support failing, Luke Skywalker placed himself into a Jedi hibernation trance, and their helpless craft drifted into the nearby asteroid belt—the site of Durga's Darksaber construction project. In his deep trance, Skywalker called out to his twin sister, who received the message and sent out a rescue mission. The *Millennium Falcon* retrieved them on the far side of the treacherous asteroid field, still without discovering the nearly completed gigantic weapon.

One of Lemelisk's new twists was the employment of a new kind of workforce, small simian creatures called Taurill, who collectively formed a hive mind. Together, these swarms of creatures assem-

*Death in the line of duty*

bled the enormous vessel according to the modified blueprints. But the Taurill were also sufficiently distractible that they generated numerous errors whenever anything extraneous caught their interest, such as the blip of Skywalker's survival ship crossing the nearby field of stars.

General Sulamar and Bevel Lemelisk worked to keep these frustrating errors and delays under control. Knowing the Emperor's history of repeatedly executing and then cloning Lemelisk, Durga threatened the engineer with a similar fate, but Lemelisk doubted the Hutt knew how to perform the resurrection process properly—and he feared a botched job even more than death itself.

After studying the tracker he had placed on Durga's ship, Crix Madine discovered the Hutt hideout in the Hoth asteroids. With a group of handpicked commandos, Madine went to spy on the secret project. Reaching the heart of the

asteroid belt and the construction site, the commandos infiltrated the industrial assembly, and Madine and his team breached the Darksaber laser housing. Madine suspected the fundamental weapon design was flawed, but before his crew could sabotage it further, he was captured; his team members died trying to buy his escape. The only survivor of the commando squad, Madine did manage to send out an alarm, via an implanted transmitter, as the Darksaber guards hauled him to face Durga the Hutt.

On the command bridge of the completed Darksaber weapon, the captive Madine, who had long ago served with distinction in the Imperial military, took one look at the puffed-up General Sulamar and recognized him as a fraud, a cowardly foot soldier pretending to be an Imperial officer. Surprised at this turnabout, Durga ordered the disgraced general into custody, as well. He then commanded that the Darksaber be powered up, moved it out of the asteroid field, and made ready to attack helpless planets. Then, as a sort of christening for his new weapon, Durga executed General Crix Madine—who died a hero to the New Republic.

As the Darksaber lumbered into motion, military fleets arrived in the asteroid field, led by General Wedge Antilles and Admiral Ackbar. They had received Madine's distress signal as they were engaged in war games near the Hutt homeworld. They issued an ultimatum to Durga and prepared to stop the new superweapon.

On board the untested and error-fraught device, engineer Lemelisk was appalled when Durga pushed the engines to the maximum and prepared to fire the superlaser. Not wanting to be executed again for failure, he slipped away and jumped ship in a small shuttle.

As Antilles and Ackbar closed in, the Darksaber fled through the asteroids. Durga, arrogant and confident as he commanded his spectacular new ship, flew into a danger zone of colliding asteroids. He intended to use his powerful new laser to clear a path through the rubble. At the critical moment, however, the weapon failed dramatically, unable even to ignite a spark; the Darksaber weapon and Durga the Hutt were obliterated in a titanic space collision.

Bevel Lemelisk's shuttle was intercepted by New Republic forces, and the engineer was taken prisoner. Later, Lemelisk was incarcerated on Orinackra—ironically, a prison where General Madine himself had been held—and tried for his crimes of genocide. He was sentenced to be executed, one of the few Imperial criminals to receive the death penalty. The sentence was carried out four years later, and Lemelisk's only comment was, "At least make sure you do it right this time."

## Assault on Yavin 4
### 12 A.B.Y.

Shortly after Kyp Durron and Dorsk 81 reached Yavin 4 to warn of Daala's impending Imperial attack, Vice Admiral Pellaeon arrived with a vanguard fleet of twelve Star Destroyers. The Imperial ships sent down assault forces, armed scout walkers, and ground assault machinery, with orders to crush the Jedi training center to dust. Daala's plan was to make this a true symbolic victory; she wanted the jungle moon to be reduced to a cinder, with every last one of the Jedi students killed. Only hours behind the vanguard force, Daala followed in her huge Super Star Destroyer, the Knight Hammer.

Even without Skywalker to lead them in the fight, the Jedi candidates defended their academy using everything they had learned. Durron, Dorsk 81, Kam Solusar, Tionne, Kirana Ti, Streen, Kyle Katarn, and the other new Jedi fought individual battles against the Empire's forces. But against such massive military strength, they had no chance.

As they gathered for a last stand at the stronghold of the Great Temple, Dorsk 81 suggested combining all their Force abilities into a single dramatic thrust, similar to the way they had defeated the dark spirit of Exar Kun. He cited Yoda's famous adage that "size matters not" and suggested they could strike directly against the Imperial battleships.

The Jedi channeled their unified push through the conduit of Dorsk 81, producing a blast strong enough to drive Pellaeon's entire Star Destroyer fleet to the fringes of the Yavin system. Though the Jedi students achieved victory, the surge of power was too great for Dorsk 81's physical body to withstand. He died, incinerated from within—one of the first true martyrs of the new Jedi Knights. But his idea had worked: the vanguard fleet was driven away and crippled.

Thus, when Admiral Daala arrived in her Knight Hammer for the second wave of the assault, she couldn't find Pellaeon or his ships. Not to be swayed, though, she launched a renewed attack on the small green moon, blasting at the jungles from orbit.

Having rescued Luke Skywalker and Callista on Hoth, the Millennium Falcon arrived at Yavin 4. While Han Solo, Chewbacca, and Leia Organa Solo remained on board to join in the space battle, Skywalker and Callista landed to assist the Jedi trainees against the ground attacks. And though Callista was still no closer to regaining her affinity with the Force, she could fight. As the Jedi continued a concerted defense in the burning jungles, Callista became separated from Skywalker.

Seeing her chance to do something significant, she stole a damaged Imperial ship and piloted it alone to the *Knight Hammer*. Bluffing her way on board the Super Star Destroyer, Callista landed in one of the rear docking bays, near the powerful engine systems. About thirty other shuttles sat there, not used for the jungle assault. Callista planted small charges on the fuel bays of each of the empty ships, set timers, then headed for the bridge. She intended to face Daala herself before the end.

As Callista had hoped, the exploding charges set off a chain reaction that ripped out the *Knight Hammer*'s engine chambers. Within moments, the Super Star Destroyer was crippled, a juggernaut with no engines and no guidance control. Pulled by the immense gravity of the gas giant Yavin, the *Knight*

*Callista*

*Hammer* nosed toward the huge orange planet.

Astonished at what had happened, Daala was helpless to prevent the total destruction of her flagship. Her only chance was to reach Pellaeon's fleet, which had been flung to the edge of the solar system. She ordered an immediate evacuation, and all personnel rushed to the escape pods while Daala stood on the bridge—a captain in danger of going down with her ship. When she went to the executive command pods to make her own escape, Daala encountered Callista, who stood waiting, lightsaber drawn.

Oddly, after all her intense and useless exercises, Callista's seething anger allowed her to feel dark tendrils, a potential for using the Force again—but only the dark side. At that moment, Callista could have used her reawakened ability, but she loved Luke Skywalker and had been trained as a Jedi Knight. She vowed not to let herself fall to the temptations of the dark side.

Daala tricked her, though, and used a moment of surprise to blast Callista with a stunner. Then Daala made her own escape as the *Knight Hammer* dived into the outer atmosphere of Yavin.

On the ground of Yavin 4, Luke Skywalker suddenly knew that Callista was on board the *Knight Hammer*, and that she had once again been able to touch the Force. In the midst of his battles, he looked up, to watch the black Super Star Destroyer plunge into the limb of the gas giant, burning as tiny dots of escape pods flew in all directions. Then the swirling clouds and crushing storms of Yavin swallowed up the battleship, dragging it down forever.

Skywalker learned later that Callista had managed to climb aboard one of the last escape pods and had made her way to safety. But after her terrifying brush with the dark side, she swore not to return to him until she regained her powers and learned how to control her anger. Skywalker did not see her again for nearly a year.

At the far edge of the Yavin system, Pellaeon regrouped his damaged Star Destroyers and retrieved as many of the *Knight Hammer*'s escape pods as he could. He rescued Admiral Daala before New Republic reinforcements could rally and come after them. Once again, Daala's grand plans had fallen to rubble. She relinquished full command to Pellaeon, in the hopes that he could lead the Empire better than she had. This transfer of power had enormous implications for the eventual settlement of hostilities between Imperial and Republic forces, seven years later.

## The Empire Regroups
### 12–13 A.B.Y.

Pellaeon wasn't the type of man to seize power, but once such a responsibility was thrust upon him, he proved extremely capable. The lessons he had learned while serving with Grand Admiral Thrawn made him an excellent tactician, while his experiences with Teradoc and Daala taught him the value of devastating psychological blows and terror strikes.

Thanks to Daala's unification efforts, the Empire was stable, though only a shadow of its former self. If anyone could restore the Empire, or at least slow its inexorable decline, Pellaeon appeared to be the one.

Daala had already pulled all the warlord fleets from out of the Deep Core, so Pellaeon abandoned that region altogether. The Outer Rim and Mid Rim offered much more favorable opportunities for harassing New Republic shipping. These systems also had more resources, better-traveled hyperspace lanes, and hundreds of thousands of worlds ripe for conquest. Pellaeon hooked up with existing Imperial fortress worlds and used his considerable fleet to carve out a well-defined Empire stretching from Wild Space to the Mid Rim, with a few scattered holdings in the other regions of the galaxy.

The moffs of the former Imperial fortress worlds threw support behind their new commander, donating carefully hoarded stores of munitions and war matériel. The most impressive acquisition was the Super Star Destroyer *Reaper*. The colossal vessel had once been the flagship of Grand Moff Ardus Kaine's miniempire, the Pentastar Alignment, before Kaine's death during Operation Shadow Hand. Pellaeon absorbed the remnants of the Pentastar Alignment and made the *Reaper* his personal command vessel.

Six months after Daala relinquished her com-

*Admiral Pellaeon*

mand, Pellaeon made an aggressive lunge at the New Republic by seizing the small planet Orinda. The New Republic was slow to respond. By the time General Antilles mounted a counterattack from the bridge of the *Lusankya*, Pellaeon had already captured six neighboring systems. In a month-long campaign, the New Republic pushed Pellaeon back, but suffered a grievous defeat in the Battle of Orinda. There, the *Reaper* destroyed most of Antilles's starfighters by annihilating the fleet carrier *Endurance*. Rogue Squadron, stationed aboard the *Lusankya*, covered the fleet's retreat. The New Republic chose to leave Orinda in Imperial hands and instead fortified the surrounding systems.

By her choice, Admiral Daala had no role in Pellaeon's effort. She had voluntarily withdrawn from the Empire and was now the president of an independent settlers group on Pedducis Chorios. Despite Pellaeon's military successes, Daala remained disgusted by the overall composition of the Empire—various pockets still under the sway of petty governors and greedy moffs. One such pocket was the Antemeridian sector, under the rule of Moff Getelles.

## Mission to Adumar
### 13 A.B.Y.

The New Republic saw the remote planet of Adumar as a key to threatening the Empire on two fronts. Located on the fringe of Wild Space, Adumar had been too distant from the centers of power to attract much notice during Palpatine's reign. Now, however, with the Empire pressed far from the Core Worlds, Adumar held a new strategic importance for both sides.

The world was maniacally militaristic, possessing a rigid duel-oriented culture and a worshipful reverence toward starfighter pilots. The first side to bring it into their fold would gain a military powerhouse, and an industrial base geared toward the manufacture of proton torpedoes. The New Republic didn't need the boost as badly as the Imperials did, but having an ally at the Empire's back door would force Pellaeon to split his forces.

Adumari culture eschewed diplomats in favor of military heroes. Consequently, General Wedge Antilles was sent to the city of Cartann to negotiate with the leadership there. His ambassadorial counterpart on the Imperial side was Turr Phennir, who had assumed command of the legendary 181st Imperial fighter group following Baron Fel's defection to the New Republic years before. Antilles witnessed firsthand the locals' love of blood sport and their ritualized death duels. Appalled by the unnecessary loss of life, Antilles made his feelings known, prompting the Cartann monarchy to lean toward an alliance with the Empire.

Unlike most civilized planets, Adumar did not possess a single worldwide government. Though

*General Wedge Antilles*

Cartann's nation was the most powerful, dozens of smaller states existed elsewhere on the planet. These states resented their larger cousin for its domineering attitude and violent culture. Representatives of the other nations contacted Antilles, who agreed to lead their combined militaries in a major offensive to break Cartann's rule.

The attack succeeded. Adumar reverted to a provisional coalition government with representatives from every nation. After due deliberation, the planet agreed to join the New Republic.

## THE DEATH SEED PLAGUE

### 13 A.B.Y.

One month after the Battle of Orinda, eight months after the destruction of the *Knight Hammer*, Chief of State Leia Organa Solo and a small fleet traveled to the backwater Meridian sector, which ran up against the Antemeridian sector and was thus situated directly on the contentious New Republic–Imperial border. Accompanied by Luke Skywalker, Organa Solo was there to meet with Seti Ashgad of Nam Chorios. Because Ashgad held no official position on his homeworld, the mission was kept a closely guarded state secret, in order to avoid political repercussions.

Ashgad had requested New Republic intervention on Nam Chorios. Seven hundred years earlier the planet had been a prison colony, but over time the original prisoners' descendants had grown into a tough, independent group of settlers. This group, the Oldtimers, had come in direct conflict with the more recent colonists, the Newcomers, for whom Ashgad was an advocate. And Ashgad claimed to be the son of the original Seti Ashgad, who had been exiled to Nam Chorios by Senator Palpatine forty years in the past.

It was all a web of lies. The man who met with Organa Solo was the *original* Ashgad, kept young and vital through stomach-turning "renewal treatments" administered by Dzym, a grossly mutated droch beetle who appeared humanoid. Ashgad's pleas—that Organa Solo force the Oldtimers into opening up their planet to outside trade—were merely a distraction from his real purpose: kidnapping the chief of state and unleashing an incurable plague throughout the sector.

Ashgad's synthdroid bodyguards carried thousands of tiny squirming drochs beneath their synthflesh coverings. Each droch carried the Death Seed plague. Dzym, the head droch, mind-controlled the contaminated swarm, spreading the

*Seti Ashgad*

malignant epidemic across the New Republic task force and killing every last member aboard. Organa Solo was stunned and brought to Ashgad's fortress on Nam Chorios. Luke Skywalker was nowhere to be found.

Ashgad was taking a terrible risk, but he had attracted powerful backers to his cause. Moff Getelles of the Antemeridian sector had long ruled his territory with a free hand and resented the fact that he now had to pay fealty to Pellaeon. Getelles had hammered out a deal with Ashgad to cripple the Meridian sector by releasing the Death Seed. The moff's sector navy would then invade, armed with automated Needle fighters from the Loronar Corporation. Loronar's CEO had also pledged to arm various revolutionary groups throughout the plague-weakened Meridian sector in return for the rights to mine Nam Chorios's valuable crystals. When all was said and done, Ashgad would be a very rich man, Moff Getelles would be an Imperial hero, and millions of innocents would be dead from the virulent Death Seed.

The unique crystals of Nam Chorios were programmable matrices used in synthdroids and Needle fighters. They were also intelligent, silicon-based creatures and were the planet's dominant life-form. Either Ashgad didn't know this, or he didn't care. He made arrangements to wrest control of the planet's defensive gun stations from the Oldtimers so the Loronar Corporation's drop ships could initiate full-scale strip-mining.

Organa Solo was kept pliant and groggy through drugs in her drinking water. Over the course of her captivity she met Beldorian the Splendid, an ancient, Force-wielding Hutt and former Jedi Knight who had been living on Nam Chorios for centuries, and she was befriended by Liegeus Vorn, Ashgad's kindhearted pilot. After a terrifying run-in with a seething mass of drochs, Organa Solo escaped Ashgad's fortress and fled across the rocky wasteland to Bleak Point, site of a planetary gun station. Among the Oldtimer settlers there, she saw a familiar face: her brother's lost love, Callista.

Luke Skywalker had been devastated by Callista's decision to abandon him following the *Knight Hammer* incident, and had spent eight months trying to track her down. He had finally uncovered hints that Callista had settled on Nam Chorios. Accompanying Organa Solo's small task force to the Meridian sector, he had departed just before the Death Seed exterminated all life aboard the fleet vessels.

Skywalker's B-wing was shot down by Nam Chorios's planetary defenses, which were manned by a religious sect of Oldtimer settlers. Limping away from the wreckage, he fell in with a group of hardworking Newcomers. Nam Chorios was an enigma to Skywalker: for a sterile desert world, it teemed with life energy—a result of the enormous crystal population. This had the peculiar effect of magnifying any use of the Force, turning a simple levitation into a potentially fatal telekinetic cyclone.

Skywalker attempted to rescue his sister from Ashgad's fortress, but she had already escaped. Instead, he hooked up with Liegeus Vorn and

rushed to Bleak Point, where they attempted to prevent Ashgad's men from destroying the cannon. They were too late. The destruction of the Bleak Point battery opened up a safe corridor into the sky and beyond. Seti Ashgad would undoubtedly take advantage of the opportunity to join Moff Getelles's Imperial invasion fleet in orbit.

Skywalker and Organa Solo rushed back to Ashgad's fortress, but failed by mere minutes to prevent his departure. While Skywalker pursued Ashgad's ship, Organa Solo was jumped by Beldorian the Hutt. The chief of state had had little time for lightsaber practice over the previous two years, and Beldorian, at nine meters, was staggeringly large even for a Hutt and possessed none of the corpulent rolls that immobilized lazy Hutts like Jabba. The old Jedi Hutt was all muscle and fire, and he slithered at Organa Solo with astonishing quickness. Fortunately, the Alderaanian princess

*Death duel*

had been raised with extensive combat training and did have a keen insight into the flow of the Force. A long, swift side cut messily ended the career of Beldorian the Splendid.

In the lower atmosphere, Skywalker's starfighter was downed by a laser barrage. Before Ashgad's ship could escape, the Jedi Master played his last card. Using the Force, he convinced the crystals of Nam Chorios—appearing as a single collective consciousness—of the danger the galaxy would face if Ashgad's plan succeeded. As Ashgad's ship neared a waiting Imperial Star Destroyer, several of Moff Getelles's Needle fighters, powered by Chorian crystals, suddenly broke formation and destroyed the vessel.

Above Nam Chorios, Getelles's fleet encountered a makeshift New Republic armada thrown together by Han Solo and Lando Calrissian. The two friends had spent weeks scouring the Meridian sector for any sign of the chief of state and had found whole planets quarantined by the Death Seed plague. Unfortunately, Solo had discovered his wife's location with scant time to prepare, and as the Battle of Nam Chorios unfolded, their ragged warships were outgunned by Getelles's modern destroyers.

One thing turned the tide in favor of the New Republic—Admiral Daala. The retired admiral had been lured away from her settlers' coalition when she had learned of Moff Getelles's glory-seeking plan. Daala was enraged and disgusted that loyal Imperials would ally themselves with schemers and madmen like Ashgad and Dzym. She gathered her own warships and helped defeat Getelles in the name of Imperial honor.

In the aftermath of the battle, Skywalker finished negotiations with the Chorian crystal mind. It agreed to send hundreds of crystals off planet to destroy every plague-carrying droch in the Meridian sector, in exchange for the eventual return of every crystal that had been unwittingly installed in a Loronar synthdroid or Needle fighter. The New Republic forced the Loronar Corporation to comply with the decree and canceled a lucrative government contract for future shipments of *Strike*-class cruisers. The move nearly sent Loronar into bankruptcy.

The culmination of an eight-month quest, Luke Skywalker's reunion with Callista was bittersweet. Skywalker had slowly come to realize that his life lay along a different path than his lover's. They didn't even exchange words—merely a warm look and a casual wave. Skywalker boarded a shuttle and left Callista behind on Nam Chorios.

Back on Coruscant, Chief of State Organa Solo had to agree to even more elaborate security precautions than she had previously endured. She was assigned a pair of bodyguards, whom she nicknamed the Sniffer and the Shooter, but she refused to have them assigned to her when she was away from the Imperial Palace.

As part of Ashgad's plot, Minister of State Rieekan had been incapacitated by poison during the crisis. One of the culprits behind the poisoning, Senator Q-Varx, was arrested and tried for treason. Rieekan's recovery was the only thing that saved Q-Varx from a death sentence, though Rieekan chose not to return to his former post. Mokka Falanthas was elected minister of state in his stead.

Admiral Daala's history following the battle was the most curious of all. While surveying the combat wreckage on the surface of Nam Chorios, Daala caught sight of Liegeus Vorn. Before Vorn had become a holo-forger and pilot for Seti Ashgad, he'd had an intense romantic relationship with Daala, years before she'd become involved with Grand Moff Tarkin. Their reunion was tender, and the two departed for Pedducis Chorios. Some New Republic officers wanted to seize Daala and try her for war crimes, while others appreciated her help in the recent battle and wanted to leave her alone. While the latter group prevailed, it appears in hindsight that the former group's instincts were correct.

Daala and Vorn briefly settled on Pedducis Chorios. They then dropped out of sight for nearly a year, during which time Daala reclaimed a leadership position with the new warlords of the Deep Core. During the Darksaber crisis, she had murdered thirteen warlords and appropriated their fleets, but she had left behind a manufacturing infrastructure and planets teeming with Imperial subjects. In the sudden power vacuum, new warlords sprang up to replace Harrsk, Delvardus, and the others. Warlords such as Foga Brill and Moff Tethys lacked military muscle but made up for it in base cruelty. Still trying to impose order, Daala tried to unite the squabbling Deep Core factions and make preparations for a unified military strike against the New Republic.

After Nam Chorios, the New Republic pressed the advantage and entered Moff Getelles's Antemeridian sector with two full fleets. Getelles was powerless to stop them, and the sector—along with a huge chunk of neighboring space—became New Republic territory. Admiral Pellaeon, initially preoccupied with a protracted campaign against Adumar, was eventually able to stop his enemy from advancing into the heart of the Empire, though the effort cost him the Super Star Destroyer *Reaper*.

# PART VIII

## UPRISINGS AND INSURGENCIES

**F**ollowing the crisis in the Meridian sector, the New Republic settled into a period of relative stability. Luke Skywalker's new Jedi Knights served as active peacekeepers and powerful symbols of the restored Republic. Chief of State Leia Organa Solo took advantage of the relative quiet to embark on a peaceful tour of remote member worlds with her three children. She wanted to show that, despite the chaos caused by the dying Empire, the New Republic still cared for the planets that had been neglected due to one crisis after another.

Tragically, the tour indicated just how fragile that peace actually was. The Empire Reborn was the first of several localized movements that would cause substantial regional troubles over the next four years.

## THE EMPIRE REBORN MOVEMENT

**14 A.B.Y.**

When Organa Solo visited the provincial planet Munto Codru, her children were kidnapped while at play. The planetary chairman, Chamberlain Iyon of the Codru-Ji people, tried to reassure the chief of state by speculating that the incident was a "coup abduction"; in Codru-Ji society, children of royal birth are routinely kidnapped and ransomed by rival political factions. The truth was much more complicated.

The children had been kidnapped by Lord Hethrir, a near-human from Firrerre. During the Empire's reign, Hethrir and his mate, Rillao, had been trained by Darth Vader in the ways of the Dark Jedi. Palpatine had been so impressed with Hethrir's abilities that he promoted him to procurator of justice—an unprecedented appointment for a nonhuman serving in the New Order. The procurator of justice was responsible for carrying out Imperial death sentences, against individuals and entire worlds. As a sign of his loyalty, Hethrir had condemned his own homeworld to death. This so horrified his mate, Rillao, that she left him in disgust. And Hethrir's office was so shadowy the Rebel Alliance was never able to connect him to the crime.

Hethrir lost his power and position in the aftermath of Endor. He fled to the Outer Rim aboard an artificial planetoid given to him by the Emperor, and began attracting wealthy backers to fund his fledgling Empire Reborn movement. His skills with the dark side of the Force, while minor compared to those of Vader or Palpatine, were enough to win over many doubters. Hethrir's core financing came through

*Lord Hethrir*

123

the sale of slaves. While serving as procurator, he had dispatched dozens of passenger freighters into deep space, each loaded with prisoners kept in suspended animation. Since he was the only one who knew the location of the freighters, Hethrir could visit them whenever funds were running low and select potential slaves at his leisure.

At the time of their kidnapping, Jacen and Jaina Solo were five, Anakin only three and a half. Hethrir told the children that their parents were dead, and smothered their Force abilities with a "wet blanket" of dark-side energy. He locked them in individual rooms aboard his worldcraft and placed them under the control of older, uniformed children called proctors. During supervised play periods they were allowed to socialize with the other young prisoners—one of whom, a centauriform girl named Lusa, would help the New Republic infiltrate the Diversity Alliance a decade later. It was Hethrir's hope that all the children would be purchased by his wealthy sponsors.

Hethrir tested the children for latent Force abilities. He had forged an alliance with an enigmatic being called Waru on the floating bazaar of Crseih Research Station, and he planned to sacrifice a Force-strong child to Waru in exchange for the creature's help. Since Anakin Solo was the most powerful of his prisoners, he was brought to Crseih as an offering.

Back on Munto Codru, breaking all protocols, the chief of state took immediate action to rescue her children. She told no one of her intentions; she simply dropped out of sight, throwing her personal staff into a panic. New Republic Intelligence worked around the clock investigating the incident, and Minister of State Falanthas stepped in to keep the government running smoothly. A curious public was told that Organa Solo had fallen ill, and the truth didn't become known until months after the actual incident.

Organa Solo, accompanied by Chewbacca, followed the kidnappers' trail in her personal yacht *Alderaan*. Eventually, she crossed paths with Rillao, Hethrir's proud ex-mate. Rillao was only too happy to provide Hethrir's name, and another contact recommended they check out Crseih Station—or, as those in the slave trade called it, Asylum.

On the way to Crseih, thanks to the Force bond that connects her with her three children, Organa Solo stumbled across Hethrir's worldcraft. Jaina Solo had already escaped from her cell and freed the other prisoners, while Jacen had used the Force to calm Hethrir's guardian sand dragon. The entire group of children had set off across the surface of the worldcraft atop the giant lizard's back. After ensuring the safety of everyone on the tiny planetoid, Organa Solo loaded her children aboard the *Alderaan* and raced for Crseih Station to save Anakin's life.

## The Power of Waru
### 14 A.B.Y.

For a decade, Hethrir had been luring investors to the Empire Reborn, eliciting scant notice from New Republic Intelligence. His sudden decision to kidnap the children of the most powerful political figure was shockingly brash. But Hethrir was not a stupid man, and he wouldn't have taken such action without feeling confident about his gamble. The key to Hethrir's gamble was the extradimensional anomaly called Waru.

Crseih Station is an ugly cluster of habitat domes and docking tubes arranged in an exotic and decadent bazaar. During the height of the Empire, Crseih had been an Imperial research center for the procurator of justice. Hethrir had authorized experiments that tested the limits of realspace, hyperspace, and a theoretical realm known as otherspace.

Following the Battle of Hoth, Crseih had relocated to a tenuous orbit near a black hole and a crystallizing white dwarf star. There, amid the region's temporal and spatial sinkholes, Hethrir's scientists succeeded in breaching the walls between dimensions and brought into existence a bizarre being—Waru—that resembled a massive slab of meat covered with shining golden scales.

A dark ichor oozed from between the plates and formed crusty stalactites around his base. Though he lacked discernable sensory organs, Waru was highly intelligent and spoke in a deep resonating voice. He possessed fantastic abilities facilitated by his unique interdimensional state. Waru could heal any disease and could open up other beings to the

*The Altar of Waru*

limits of the Force. Unfortunately Waru's appetite was as massive as his power: he consumed life essences in the hopes of gaining enough power to return to his own dimension.

When Crseih Station became a freewheeling traders' plaza and slavers' market, Waru rose to prominence as a healer of the infirm. Religious worshipers began making pilgrimages to Crseih to cure their sick at the Altar of Waru. Eventually rumors of this powerful healer reached Jedi Master Skywalker. Hoping that the rumors indicated the existence of another latent Jedi Knight, Skywalker left the academy in the hands of Tionne and journeyed to the space station with Han Solo and C-3PO.

Their contact on Crseih was none other than Xaverri, the master illusionist and an old flame

who had helped Han Solo seventeen years earlier at the Battle of Nar Shaddaa. Xaverri took the newcomers to one of Waru's nightly "healing" sessions, where pleading supplicants approached the creature one by one. Waru encased each diseased victim in a golden sphere, then broke it open, revealing either a miraculously cured patient or a cold, broken corpse. In the latter instances, Waru spoke with great sorrow and claimed to have done all he could.

Before long, Hethrir arrived with a retinue of wealthy supporters. Hethrir knew that regular life essences provided Waru little energy. In order for Waru to achieve maximum strength, he would need to devour a Force-strong individual, and young Anakin Solo—the grandson of Darth

Vader—would make a fitting prize. In return, Hethrir hoped to receive omnipotent Force powers, once Waru bestowed upon him his extradimensional energy.

Solo, Skywalker, and Organa Solo disrupted the depraved sacrificial ritual, and Anakin was rescued. But Skywalker remained in front of the altar, as Hethrir shrieked that Luke Skywalker was even more powerful—he was Vader's actual *son*—and Waru lurched forward greedily. Skywalker sank into a golden pool and was absorbed into the creature's shining essence.

Heedlessly, Organa Solo leapt in after her brother. Solo quickly followed and found himself swimming through a golden light. Deep below, Skywalker and Organa Solo were being drawn into a dark whirlpool, a vortex that led to the alternate dimension from which Waru had come. After a struggle, the two siblings broke Waru's seductive spell and swam away from the swirling mass. All three emerged safely back into the offering chamber.

The Waru creature was enraged. Since Hethrir had given him nothing, he decided to consume Hethrir instead. Waru engulfed the wailing Firrerreon with his massive body, trapping him in a golden sphere, which contracted to the size of a fist and then a grain of sand, before disappearing with a tiny pop. Waru and Lord Hethrir vanished from the known universe.

Simultaneously, outside Crseih Station, the white dwarf star had reached the final stages of "freezing"—its compression into an unstable quantum crystal. The crystal star was falling under the adjacent black hole's gravitational pull and rapidly approaching its event horizon. The catastrophic fragmentation of the star would take less than three hours and would destroy everything in local space.

Crseih Station's long-dormant hyperdrive was fired up with only minutes to spare. The space city jumped to lightspeed as the crystal star shattered into quantum fragments, destroying any possibility of recreating the conditions under which Waru had slipped into realspace. Crseih Station arrived at Munto Codru, where most of its passengers were off-loaded for questioning by New Republic Intelligence. The movable space bazaar remained in

business, however. After Chamberlain Iyon of the Codru-Ji lodged a formal protest with sector authorities, the denizens of Crseih moved their vice den to the neighboring Pakuuni system, where it has remained to this day.

The most tangible side benefit of the Empire Reborn incident was the acquisition of Hethrir's worldcraft. This astonishing structure, a movable planetoid with a forested surface and a blue sky, has been scoured by teams of researchers since its arrival in a classified safe system. Even Death Star designer Bevel Lemelisk, before his execution, was briefly granted a temporary research furlough from the maximum security prison on Orinackra to study the captured vessel. The worldcraft retains its atmosphere with a force field and maintains a standard gravity via buried gravfield plates. The heart of the planetoid is a massive reactor that feeds the hyperspace engines and powers the tractor beam that holds its own miniature "sun" in position.

The New Republic has stated that it has no interest in replicating the ridiculously expensive design. The fact that Hethrir was able to keep it operational for a decade is testament to his formidable resources. Rather, New Republic researchers assigned to the worldcraft project continue to gain insights into engineering and energy management issues. One beneficiary of this information was the New Class warship development program.

The eight new starship designs of the New Class had been commissioned following the victory over the resurrected Emperor. New flagships were completed in different years and passed into service as they were finished. The last of the ships, the *Nebula*-class New Republic Star Destroyer, was christened eleven years after Endor, more than a year after the Empire Reborn incident. Since this was the quietest year since the New Republic's founding, it was a poor time to introduce a new weapon of war. During such surface tranquility, public opinion was sharply divided over the need for an expanded military. One year later, enough of the New Class had been produced at the Kuat yards to make an entire armada, the New Republic Fifth Fleet. Immediately, some senators began to question the chief of state, even going so far as to compare construction of the Fifth Fleet to the sweeping military expansions of Emperor Palpatine.

# THE BLACK FLEET CRISIS

### 16–17 A.B.Y.

The genesis of the Black Fleet Crisis began eight months after the Battle of Endor, during the Imperial Black Sword Command's retreat from the Koornacht Cluster. Yevethan dockworkers at N'zoth rose up, murdered their captors, and seized the Black Fleet armada for themselves. Over the next twelve years the Yevetha learned to operate their captured warships, including the Super Star Destroyer *Intimidator*. Nil Spaar, chief commando behind the uprising, became the leader of the Yevetha and head of the Duskhan League, a political federation of pure Yevethan colony worlds.

Twelve years after the fall of the Empire, the New Republic was in a tranquil state of relative peace. Other than Hethrir's kidnapping of the Solo children, the galaxy had experienced no serious crisis since the power struggle in the Meridian sector. As a sign of the times, a placard hung outside the governmental offices: "882 DAYS WITHOUT A SHOT FIRED IN ANGER."

Leaving her husband, Han Solo, with the day-to-day responsibilities of raising three school-age children, Leia Organa Solo engaged in a series of peaceable talks with Nil Spaar. The chief of state knew nothing about her guest's terrorist past and chose to ignore the misgivings expressed by her advisers, including Defense Council Chairman Behn-kihl-nahm.

Admiral Hiram Drayson, head of a covert New Republic intelligence agency, suspected Spaar was hiding something and arranged for an unarmed scout ship to make a reconnaissance run deep into the Koornacht Cluster. The ship was blown to bits, and Spaar seized upon the incident as proof of Organa Solo's "warmongering" and begged to be left in peace by the obviously reckless New Republic military. Organa Solo was stunned at the sudden turnabout. Spaar played politics like a born master, milking the tragedy for all it was worth. A citizenry weary of war expressed general outrage over Organa Solo's apparent callousness. Several member worlds went so far as to submit articles of withdrawal from the New Republic.

It was the perfect time for the Yevetha to make

*Yevethan Viceroy Nil Spaar*

their move. In a series of lightning raids, they used stolen Black Fleet warships to strike at all non-Yevethan colonies within the Koornacht Cluster. Their fanatical troops captured more than a dozen planets, murdering thousands of innocent homesteaders and wiping away all traces of their once-hopeful settlements. To the Yevetha, this act of genocide was merely the extermination of "alien vermin." They proudly labeled their bloody crusade the Great Purge.

When word of the incident leaked out, Nil Spaar claimed to be defending his borders against New Republic aggression. He warned the chief of state that if she didn't back down immediately and allow the Yevetha this victory, it would lead to all-out war.

Organa Solo faced a political disaster. Unlike the high-profile strikes of Thrawn and Daala, the Yevetha's Great Purge failed to agitate the electorate. Koornacht was too isolated: most citizens were unwilling to risk New Republic lives to defend worlds they'd never visited, and were angry with their chief of state for suggesting they should.

*The Battle of Doornik-319*

Regardless, Organa Solo delivered an ultimatum to Nil Spaar, ordering the Yevethan leader to surrender the planets he had seized. If he refused, the New Republic would force him out.

Spaar called her bluff. Armed conflict was inevitable. At a Cluster colony world called Doornik-319, the Yevethan fleet and the New Republic armada clashed. But as New Republic K-wing bombers lined up for strafing runs against enemy thrustships, the Yevetha broadcast a signal across all wavelengths—the pleading cries of recently seized hostages who begged for New Republic restraint lest they be killed along with their captors.

The devious tactic succeeded. Enough K-wings hesitated, and the carefully planned attack runs failed. The New Republic retreated in shameful defeat.

Angry and embarrassed over the debacle, several senators petitioned a recall against the chief of state on the basis of general incompetence and for needlessly endangering the lives of brave Republic soldiers. The petition failed, but it was an ominous harbinger of things to come.

Leia Organa Solo wasn't willing to back down. If anything, the disaster only deepened her legendary resolve. Several recon flights went into the heart of the Koornacht Cluster, finally revealing the long-buried truth that every warship in the "lost" Black Fleet was in the hands of the Duskhan League, including the Super Star Destroyer, which had been rechristened *Pride of Yevetha*.

In response a massive New Republic force was sent off to patrol the Cluster's borders. Han Solo, given the temporary rank of commodore, was placed in charge of this task force. On his way to take command, Solo's shuttle was yanked from hyperspace by a Yevethan Interdictor cruiser. Captured, bound, and beaten, Solo was taken as a prize to the spawnworld of N'zoth and brought before a gloating Nil Spaar.

Even as Organa Solo received the devastating news of her husband's capture, one of her closest friends in government, Senator Beruss of Illodia, asked her to voluntarily resign her post, or face full recall proceedings before the entire senate. With her husband a prisoner of Nil Spaar, some believed that the chief of state might risk the lives of New

Republic soldiers in an ill-advised attempt to free him. Many senators thought she should be replaced with someone "less involved."

Organa Solo adamantly refused quick-fix solutions, such as ordering Luke Skywalker's Jedi Knights on an infiltration-and-rescue mission. "The Jedi are not the New Republic's army," she said, "or its mercenaries, or its secret weapon." She stubbornly continued the fight, but on two contentious fronts—the battlefield and at home.

Han Solo, in prison on N'zoth, was offered a bargain by Nil Spaar. The Yevethan dictator promised an end to the hostilities if Solo would convince his wife to back down. Solo, of course, refused the offer in his usual colorful fashion. Spaar warned his enemy that the New Republic was destined to lose; they had never faced an enemy like the fanatical Duskhan League. The Yevetha would never surrender and would fight to the last man. Solo was transferred to a holding cell on the *Pride of Yevetha* with added security.

For the second time during the Black Fleet Crisis, the New Republic forced a military confrontation. Fortunately, this clash had a much more favorable outcome than at Doornik-319, and the Republic fleet demolished the Yevetha's Black Nine shipyards.

Nil Spaar was livid. Without delay, he transmitted a private hologram to the chief of state in which he savagely beat and kicked a trussed-up Han Solo for an excruciating twenty minutes. Only three words were spoken throughout the whole stomach-turning display: "Leave Koornacht now."

Revealing his naked cruelty and utter depravity, the hologram was the worst tactical mistake Spaar could have made. Organa Solo's advisers closed ranks behind her. With righteous fire in her heart, the chief of state addressed the senate regarding Doman Beruss's misguided petition of no-confidence. She calmly announced that, mere hours earlier, the New Republic had officially declared war on the Duskhan League. A hush fell over the assemblage as Organa Solo asked the gathered senators to remember the thousands of innocents murdered during the Great Purge. To do nothing, she argued, would dishonor their memories. Her moving and inspirational speech, which has been accorded a place in the annals of modern oratory, brought the entire hall to its feet in a resounding ovation.

The most remarkable thing about Organa Solo's declaration of war was her selfless decision to put the needs of the Great Purge victims above her own desires. Fortunately, a nearly unstoppable strike team was already planning a rescue. Several Wookiees, including Chewbacca and his young son, exhibited typical Wookiee subtlety by charging at the *Pride of Yevetha* with all guns blazing. The *Millennium Falcon* attached itself to the Super Star Destroyer and cut through its hull, allowing Chewbacca and his son to rescue Han Solo from his holding cell.

With Spaar's bargaining chip eliminated, it was time for a decisive strike against the Duskhan League. The New Republic fleet leapt into the heart of the Koornacht Cluster and squared off against the enemy. The clash grew into a savage brawl, but the New Republic received unexpected reprieves from two surprising sources.

A phantom fleet appeared, causing the New Republic forces to seem far superior. Brought by Luke Skywalker, the phantom fleet caused no outright damage, but caused the Yevethans to fire uselessly at illusions.

Every ship in the Black Fleet was partially crewed by Imperial prisoners of war, captured years earlier during the shipyard uprising at N'zoth. While the Imperials had no love for the Rebels, they despised their Yevethan captors more. The human captives activated a hidden slave-circuit web they had installed piecemeal in the Black Fleet's control boards over the previous decade. The Imperials stopped the warships dead, brought them about, and jumped every last Star Destroyer in the direction of Byss in the Deep Core. Nil Spaar, aboard the *Pride of Yevetha*, disappeared along with them.

Many Yevethan thrustships remained, but the battle was essentially over. Even so, the Yevethans fought to the bitter end and took a tragic number of New Republic vessels down with them. The Battle of N'zoth was a victory, but a costly one.

The Black Fleet found nothing but rubble when it finally arrived at Byss. The Imperial prisoners had been isolated for years, and while they had heard rumors that the Rebels had captured Coruscant, they had nevertheless assumed the Emperor's hidden

throneworld would still be a stronghold. Instead they discovered a scorched asteroid field still expanding in Byss's orbit six years after the planet's destruction by the Galaxy Gun.

Adding to the Imperials' troubles, the Black Fleet was running on less than a skeleton crew. Most of the Yevetha, including Nil Spaar, had been executed, and the remaining alien prisoners refused to assist their enemies. Within a month, the vast majority of the Black Fleet had accepted the reality of their situation and defected to the New Republic. Four *Victory*-class Star Destroyers hooked up with Daala's warlords in the Deep Core, and two of the most advanced Star Destroyers, as well as the experimental weapons test bed *EX-F*, chose to join Admiral Pellaeon's shrinking empire in the Outer Rim.

The *Pride of Yevetha* vanished entirely. The Super Star Destroyer was discovered four years later, drifting abandoned near the Unknown Regions and damaged beyond repair.

## Master Skywalker and the Fallanassi
### 16–17 A.B.Y.

The resolution to the Black Fleet Crisis would not have been possible without the intervention of a mysterious group of women known as the Fallanassi. The members of this reclusive religious order practice pacifism and follow the White Current. Similar to the Witches of Dathomir or the disciples of Ta-Ree, the Fallanassi use the White Current in much the same way that Jedi Knights manipulate the Force. As Luke Skywalker has said, "The Force is a river from which many can drink, and the training of the Jedi is not the only cup which can catch it."

Just prior to the Crisis, Skywalker had reached a crux point in his understanding of the Force. Still smarting from the psychic wounds inflicted on him by the cloned Emperor, he decided that the key to greater knowledge was to isolate himself from the "noise" of everyday demands. Turning from his duties at the Jedi praxeum, he left the training of his students in the hands of an unlikely successor—Streen, the cloud-prospecting hermit from Bespin who had been one of Skywalker's first Jedi trainees.

Then, on the shores of Coruscant's artificial Western Sea, he erected a private hermitage upon the ruins of Darth Vader's former meditation retreat.

After only a few days of isolation he was visited by Akanah Norand Pell, a sister of the Fallanassi. As a child Akanah had been forced to leave her people and was embarking on a search to pick up their trail. To secure Skywalker's help, she dangled an irresistible tidbit of information, implying that his long-lost mother, Nashira, had once been a Fallanassi herself. Everything about Akanah's story turned out to be counterfeit, including the name Nashira, but Skywalker had no way of divining the truth. Leaving Streen in charge of the latest batch of recruits at the Jedi academy, Skywalker accompanied Akanah.

The trail of the Fallanassi led to Lucazec, then Teyr, then Atzerri, and finally to J't'p'tan in the heart of the contentious Koornacht Cluster. Sadly, it appeared that the fanatical Yevethan army had gotten there first. J't'p'tan's only settlement had been bombed into a lifeless, smoking ruin.

The Fallanassi, however, proved quite skilled at manipulating perceptions and generating illusions. Akanah showed Skywalker how to slide beneath the surface of the White Current; there, in that altered state, the temple was intact and thriving. Hundreds of workers and pilgrims wandered to and fro. Akanah's people were waiting to welcome their lost sister back with open arms.

Skywalker realized the astonishing implications of the hidden temple and convinced the Fallanassi to lend assistance to the New Republic by creating an illusory "phantom fleet" at the Battle of N'zoth. The Fallanassi, pacifists by nature, initially resisted the offer, but grudgingly accepted when they realized that their imaginary vessels would draw fire away from the true targets and ultimately save hundreds of lives. As expected, the phantom fleet did not frighten the frenzied Yevetha, but it did split their

fire and allow the New Republic to take out the thrustship armada with far fewer casualties than originally expected.

Following the battle, the Fallanassi departed on their private starliner. They have not been heard from since.

## The Teljkon Vagabond
### 16–17 A.B.Y.

Considering how quickly Lando Calrissian's fortunes have changed, it is remarkable that at the time of the Black Fleet Crisis he had kept his spice mining operation on Kessel going for five mostly profitable years. In fact, the operation ran so smoothly that Calrissian went looking for a little excitement. He got more than he wished for: an enigmatic alien "ghost ship," code-named the Teljkon vagabond due to a previous sighting in the

*Exploration of the vagabond*

Teljkon system, reappeared near Gmar Askilon. Calrissian and the cyborg Lobot accompanied a New Republic task force to investigate.

Calrissian and his companions boarded the strange, organic craft and were whisked along for the ride when the vessel abruptly jumped to hyperspace. For weeks they floated through the ship's empty corridors, with dwindling air supplies and minimal food. The baffling ship appeared to be a product of the long-extinct Qella species, but the insight was of little use in their search for the craft's command center.

The Teljkon vagabond emerged in the Deep Core, where it was fired upon by Imperial warships under the command of Foga Brill. The vessel escaped, but suffered such grievous damage it immediately hopped to its "home"—the lifeless ice-enshrouded ball of Qella.

At Qella the vessel was finally located by a New Republic chase team. Skywalker, fresh from the Battle of N'zoth, rescued Calrissian and his com-

panions and used his Jedi powers to learn more about the vagabond. The ship indeed had been built by the Qella just before their twin moons tumbled from orbit and brought about a catastrophic ice age on their homeworld. But the craft wasn't an escape pod, or even a vast floating museum. Instead, the vagabond was a "tool kit" for use in melting a frozen planet. Beneath the kilometer-thick ice, thousands of Qella lay in hibernation, waiting for the thaw. Master Skywalker jump-started the ship's heat rays.

Thus, more than twenty-one years after the founding of the New Republic, the vagabond is still in orbit, carrying out its assigned task flawlessly. New Republic scientists aboard Qella's orbital research station estimate that a complete thaw will be achieved within three years. The Teljkon vagabond ranks as one of the most significant archaeological discoveries of the past century, alongside the Corellian planetary repulsors, the cities of the Sharu, and the Jedi library on Ossus.

## UPRISING AT ALMANIA

**17 A.B.Y.**

The Black Fleet Crisis had serious long-range repercussions for galactic peace. The Yevetha were an isolated and numerically insignificant foe, yet they had caused the New Republic more grief than anyone since Admiral Daala. Other groups, including the remnants of Pellaeon's empire and the Deep Core warlords, began to reconsider armed conflict against their old foe. Even member worlds started to question the government's authority, particularly the leadership of the chief of state. To add more fuel to the fire, the senate passed a measure allowing former Imperial officials to hold elective office.

The measure's most vocal opponents predicted, correctly, that admitting unrepentant Imperial loyalists into the senate would cause the government to dissolve into partisan gridlock. The ex-Imperial senators delighted in opposing Organa Solo at every turn. Legislation was held up in committees, and the senate floor became a stage for grandstanding and inflammatory rhetoric. On the fifty-

first day of the new term, when Organa Solo stepped into the Senate Hall to address the body, a tremendous explosion knocked her off her feet and shot deadly shrapnel in every direction.

The chief of state survived with minor injuries, though dozens of senators were killed instantly. More died over the following days. Emergency elections were held to fill the sudden vacancies. Senate Hall was declared a ruin, closed off to visitors as construction began on its replacement, the Grand Convocation Chamber. Luke Skywalker himself investigated the bomb scene, and among the wreckage he sensed the echoes of a familiar presence—Brakiss, one of his failures from the Jedi academy on Yavin 4.

Brakiss, a former Imperial spy who had unsuccessfully tried to infiltrate the praxeum, was in league with Dolph, another fallen Jedi trainee. Years earlier, Dolph had abandoned his training to fight the despotic Je'har regime on remote Almania. He rose to prominence among the resistance, assuming the name Kueller and hiding his identity behind a formfitting death's-head mask. Over sev-

*Senate Hall following the bombing*

eral years Kueller employed dark-side skills to exterminate the Je'har and become Almania's undisputed leader. Then he set his sights on the New Republic.

Brakiss had fled the Jedi academy when Skywalker had forced him to confront the darkness in his heart. Kueller had helped put him back together, and Brakiss served the powerful man out of gratitude and fear. For two years, Brakiss had been the sole operator of the Telti droid factories, and he had secretly rigged the manufactured droids with explosive detonators. These were Kueller's secret weapons—unexpected, unseen, and completely devastating.

In addition to the senate bombing, Kueller used rigged droids to obliterate the populations of Pydyr and Auyemesh, two of the three inhabited moons orbiting Almania. He used the moons' wealth to fund his military operations and consolidate his stranglehold over his corner of space. Though Almania had never been a member of the New Republic, pro-Imperial observers issued rhetoric that dubbed this struggle between mismatched opponents "the new Rebellion."

Luke Skywalker investigated Brakiss's droid-manufacturing plant on Telti and set out for Almania. His X-wing had been sabotaged, though, and while he was passing the devastated moon of Pydyr, the X-wing exploded. Skywalker bailed out and found himself stranded on Pydyr, with third-degree burns on his back and a shattered left ankle. His left leg had been weak ever since his ordeal aboard the *Eye of Palpatine*, and he found himself unable to move without assistance.

Kueller was unable to resist such a rich prize as a wounded Jedi Master. He traveled to Pydyr, where Skywalker recognized the skull-masked nightmare as Dolph, his former pupil. Skywalker tried to reach the core of goodness inside Kueller, but failed. The Almanian autocrat forced a lightsaber duel and easily defeated his hobbled opponent. Skywalker was taken back to Almania to serve as bait.

Back on Coruscant, the chief of state presided over the political equivalent of a ticking thermal detonator. Emergency elections had ushered in even more ex-Imperial officials, giving her opposition a simple majority in the senate. With the Yevethan incident and the Senate Hall bombing

*Kueller and Brakiss*

fresh in everyone's minds, a no-confidence petition was filed by a group of hostile senators.

In the midst of this turmoil, Kueller contacted Organa Solo and demanded that she turn the reins of the New Republic over to him. If she refused, he would kill her brother. For Organa Solo, the solution was clear: she immediately resigned her position as chief of state. This nullified the no-confidence vote and meant that her family members were less likely to become targets in Kueller's power grab. It also freed her to go after this murderous madman on her own, without having to worry about the political implications. Mon Mothma, one of Organa Solo's oldest friends, returned to lead the New Republic until new elections could be held.

Mon Mothma sent a small fleet under the command of General Antilles to provide firepower for Organa Solo's rescue mission. While the action seems controversial in hindsight, Mon Mothma's strategy was quite canny. If the rescue effort had failed, she would have denounced the group as unsanctioned loose cannons and thereby held on to most of her political credibility. Leia Organa Solo left for Almania in her personal ship, accompanied by Antilles in a Mon Calamari star cruiser and a number of smaller warships.

When they arrived in the Almanian system, three *Victory*-class Star Destroyers rose from the planet, unleashing scores of deadly TIE fighters. Antilles steamed into pitched battle with Kueller's armada, while Organa Solo slipped through the fighter screen and landed on Almania's surface.

General Antilles's battle group took heavy losses from the guns of the Star Destroyers, but in a flash of insight that turned the tide of the battle, Antilles realized the reason for the enemy ships' oddly precise maneuvers: they were crewed entirely by droids. The general ordered his ship's gunners to fire on the other New Republic warships, not enough to do serious damage, but enough to convince the enemy computers that his vessel must be one of their own. The robotic Star Destroyers dropped into a protective flanking position around Antilles's flagship, and he promptly crippled them with precise turbolaser hits.

On Almania, Organa Solo rescued her brother and helped him back to her ship, but they discovered Kueller standing between them and freedom. Kueller had decided to kill them both, in order to become the most powerful Force user in the galaxy. He ignited his energy blade and lunged at Skywalker, and as the furious swordplay ground on, Skywalker suddenly realized that his aggression was only making Kueller stronger. Recognizing the master-to-student parallels with Kenobi and Vader's showdown aboard the Death Star, Skywalker prepared to sacrifice his own life in a similarly heroic fashion. If Kueller chose to strike him down, Skywalker would return in spirit form and guide Organa Solo to ultimate victory.

But as Skywalker raised his lightsaber in a passive salute, a surprising participant entered the fray. Kueller became disoriented and completely lost his advantage when a furry native animal called a thernbee lumbered nearby. Only a few minutes earlier, the creature had swallowed several nutrient cages containing Force-repelling ysalamiri. A Force-empty bubble was generated, and it swept over both combatants.

In a blind rage, Kueller pulled a master detonator control from his robes—a device that could

trigger the explosion of every droid manufactured on Telti in the past two years. Before anyone could stop him, he stabbed his finger on the button.

While this was occurring, the droids C-3PO and R2-D2 had continued to investigate the Senate Hall bombing, and the clues led them to Telti, as well. After convincing the mechanic and pilot Cole Fardreamer to take them to Brakiss's droid factories, they succeeded in breaking into the control room, assisted by an army of astromechs. Jacking into a computer terminal, R2-D2 intercepted Kueller's master control signal and deactivated all the remote detonators at the last instant.

Organa Solo had no way of knowing whether Kueller's bombs had been discharged, so she took the quickest possible route to prevent further trickery. Drawing a blaster, she shot Kueller, and the would-be emperor crumpled to the ground. When she removed his death's-head mask she uncovered the smooth, innocent features of a mere boy. Was her deed—a violent killing committed in anger—an act born from the dark side of the Force? By her own account, at that moment, she didn't care.

Organa Solo, Skywalker, and Antilles returned to Coruscant as heroes. Mon Mothma gladly stepped down, and Organa Solo returned to her former position, which was ratified without dissent. The no-confidence vote was called off. The chief of state addressed the congress in the temporary senate hall, vowing to make this new term one of unity and strength.

Almania remains a trouble spot. Millions of Almanian citizens were killed during the Je'har purges and Kueller's genocidal counterattack, and the survivors have little to call their own. The New Republic opened negotiations with one of Kueller's lieutenants, Yane, but he was soon overthrown by a rival, Gant. Leadership has dissolved into a military junta that changes hands often, and the New Republic has given up on accepting Almania as a member world for the foreseeable future.

In the wake of his failure on Telti, Brakiss fled the droid-manufacturing moon. He disappeared for several years and was later discovered serving as a neutral intermediary between the warlords of the Deep Core. Eventually Brakiss rose to a leadership position with the Second Imperium, a group that caused significant headaches for the New Republic during the later years of Imperial–New Republic peace. He founded a training center for dark Jedi, the Shadow Academy, with the intention of creating evil Force warriors in the continuing battle.

## Smuggler's Run
### 17 A.B.Y.

Though Han Solo is considered one of the greatest heroes of the Rebellion, and his loyalty and heroism would seem beyond reproach, his former life as a smuggler occasionally has come back to haunt him. Such was the case during the uprising at Almania, when some of the more hard-line senators, many of them former Imperial officials, attempted to pin the blame for the horrific senate bombing on Solo himself. Their most explosive piece of evidence was an intercepted and highly suspicious transmission.

The vaguely worded message implicated Solo, but proved nothing; some said it was merely a distraction or smear tactic. But many citizens were all too willing to go looking for character flaws in their public figures. For a time, Solo's future was genuinely at risk, and the fact that the unorthodox Corellian spent almost the entire crisis hiding out in Smuggler's Run certainly didn't help his case.

Smuggler's Run is a dense asteroid belt near Wrea and has served as a smugglers' haven for generations, despite attempts from the Wreans and the Empire to flush out the squatters. Just prior to the bombing of the Senate Hall, Solo was informed that many of his former associates had been selling junked-out Imperial equipment to a mysterious buyer, who turned out to be Kueller of Almania. Solo and Chewbacca, aboard the *Millennium Falcon*, braved the treacherous asteroid field to investigate the Run.

Though the place had changed a great deal since he had last visited, Solo learned that the smugglers had been obtaining secondhand Imperial equip-

*Calrissian's dilemma*

ment, which was then repaired by Jawas at much cheaper prices than a mechanic would have charged. While it is true that a Jawa repair is often worse than no repair at all, Kueller was more concerned with appearances than with function.

Lando Calrissian followed Solo to warn him of the unfolding campaign to frame him. Calrissian's selflessness was remarkable in light of the fact that the crimelord Nandreeson, a fire-breathing Glottalphib who resided at Smuggler's Run, had placed a hefty price on his head. Twenty years prior, Calrissian had stolen a cache of Nandreeson's treasure, and the old gangster had hated him ever since.

Calrissian was captured and brought to the crimelord. In Nandreeson's personal quarters—a mossy, water-filled cavern buzzing with parfue gnats and Eilnian sweet flies—the gambler was tossed into a deep pool and ordered to tread water until he drowned.

Solo and Chewbacca threw together a rescue squad consisting of many of their former smuggling comrades, but their "friends" betrayed them when they infiltrated Nandreeson's hideout. Together in the pool, Solo, Chewbacca, and Calrissian ducked below the water as the traitors opened fire. In the ensuing chaos, Calrissian got his hands on a blaster and disturbed a nest of watumba bats. Since the bats consume fire, they swept down on the fire-breathing Glottalphibs and left behind cold, desiccated corpses.

As the comrades prepared to leave Smuggler's Run, dozens of droids exploded simultaneously throughout the inhabited asteroids. These droids, booby-trapped products of Telti, had originally been slated for service aboard the Coruscant Fleet, until they were stolen by a group of pirates. Though their devastation of the Run resulted in hundreds of deaths, if the droids had been installed aboard fully crewed warships, the New Republic task force at Almania would have been destroyed, and Kueller would have remained a galactic menace.

It was at this point Solo learned that his wife had gone to Almania, and he arranged for Talon Karrde to provide him with a cargo of Force-blocking ysalamiri to neutralize Kueller's Jedi talents. The ysalamiri proved extremely useful —though not quite in the manner he had intended—and Han Solo was lauded as a hero in the newsnets. The editorials calling for his arrest vanished as quickly as an icicle on Tatooine, and the incident has since been depicted as nothing more than slander initiated by Imperial loyalists seeking political gain.

## Imperial Skirmishes
### 17–18 A.B.Y.

Hot on the heels of the Almanian uprising, both the Deep Core warlords and Pellaeon's empire attempted to reclaim formerly held sectors. They gambled that the New Republic wouldn't put a full effort behind stopping them, for fear of inspiring another public-relations debacle like the Yevethan conflict at Doornik-319. They were mistaken.

The New Republic added the Super Star Destroyer *Guardian*, captured during the previous year from the rogue Imperial Admiral Drommel, to the third fleet, then sent both the third and fifth fleets out to engage Pellaeon in several major brawls.

When the dust from these conflicts finally settled, Pellaeon's empire had been pushed back into a mere eight sectors of a strategically barren section of the Outer Rim.

The Deep Core warlords fought on the opposite edge of space, but didn't present a unified front. Therefore, they crumpled under a series of deadly perimeter assaults launched by the Republic's fourth fleet. In one of the final assaults, General Bel Iblis attempted to capture Admiral Daala in a pincer movement utilizing a pair of CC-7700 gravity-well frigates. In a shocking move, Daala's lead frigate rammed one of the CC-7700s, destroying it. Her badly damaged flagship then escaped into hyperspace and has not been encountered since. New Republic Intelligence has been tempted to declare Daala killed in action, but it has learned from experience never to presume an enemy's death—especially not hers.

The New Republic's enemies were in retreat, their navies spent. No further galactic conflicts loomed on the immediate horizon. Ackbar took advantage of the temporary respite to order most warships into dry dock for repairs and upgrades. Those fleet vessels not affected by the recall were put to work patrolling the borders of the Empire and the Deep Core.

# THE CORELLIAN INSURRECTION

**18 A.B.Y.**

During the lull, Chief of State Leia Organa Solo scheduled a visit to a major trade conference on Corellia. The Corellian sector had been one of the most influential regions of space since the dawn of the Old Republic. The system itself contains five inhabited planets—Corellia, Drall, Selonia, and the double worlds of Talus and Tralus—which some theorists claimed had been transported into their orbits by some ancient and unknown power.

As the home of major conglomerates such as the Corellian Engineering Corporation, and the birthplace of famous Republic heroes such as Han Solo and Wedge Antilles, the Corellian sector was respected throughout the galaxy.

In the post-Palpatine era, however, the sector surrounded itself in airtight isolation. Having fed upon the Corellians' natural sense of independence and self-reliance—some might have said arrogance—the ruling Corellian diktat vanished, and the sector became inward focused and inward thinking. Lucrative trade routes dried up, and businesses relocated elsewhere.

The New Republic had little power to affect the Corellian system, though, so when they installed a Frozian named Micamberlecto as Corellia's governor-general, he was greeted as an outsider bureaucrat and could do little to control the discontented populace.

Thus, the chief of state hoped this trade conference would be the first step in bringing the sector more fully into the fold.

Organa Solo arranged for her family to accompany her, without a large official party. Luke Skywalker declined the invitation, though he was no longer needed full-time at the Yavin academy, since many of his earliest students now taught new classes. Skywalker gave his sister a farewell present, though—a new red-bladed lightsaber to complement the weapon she had constructed prior to the campaign of Grand Admiral Thrawn. The two siblings engaged in an impromptu practice duel, and Organa Solo disarmed her surprised brother, thus showing how her Force skills had been improving.

Lando Calrissian, meanwhile, decided to turn over regular operation of the Kessel mines to Nien Nunb, his Sullustan copilot during the destruction of the second Death Star at Endor. While lucrative, the spice mines had caused Calrissian too many headaches. The recent Imperial–New Republic fighting in the Outer Rim had emboldened several pirate groups. With New Republic forces preoccupied, the pirates had struck at Kessel and made off with billions of credits' worth of unrefined glitterstim. At the same time, subterranean tremors had disturbed a nest of aggressive spice spiders and made deep-tunnel mining temporarily impossible.

Hoping to cut his losses, Calrissian sold partial ownership to Nien Nunb and invested the funds in an underground housing project on Coruscant called Dometown. But Dometown didn't satisfy the gambler's yearning for a quick score, so he turned to the easiest and oldest method of getting rich quickly: marry into money.

Calrissian conned Skywalker into accompanying him on his "wife hunt." A candidate on his list was Tendra Risant, a wealthy heiress from Sacorria, in the backwater fringes of the Corellian sector. Risant was warm, friendly, and genuine, and Calrissian actually became interested in her for more than her credit account. But their budding romance was cut short when Calrissian and Skywalker were both expelled from Sacorria by the planet's repressive government, called the Triad.

Neither man realized at the time that the masterminds of an imminent Corellian insurrection were operating right under their noses. The Triad of Sacorria had orchestrated a plot to break away from the New Republic and have the Corellian sector recognized as an independent state. The key to their scheme was Centerpoint Station, a Death Star–sized space depot located at the balance point between the twin worlds of Talus and Tralus. Centerpoint was an unimaginably ancient alien artifact, having existed in isolation in the Corellian system since before recorded history. Millions of citizens lived in its labyrinthine corridors and along the spherical walls of its hollow interior. After more than thirty thousand years, the Triad had at last uncovered Centerpoint's purpose and origin.

Centerpoint Station is a massive hyperspace

tractor-repulsor, and the entire Corellian system is an artificial construct assembled eons ago by an incomprehensibly powerful alien species. Centerpoint was the "engine" that pulled the planets through hyperspace; vast repulsor chambers buried beneath the crust of each world nudged them into stable orbits around the star. The identity of the architects remains a mystery, though it is possible they were the same entities who forced the Sharu of the Rafa system into intellectual dormancy. The Centerpoint revelations have also reopened the debate over whether the Maw black hole cluster is natural or artificial.

The Triad realized that Centerpoint, and its individual planetary repulsors, could be used as powerful weapons. They backed various insurgent groups on each planet—the Human League on Corellia, the Overden on Selonia, the Drallists on Drall—and ordered them to find their respective planetary repulsors, thus preventing the devices from being used against the Triad.

They also learned how to make Centerpoint Station fire hyperspace repulsor bursts to trigger supernovas in distant stars. Their first two targets—an unnamed, uninhabited test system, and the colony system of Thanta Zilbra—were utterly destroyed. Finally, the Triad discovered that Centerpoint could generate an interdiction field that encompassed the *entire* star system. With Chief of State Organa Solo trapped by the interdiction field, and a supernova countdown as their nonnegotiable ultimatum, the Triad planned to create a breakaway miniempire.

Unfortunately, the Triad made a fatal mistake by approaching Thrackan Sal-Solo, the treacherous leader of Corellia's antialien Human League. When Organa Solo arrived at the trade conference, the Triad triggered the interdiction field. Sal-Solo, however, double-crossed his masters and activated Centerpoint's massive jamming field, as well, preventing the Triad from negotiating with the chief of state. Sal-Solo declared himself diktat and claimed to be the brains behind the plot, figuring he could grab most of the Corellian system for himself before the Triad could move against him.

What was supposed to have been a quiet trade conference had turned into a catastrophe. The chief of state was held captive by Human League troops.

*Thrackan Sal-Solo*

Chewbacca and the three Solo children, along with their Drallish tutor Ebrihim, escaped Corellia on the *Millennium Falcon* but were trapped in-system by the interdiction field. Han Solo was captured by Thrackan Sal-Solo, and in the underground headquarters of the Human League the two men confronted each other. Solo's worst fears were confirmed: Thrackan was indeed his cousin, returned after a thirty-year absence.

Han Solo was imprisoned, and his cellmate was Dracmus, a furred Selonian. The Selonians follow an insectlike hive social structure, and each den controls a patch of territory. Dracmus's people were struggling for dominance against the Triad-backed Overden. Several Selonians broke the prisoners out of jail, and Solo was loaded aboard a coneship for transport to Selonia. Dracmus and her den members planned to use the New Republic hero as a bargaining chip in their negotiations with the Overden.

Leia Organa Solo escaped her own house arrest with help from fellow prisoner Mara Jade, who had been drawn to the conference by an intercepted Human League message—one which was intended to trap her and Leia. A hidden slave-circuit control roused Jade's yacht from its parked position at the spaceport, and both women escaped just ahead of angry Human League troops.

Chewbacca piloted the *Falcon* to Drall, where he and the children were taken in by Ebrihim's stubborn but level headed Aunt Marcha. Jacen, Jaina, and Anakin Solo soon located Drall's planetary repulsor, a vast shining chamber more than a kilometer deep. Anakin mistakenly activated the ancient device through an unconscious manipulation of the Force. The repulsor burrowed its way upward, pushing out into open night air.

On Coruscant, the New Republic strategists couldn't contact the chief of state or anyone else in the Corellian system. And because of the interdiction field, they couldn't order a scout ship to investigate. The only solution appeared to be to send a task force in at sublight speeds, a mind-numbingly slow journey that would take more than two months.

Mon Mothma offered a better solution. Almost every capital warship in the New Republic navy was in dry dock or otherwise occupied near the Empire and the Deep Core. While Ackbar could have spared a few vessels from Coruscant's home defense, Mon Mothma had intelligence information indicating that the Bakurans had succeeded in developing a foolproof interdiction-field countermeasure. Luke Skywalker was dispatched to Bakura to "borrow" their fleet.

It had been fourteen years since the historic truce at Bakura, but the planet's inhabitants hadn't lowered their guard against a possible Ssi-ruuk return. They had built four powerful cruisers, each equipped with experimental devices that allowed them to escape from interdiction fields. None of the gadgets were designed to handle a monstrously large field like the Corellian one, but they would get the fleet in quite far before they overloaded and shut down.

Skywalker met with Gaeriel Captison, now a councilor and retired politician. Grateful for the assistance the Rebel Alliance had given her planet during the turbulent Ssi-ruuk invasion, Captison agreed to help. With Captison along as a Bakuran representative, the four war cruisers set out to break through the Corellian interdiction field, stage a diversionary assault at Selonia, then move on to Centerpoint Station to shut it down.

The small armada leapt blindly into the system's heart. The unique anti-gravity-well devices allowed the ships to force their way in quite a distance. The fleet gained a nice head start, but one ship, the *Watchkeeper*, was heavily damaged during realspace reentry and would be useless in the upcoming battle. That ship was evacuated for use as a remote decoy as they slowly approached Selonia.

As expected, when they neared the planet, an invisible blow from the Selonian planetary repulsor slammed into the decoy vessel, reducing it to a loose jumble of bolts, rivets, and hull plates. The remaining three ships retreated from Selonia and proceeded to their true target: Centerpoint Station.

The colossal structure was abandoned, save for its chief operations officer. Following two "flare-ups" by the station's artificial sun, all residents had been evacuated to Talus and Tralus. During these incidents, Centerpoint's sun had swelled with such intensity that the city's lakes had burned away and its buildings had been charred to blackened ash.

The flare-ups were actually a by-product of Centerpoint's starbuster firing process. The Triad, having already destroyed two systems, had targeted a third—Bovo Yagen, inhabited by millions. The New Republic investigators discovered they were in a race against the clock.

Lando Calrissian deduced that the only sure countermeasure against an unfathomable alien technology was more of the same; in order to stop Centerpoint, they needed to take control of one of the planetary repulsors.

On Selonia, Han Solo was trying to do just that. Solo had been reunited with his wife, and the two of them tried to aid Dracmus's den in seizing the planetary repulsor from the Overden—but without success.

On Drall, however, the Solo children had successfully uncovered the Drall repulsor. Unfortunately, their actions attracted the attention of Thrackan Sal-Solo, whose ruthless thugs were more than a match for a Wookiee, two Drall, and three young children.

Thus Sal-Solo possessed two invaluable prizes—the Solo children, who he could use to secure concessions from the New Republic, and the Drall repulsor, which he could use to hold the starbuster plot hostage from his Triad "masters." But, to

*Destruction of the* Watchkeeper

unveil his new hostages, Sal-Solo brought down the systemwide jamming field. His broadcast was a predictable terrorist screed, demanding that the New Republic recognize an independent Corellian sector, with him at its head. Organa Solo refused to bow to his threats.

Thankfully, the Solo children escaped from under Sal-Solo's nose. They fled Drall aboard the *Falcon* and were quickly recovered by one of the Bakuran ships. The entire New Republic contingent prepared for imminent battle, as the Triad at last decided to show its face. Enraged by Thrackan Sal-Solo's broadcast, the Triad dropped the systemwide interdiction field. Moments later, a massive Triad war fleet leapt into the Corellian system in an assault designed to crush the New Republic interlopers and chastise their renegade underling.

The New Republic's greatest heroes went into battle against the Triad armada, piloting some of the most familiar ships in recent history—the *Millennium Falcon*, Lando Calrissian's *Lady Luck*, and Luke Skywalker's X-wing fighter. Seven-and-a-half-year-old Anakin Solo, whose Force abilities seemed tailor-made for manipulating unfamiliar technology, went to Drall to activate its planetary repulsor.

The Triad fleet quickly gained the upper hand through the use of robot ramships—solid metal projectiles built for suicide runs. Four of the ramships made a breakneck dive on the Bakuran flagship. By the time the gunners realized what was happening, it was too late. The ramships plowed into the ship, crippling it beyond repair.

Gaeriel Captison and Admiral Ossilege were on the flagship's bridge when the ramships hit. Both were severely wounded by the explosion and realized they could never make it to the escape pods in time. In a heroic act of self-sacrifice, Captison triggered the ship's self-destruct mechanism. The fiery blast tore a hole into the heart of the Triad

*Hollowtown devastated*

formation. Minutes later, Admiral Ackbar plowed into the fray with a host of New Republic reinforcements to mop up the stragglers.

The enemy fleet was smashed, but Centerpoint still geared up for its unavoidable shot at Bovo Yagen. On the surface of Drall, at the last possible instant, young Anakin Solo fired an invisible repulsor burst that splashed into Centerpoint and disrupted the station's firing process. The star-smashing shot dissipated harmlessly.

The aftermath of the Corellian insurrection was choked with thorny issues. Corellians have always been a self-reliant lot, and while most disapproved of the Triad's extreme methods, many sympathized with the reasoning behind it. An independent Corellian state was an appealing concept to the local citizens.

Once again the New Republic was criticized for butting in where it wasn't welcome, and the chief of state was roundly vilified for letting the situation progress as far as it did. Organa Solo knew she had done everything possible under the circumstances. With no-confidence motions filed against her during the Black Fleet Crisis and the uprising at Almania, this latest round of faultfinding was the branch that broke the bantha's back.

To her advisers, Organa Solo privately declared that she was disgusted with politics. She insisted on, and was granted, an indefinite leave of absence. Interim elections were held, and the Calibop senator Ponc Gavrisom was elected the new chief of state and president of the senate.

The Corellian sector was given a new governor-general, Marcha of Drall. Despite the fact that she was a New Republic appointee, Marcha was widely accepted by the Corellian populace because she was a native of one of the Corellian worlds. The transition has not been easy, but Marcha has remained in power in the Corellian sector, seven years after the violent insurrection.

# PART IX

## A LASTING PEACE

**A**t its peak, Palpatine's Empire was an awe-inspiring example of omnipotence. But fifteen years after the death of its ruler, the Empire was little more than a pitiable curiosity. Pushed into the wild fringes of the Outer Rim, consisting of eight small sectors and only a thousand inhabited systems, Imperial dominion was little threat to anyone—certainly not the prosperous worlds of the ever-growing New Republic. Admiral Pellaeon, commander of the Imperial Fleet, was smart enough to realize he'd been beaten.

### The Caamas Document
### 19 A.B.Y.

After Admiral Daala had promoted him following the disastrous attack on Yavin 4, Pellaeon had put his best efforts into halting the erosion of the Empire's borders. But despite a few scattered victories, including the Battle of Orinda and the reacquisition of his flagship *Chimaera* at the Battle of Gravlex Med, he had been unable to stop the march of history. Pellaeon met with the remaining moffs on the capital world of Bastion and broached the unthinkable: an Imperial surrender. The moffs met his plan with understandable resistance, but eventually agreed that a conditional capitulation was the only way to guarantee the Empire's continued survival.

One of the moffs, however, had other plans. Ambitious and amoral, Moff Disra was a political genius, and he was just one member of a secret triumvirate determined to scuttle Pellaeon's weak-willed submission strategy and restore the Empire to its former grandeur.

Disra's aide, Major Tierce, was an expert on military tactics and claimed to be one of Palpatine's

*Sinister Triumvirate: Moff Disra, Major Tierce, and Flim*

former Royal Guardsmen. Tierce was the one who had executed Rukh following the Noghri traitor's assassination of Grand Admiral Thrawn. But it was a third player—a simple con man named Flim—who was the key to Disra's plan. Flim bore an uncanny resemblance to the late Thrawn, and with blue makeup and glowing corneal inserts, the likeness became nothing short of astonishing. Flim, or rather, "Thrawn," would be used as an inspirational figurehead, a badly needed propaganda tool that would breathe flame into the dying embers of the Empire.

Disra's first move was to intercept and capture Pellaeon's envoy before the man could deliver the offer of peace. The envoy's corvette was captured by one of Disra's Star Destroyers at Morishim, and the New Republic leadership had no way of knowing just how close they'd come to a peaceable resolution to the decades-long Galactic Civil War. Furthermore, Pellaeon remained unaware of Disra's treachery; he assumed his enemies had received the Empire's offer and were contemplating its implications. Pellaeon headed off to his chosen rendezvous point, the deserted gas giant Pesitiin, and waited fruitlessly for a New Republic delegation that wasn't coming.

Disra's second step was more devious. A private performance by "Grand Admiral Thrawn" was enough to convince several Imperial fleet captains that their beloved leader had miraculously returned from the grave. On Thrawn's orders, three Star Destroyers were fitted with cloaking devices and sent to Bothawui. There, high above the Bothan homeworld, the invisible ships anchored themselves to a passing comet and waited patiently for the signal to attack.

Disra's target hadn't been a random selection. A few weeks earlier, Leia Organa Solo, now holding the position of councilor, had been visiting a Noghri relocation settlement on Wayland when a Devaronian treasure hunter had uncovered a shocking item from the ruins of Palpatine's storehouse inside Mount Tantiss. The item was an unremarkable black data card, but its scandalous contents gave full historical details on the decades-old devastation of Caamas. The wholesale destruction of this peaceful world has long been considered one of the galaxy's great tragedies, but for years no one was sure who had been behind the vicious and indiscriminate slaughter. Now the painful truth was laid bare: the aggressors had included a group of Bothan saboteurs.

Many galactic citizens resented the Bothans due to their notoriously devious politics, and now those citizens had a lightning rod on which to focus their fury. Angry denunciations began in the New Republic Senate, with opposing parties speaking out in support of the species, or at least pointing out that modern Bothans shouldn't be held responsible for the transgressions of their ancestors. However, it was argued, though many decades had passed, some of the perpetrators might still be alive

and should be tracked down. And any implicated Bothan individuals or institutions could be forced to make restitution.

The battle lines were drawn, and the divisive issue threatened to tear the New Republic apart. The only solution would be to discover the identities of the actual Bothans who had participated in the incident, and put them on trial for war crimes.

But such a list, designated the Caamas Document, was nowhere to be found in any current databases. A call went out to all top New Republic officials: *Find a copy of the Caamas Document.*

Leia Organa Solo and her husband, having just recovered from a recent confrontation with Boba Fett on Jubilar, hoped to prevent the Bothan incident from boiling over into violence. The two visited Bothawui to inspect governmental financial records, but were swept up in an anti-Bothan riot. Twenty-seven rioters were killed in the fiasco, and Solo was framed as a murderer.

Just when things looked as if they couldn't get much worse, Lando Calrissian, taking a break from his latest mining operation on Varn, was intercepted by an Imperial Star Destroyer commanded by "Grand Admiral Thrawn." Although a skilled con man himself, even Calrissian was duped and had to admit that the rumors of Thrawn's death seemed to have been greatly exaggerated. Calrissian was released without harm, and he quickly carried the bleak tidings to the leaders of the New Republic.

The news hit the galaxy like a pressure bomb. Agitation over the Bothan incident built to a fever pitch with the astonishing possibility of an Imperial military resurgence, and the New Republic came to the brink of civil war.

Far from the galactic hubs of information, in lonely orbit around the gas giant Pesitiin, Admiral Pellaeon began to suspect that the New Republic had never received his overtures of peace. He was considering abandoning the rendezvous altogether when a substantial armada of battle cruisers leapt from hyperspace and moved into attack formation. The warships were pirates hired by Moff Disra, painted with insignia to make it appear as if the New Republic had rejected Pellaeon's truce and had arrived to exterminate him. Pellaeon was wise enough to realize that such underhanded tactics weren't his enemy's style. After defeating the attackers in pitched battle, he understood that someone had tried to set him up.

In all other respects, though, the grand scheme hatched by Moff Disra, Major Tierce, and Flim was working to perfection. "Thrawn" made numerous appearances, convincing even the most skeptical observers that the most brilliant of Palpatine's grand admirals had found a way to cheat death. With the New Republic dissolving into fratricidal squabbling over the Bothan incident, the newly animated Empire began to look powerful and attractive. Many planetary leaders still remembered how close Thrawn had come to conquering the galaxy a decade earlier, and this time they wanted to ensure that their homeworlds landed on the winning side. Soon, dozens of systems were clamoring for voluntary readmittance into the Empire.

Still trying to obtain a copy of the Caamas Document, the New Republic threw together numerous plans. In a seemingly unrelated incident on Pakrik Minor, Han Solo and his wife were ambushed by Imperial fighters, but quickly rescued by a group of Imperial clones. This small sleeper cell of clones, grown from the legendary Baron Fel fighter-pilot template, had been deployed a decade earlier by Thrawn, for purposes unknown. But after ten long years waiting for orders, the clones were no longer interested in serving their Imperial masters. One of their number agreed to obtain the top secret coordinates for the Imperial capital world of Bastion. Solo, Calrissian, and Lobot headed into the fortified heart of the Empire to secure the Caamas Document from Bastion's information libraries. They failed.

Fortunately, the New Republic had a backup plan. Yaga Minor was a heavily fortified ship-building center and intelligence base, one of the last jewels in the Empire's crown. An assault there would be perilous and costly, but it appeared to be the only place that might still possess a duplicate of the Caamas Document. Admiral Ackbar and General Garm Bel Iblis drew up plans for a swift raid that would catch the Imperials unawares. The key to their assault was Booster Terrik's Star

Destroyer, captured more than a decade earlier at the conclusion of the Thyferran Bacta War and operated by the smuggling captain as a floating bazaar ever since. Such an Imperial-built warship would presumably be able to slip past Yaga Minor's outer defenses.

Leia Organa Solo, meanwhile, learned that Pellaeon's attempt to deliver an armistice message had not been completely unsuccessful. A few bits of the transmission had leaked out before the courier's corvette had been overtaken by Moff Disra's Star Destroyer, and the garbled fragment was at last deciphered. Realizing that Pellaeon's invitation was already weeks old, Organa Solo rushed to the rendezvous point and caught the Imperial admiral just as he was preparing to leave. The two held talks aboard the Chimaera that were amicable, if inconclusive. Pellaeon headed back to the Empire to deal with Disra and investigate the reports of Thrawn's incredible resurrection.

But back in the New Republic, passions over the Bothan incident had reached a breaking point. In orbit over the Bothan homeworld, ragtag battleships from dozens of pro- and anti-Bothan factions finally exploded into armed conflict, triggered by the sudden destruction of the Bothawui planetary shield generator by Imperial saboteurs. As ships fired on the planet's surface and on each other, Organa Solo struggled to impose order.

Han Solo inadvertently found the solution. Investigating a suspicious comet on close approach to Bothawui, Solo was startled when the Millennium Falcon dipped beneath the invisibility screen of a cloaked Imperial Star Destroyer. Their ambush spoiled, the three Star Destroyers abruptly dropped their cloaks and charged forward to decimate the survivors of the New Republic's fratricidal bloodbath. Unfortunately for them, the appearance of an external threat was sufficient to unite the squabbling fleets against their common foe. Lando Calrissian led the hastily assembled armadas to victory.

At Yaga Minor, Booster Terrik's vessel prepared for its information raid on the data libraries. The disguised Star Destroyer successfully cleared the outer planetary defensive ring, but was trapped by dozens of heavy industrial tractor beams as soon as

*The end of an era*

it passed the point of no return. Moff Disra, Major Tierce, and Flim were all at Yaga Minor at the time of the failed attack, and "Thrawn" smugly contacted his helpless prey to demand Terrik's unconditional surrender.

But an uninvited guest crashed the trio's private party. To the gasps of the watching pit crews, Admiral Pellaeon strode onto the bridge of the false Thrawn's command ship. Of all those present, Pellaeon had known Thrawn best, and the room held its collective breath, waiting for the admiral's judgment. In a cool matter-of-fact tone, Pellaeon dropped the explosive news that the glorious return of Grand Admiral Thrawn had been nothing more than a parlor trick.

Pellaeon's assertion was confirmed when he provided data regarding Flim's origins and current whereabouts. Major Tierce attempted to deny the facts, but Pellaeon had an even more startling revelation regarding the former Royal Guardsman. Far from being the last of Palpatine's original bodyguards, as he'd claimed, Tierce was in fact merely a clone of the true Grodin Tierce, grown during Thrawn's original military campaign. Enraged, Tierce attempted to attack Pellaeon and was killed instantly. Their coup an utter failure, Flim and Disra were taken into Imperial custody.

Luke Skywalker secured a copy of the Caamas Document. The surviving guilty Bothans were located and brought to trial, bringing an end to most of the internal New Republic discord. No obstacle remained to forestall an official treaty negotiation between the Empire and the New Republic. Within weeks, the historic peace accords were signed aboard the *Chimaera* by Admiral Pellaeon and acting Chief of State Ponc Gavrisom. After more than two decades, the galaxy's most devastating war ended with the muted mark of a writing stylus.

## The Hand of Thrawn
### 19 A.B.Y.

Just prior to the hunt for the Caamas Document, Luke Skywalker left his Yavin academy and investigated a disturbing trend: increasing numbers of cloned crewmen had been appearing aboard outlaw pirate vessels. Ten years earlier, the New Republic

had concluded that the clone threat was effectively over, following the destruction of the Mount Tantiss facility. The presence of new clones indicated that someone had found a way to activate Thrawn's sleeper cells of clone soldiers.

While scouting out a pirates' nest in the Kauron asteroid field, Skywalker was ambushed by bloodthirsty buccaneers and nearly killed in their ingenious "Jedi Trap." Skywalker managed his narrow escape only through the timely arrival of Mara Jade. On her way to the nearest New Republic medical facility, Jade noticed a strange alien craft. The mysterious bystander broadcast an unintelligible garbled signal, then vanished into hyperspace.

Mara Jade dropped Skywalker off at a medcenter, then paid a visit to her longtime employer Talon Karrde. While there, she encountered another of the enigmatic alien ships. It jumped into hyperspace, but now Jade had two hyperspace exit vectors. By plotting them as straight-line paths, she found the convergence point—a jaw-droppingly remote star system near the Unknown Regions, dutifully logged in the navigational charts as Nirauan. On Nirauan, Jade investigated a shadowy cave and encountered a thick swarm of tiny winged creatures—half bat, half mynock. Jade lost her footing and was knocked unconscious when her head struck a craggy rock outcropping.

At the urging of Talon Karrde, Luke Skywalker came to the rescue, piloting the heavily armed yacht *Jade's Fire*. Skywalker swooped down to the planet's rugged surface, where he was saved from having to search for Mara Jade on foot when one of the planet's batlike natives led them inside a dank, uninviting cave.

The cave dwellers he found there were known as the Qom Jha, and the bat he had initially encountered was of a different tribe, the Qom Qae. Both races were cautiously friendly and requested the humans' assistance in eliminating a menace that lurked in the High Tower, a foreboding black castle perched atop a nearby promontory. Skywalker and Jade agreed.

The safest path to the tower lay beneath hundreds of meters of rock. Skywalker and Jade picked their way through dripping underground tunnels, using their lightsabers to clear stalagmites and foil predators. Eventually they reached their destination

*Infiltrating the Hand of Thrawn*

and discovered the High Tower's true purpose.

Nirauan's High Tower was Thrawn's secret weapon—an information repository sometimes referred to as the Hand of Thrawn. The stone fortress had been the grand admiral's base of power, back when he had been sent by Emperor Palpatine to scout the Unknown Regions. Thrawn had succeeded beyond the Emperor's wildest dreams: an immense new swath of previously undiscovered territory had been meticulously mapped and cataloged, representing a bottomless new source of resources that could turn the Empire from victim to vanquisher in a single day. And the Hand of Thrawn's occupants had every intention of turning their closely guarded prize over to the current Imperial leadership on Bastion.

The stronghold was run by Admiral Voss Parck, a longtime associate of Thrawn's from the Empire's early days, and was operated by the Chiss, the blue-skinned, red-eyed people from Thrawn's homeworld. The group had been waiting on Nirauan for a decade, anticipating their leader's triumphant return. For Thrawn had always promised his followers that if he should ever be killed, he would come back to them in ten years' time. Now, in light of the rumors that someone matching Thrawn's appearance had begun to rally the Empire's remnants, it appeared the prophecy had at last come true.

Skywalker and Jade realized that they couldn't allow Parck to contact Bastion. The two Jedi escaped the castle in a stolen alien fighter, and Jade used the beckon call installed aboard the *Jade's Fire* to rouse her cherished ship and guide it directly into the Hand of Thrawn's hangar bay. The yacht exploded with stunning violence, destroying every craft on the launching pad and eliminating Parck's ability to get any word to the outside galaxy.

But that wasn't enough, and they both knew it. Skywalker and Jade returned to the enemy citadel, this time to a series of chambers far beneath the structure's foundation. There, in a room so protected that not even Parck knew about it, they found a Spaarti cloning cylinder. And floating inside the cylinder was a fully grown clone of Grand Admiral Thrawn.

Their difficult moral choice—to execute a helpless being in cold blood, or to stand aside and allow a new Thrawn to resubjugate the galaxy—was decided for them when the droid R2-D2 jacked into a computer system to download data. The room's automated defensive systems came on-line and focused hot blaster fire on the intruders. Jade's expert lightsaber work eliminated the threat but fatally weakened the chamber's rock wall in the process. With an angry gurgle, thousands of gallons of lake water smashed through the damaged barrier, flooding the room in a churning vortex of icy liquid and nullifying the Thrawn clone's impending birth. Skywalker and Jade narrowly escaped, a little waterlogged, but very much alive.

Over the previous decade Skywalker and Jade had progressed from enemies to friends to fellow Jedi, and their experiences on Nirauan marked a turning point in their relationship. After surviving near-death experiences and struggling side by side against overwhelming odds, they began to realize that they seemed matched in ability and in attitude, in strength and in spirit. Though they didn't always see eye-to-eye, their differences complemented one another perfectly. Their hearts meshed together peak-to-valley in a hold that was far stronger than either heart could be standing alone. Luke Skywalker proposed marriage. Mara Jade accepted.

The two left Nirauan behind in a stolen alien starship and headed back to the New Republic with an unexpected find more valuable than ten cargo carriers of glitterstim. During his electronic link with the cloning center computer, R2-D2 had downloaded reams of data from Thrawn's personal archives, and one of the files was a complete, untouched, and entirely accurate copy of the Caamas Document.

Skywalker made preparations for his impending wedding. Three months later, the two Jedi were married in a private ceremony in Coruscant's Reflection Gardens.

After his wedding, Luke Skywalker decided to alter the instruction schedule of his Yavin training center, allowing a portion of the training to focus on younger pupils with developing Jedi skills. After all, Yoda had stated that younger students were easier to teach in the ways of the Force. Some of the more advanced trainees left Yavin 4 to engage in one-on-one teacher-student relationships throughout the galaxy, among them the more mature Jedi Kam Solusar, Kyp Durron, and Streen. Tionne took over many of the historical chores, enriching the legacy of the Jedi Knights. Mara Jade insisted she was no teacher, and spent very little of her time on the jungle moon, even when her husband returned to the praxeum to address his students.

All together, with peace finally declared between the New Republic and the formal remnants of the Empire—though many dissatisfied splinter groups still remained—and with great numbers of new Jedi Knights spreading out into the galaxy, the future looked bright at last.

# PART X

## GENERATIONS OF JEDI KNIGHTS

**T**he armistice brought about by the Pellaeon-Gavrisom treaty was a durable peace. Three quiet years passed, blissfully uninterrupted by Imperial schemes, mad Jedi, local brushfires, or unexpected alien invasions.

After more than a decade of labor, Luke Skywalker had many successes in his Jedi praxeum on Yavin 4. He had found many new trainees, some human and some exotic. However, because Skywalker was frequently called away on his own adventures and also because he wanted to spend time with Mara Jade, one of his first trainees, the scholar and minstrel Tionne, took over his duties.

Interplanetary squabbles and trade conflicts were as much a constant as always. At the urging of her friends in the government, Leia Organa Solo ran again for the post of New Republic chief of state and was elected back into that office seventeen years after the Battle of Endor.

Organa Solo's three children—the twins, Jacen and Jaina, and her younger son, Anakin—all exhibited a strong talent in the Force. Though burdened with her immense political duties, Organa Solo and her husband tried to spend as much time as possible with their children. However, because of the Skywalker legacy, the three youths also spent much time at the Jedi praxeum on the jungle moon.

## THE GOLDEN GLOBE AND KENOBI'S LIGHTSABER

**22 A.B.Y.**

The surviving Jedi Holocrons offered few lessons regarding the training of extremely young children, and no specific rule for the age at which a talented person could begin to learn the ways of the Force. Anakin Solo came to the Jedi academy when he was midway through his eleventh year. Different from his outgoing twin siblings, Anakin was studious and reserved, often a loner. He liked puzzles, mysteries, mental challenges, and brainteasers—and he specialized in finding ways to go where he wanted, even if he lacked permission.

On Yavin 4 he befriended a young girl named Tahiri, the daughter of a moisture-farming family from Tatooine, who had been orphaned and captured at the age of three in a raid by the ferocious Sand People. She grew up leading a nomadic life in the desert, keeping her face fully bandaged, breathing through metal filters, but the Jedi instructor Tionne discovered her on a journey to Tatooine. Surprised to find that the young girl had Jedi potential, Tionne brought her back to Yavin 4, though Tahiri promised the leader of her Tusken tribe that she would return.

On one occasion, despite protests by Skywalker's droid R2-D2, who had been assigned to guard the young trainees, Anakin and Tahiri crossed a jungle river near the academy and trekked to the Palace of the Woolamander, a crumbling ruin abandoned ages ago. Both young trainees had been drawn there by identical dreams. As they explored the dim ruins, they broke into a sealed chamber that contained a glowing sphere of golden light. They sensed its power and seemed to hear voices. Curled up at its base lay a mysterious furry creature, deep in sleep, whose coloration seemed as adaptable as a chameleon's. It had large eyes, floppy ears, and simian features. The creature stirred, awoke, and followed them, but Anakin experienced a powerful

**Anakin Solo and Jedi Master Ikrit**

dread and warning, so he and Tahiri fled back to the Great Temple.

That night, Anakin was awakened by movement at his window—the creature, sneaking into his room. There, in the quiet darkness, the furry being began to talk, explaining that his name was Ikrit. He was a Jedi Master who had come to the jungle moon to study the Massassi temple ruins four centuries earlier. He had discovered the golden globe, but could not break its curse, and had been hibernating ever since. He believed, though, that Anakin could succeed where Ikrit had failed.

Journeying to the nearby moon Yavin 8, Anakin and Tahiri discovered a message in ancient writing on a deep cave wall. They translated the words and learned that the golden globe contained trapped spirits of young Massassi victims of Exar Kun's experimentation, thousands of years earlier. The spirits remained imprisoned, much like the spirits of miners devoured by the leviathan of Corbos, who had been freed by Kyp Durron and other Jedi Knights. According to the inscription, the prisoners

were blocked by Sith magic that could be defeated only by "children, strong in the Force."

Before Anakin and Tahiri could learn how to break the curse, the leader of the Sand People tribe that had raised Tahiri demanded that she return to Tatooine. Without a choice, she went back to the desert world to face an ordeal and save the man who had been her surrogate father. Accompanied by Anakin, she rejoined the Sand People and learned of her real parents, Tryst and Cassa Veila, who were strong in the Force but had accidentally been killed in a Tusken raid. Tahiri was tested in the harshest deserts of the Dune Sea, but she and Anakin survived by using their growing Jedi powers.

Finally, when they returned to Yavin 4, the two trainees were confident enough to reenter the Palace of the Woolamander and face the Sith barrier surrounding the golden globe. Anakin and Tahiri broke past the barricades erected long before by Exar Kun, and freed the trapped Massassi spirits.

When they emerged from the temple, the two youngsters found Luke Skywalker waiting for them, standing beside Ikrit; the strange creature had revealed his true identity to the Jedi Master and promised to assist Anakin in his training.

Anakin remained troubled by dreams that showed him as a Dark Jedi, by his heritage as the grandson—and namesake—of Darth Vader. When Leia Organa Solo was pregnant with Anakin, the resurrected Emperor had touched her and tried to take over the unborn child. To make certain that he didn't have the potential for evil inside him, young Anakin asked if he could go to the cave on Dagobah, as Luke Skywalker had done, and face himself. It was arranged for Tahiri to accompany him, and Master Ikrit offered to take charge of the children, claiming he had wanted to go to the swamp planet for his own reasons.

Before arrangements could be made, a stowaway teenager was found on one of the supply ships to the Jedi academy. The young man, Uldir, begged Skywalker to train him as a Jedi, though when tested, Uldir showed no Force potential whatsoever. When Anakin, Tahiri, and Ikrit traveled to Dagobah, Uldir stowed away again and got himself into trouble with the swamp creatures on Dagobah, though the young trainees and Ikrit saved him.

The group finally reached the cave where

*Anakin Solo and the image of his grandfather, Darth Vader, in Bast Castle on Vjun*

Skywalker had faced his own dark side during his training with Yoda. Though neither Tahiri nor Uldir found anything in the cave, young Anakin faced down the manifestations of his own doubts and fears and emerged stronger and confident at last.

Before departing Dagobah, the group visited the site of Yoda's old house, where Ikrit revealed that Yoda had been his own Jedi Master, centuries earlier. Though still powerless in the Force, Uldir convinced himself more than ever that he could become a Jedi if he only had the same opportunities and "lucky breaks" as Anakin and Tahiri.

Meanwhile, the Jedi historian Tionne returned to Yavin 4 with an interesting discovery: after the murder of Obi-Wan Kenobi on the Death Star, Darth Vader had retrieved his old Master's lightsaber and stored it at his stronghold, Bast Castle on the planet Vjun. Because an information broker had sold her this story, though, others might have found out about it, and Tionne made the case to Skywalker that they had to act quickly. Thinking it would be a simple journey and time for training, she allowed Anakin and Tahiri to accompany her, along with Uldir and the Jedi Master Ikrit.

When they arrived on stormy Vjun, they discovered another ship, empty, and feared that someone had gotten there before them. The group worked through booby traps and automatic defenses into the fortress, and finally discovered Kenobi's lightsaber on display in a protected alcove.

As soon as they had retrieved the artifact, though, a group of mercenaries and pirates attacked them, led by a cloaked man named Orloc, who called himself a mage with great powers. The thieves stole the lightsaber and fled, so the Jedi pursued them through the winding fortress. In a brief confrontation, Orloc tempted Uldir, promising the powerless boy that he could grant him all the Jedi skills he wished. But Tionne, Ikrit, and the others rescued Uldir and retrieved the artifact, as well as a precious historical Holocron filled with Jedi knowledge. Orloc fled.

When they returned to Yavin 4, Tionne delved into the information within the Holocron. Uldir, though, remained obsessed with what the mage had told him. No one at the Jedi academy had been able to awaken Force powers in him, and so he stole the Holocron, the lightsaber, and a ship, and fled to find Orloc.

Anakin, Tahiri, Tionne, and Ikrit pursued him, and the trail led to an ancient ghost city in space, Exis Station, where Nomi Sunrider had long ago called a great Jedi convocation, and where Tionne herself had met Luke Skywalker in her search for artifacts. There, Mage Orloc had set up his base and had taken Uldir as a new recruit. Orloc actually had no Force talent himself, but used high-tech gimmicks to fool others with demonstrations of "power." Uldir was completely duped.

Tionne, Ikrit, Anakin, and Tahiri confronted Orloc and tried to show Uldir that the mage was a fraud. In a battle of Force versus fake technomagic, Tionne was injured. Ikrit—who had sworn not to use a lightsaber until he found worthy students—made his decision and joined the battle, along with young Anakin and Tahiri. Seeing true Jedi power in action, Uldir admitted to himself that he had been tricked and helped to defeat Orloc at his own game. Together, they retrieved the Holocron and Kenobi's lightsaber and left Exis Station. They returned to the Jedi academy, knowing they still had much to learn, and many years yet in which to do it.

## THE SHADOW ACADEMY AND THE SECOND IMPERIUM

**23 A.B.Y.**

The Solo twins—Jacen with his quirky sense of humor and his rapport with animals, and Jaina with her aptitude for mechanics—became two of the most talented and best known of the new generation of Jedi Knights. Together with their companions Tenel Ka, warrior daughter of Prince Isolder of Hapes and Teneniel Djo of Dathomir, and Lowbacca, the Wookiee nephew of Chewbacca, they fought for the New Republic with as much bravery as the legendary Jedi Knights of old.

During a training exercise in the jungles of Yavin 4, the young Jedi Knights discovered the

*Jacen and Jaina Solo*

wreckage of a TIE fighter, which had crashed there years before during the Rebel defense against the first Death Star. Inspecting the hulk, which was overgrown with weeds, Jaina believed that with a little work she could restore the ship. The others helped her, eager to have a showpiece spacecraft of their own. They were unaware that the original pilot, a grizzled old man named Qorl, had survived the crash and for decades eked out a living in the wilderness. Seeing the quartet completing repairs on his ship, he recognized a chance to return to the Empire.

Armed with an Imperial blaster, Qorl attempted to capture the companions as hostages; Lowbacca and Tenel Ka managed to escape, but Jacen and Jaina remained prisoners, forced to complete the final repairs so the shipwrecked pilot could flee the jungle moon. The twins told the Imperial pilot what had happened in the twenty-three years he had been stranded, and though his heart softened somewhat, he refused to believe them.

Lowbacca and Tenel Ka, running in separate directions, tried to get back to the academy where they could arrange for a rescue. Qorl, though, climbed aboard his TIE fighter and soared off into space before reinforcements could arrive. The TIE

fighter swooped over the Massassi temples in a perfunctory attack, but Jaina had deactivated the ship's weapons systems. Not wishing to be recaptured, Qorl flew off to rejoin the Empire—wherever he could find it.

Months later, as the new Jedi Knights continued their training, Jacen, Jaina, and Lowbacca accompanied Lando Calrissian to his new Corusca-gem mining facility *GemDiver Station*, in the atmosphere of the gas giant Yavin. While Calrissian showed them his fantastic operations, the station came under attack by a crack Imperial commando squad. Calrissian and the miners defended themselves, but the stormtroopers—led by a frightening black-clad woman, Tamith Kai, one of the Nightsisters of Dathomir—were intent on the capture of the Jedi trainees. Jacen, Jaina, and Lowbacca were stunned and taken prisoner.

They awoke on board a cloaked Imperial station, a gigantic facility known as the Shadow Academy, a dark counterpart to Skywalker's Jedi academy. There Imperial trainees were taught to use the dark side of the Force. The Shadow Academy was run by Brakiss, a former student of Skywalker's who had once been planted on Yavin 4 by the remnants of the Empire. Skywalker had tried to make Brakiss confront his own nature, but the Imperial spy had fled. He had joined Kueller in his new rebellion against the Coruscant government, worked at the droid factories on Telti, and escaped again when Kueller's plans failed.

So Brakiss had joined up with another resurgent movement, the Second Imperium, and he had sworn to provide Dark Jedi for the reconquest of the galaxy. He and his followers refused to recognize the sham peace accords Pellaeon had signed. The Nightsister Tamith Kai, along with the TIE pilot Qorl, had captured Jacen, Jaina, and Lowbacca as powerful recruits for Imperial brainwashing.

Master Skywalker joined with Tenel Ka to track down where the missing students had been taken. Their search led them to the seedy asteroid station Borgo Prime and then to Tenel Ka's primitive planet, Dathomir, where they encountered other Nightsisters who were also involved in the Shadow Academy. Armed with the knowledge they needed, Skywalker and his student went to the last known coordinates of the cloaked Imperial station.

Meanwhile, the captives resisted all attempts to convert them to the dark side. Employing a Corusca gem Jacen had taken from Calrissian's *GemDiver Station*, as well as Lowbacca's computer expertise, they escaped—with surprising assistance from the troubled TIE pilot Qorl, whom they had tried to befriend in the jungle. They attempted to flee the station, just as Skywalker and Tenel Ka arrived to rescue them. Brakiss saw Skywalker and viewed him as a mortal enemy, and they dueled with their lightsabers. Tenel Ka fought against the other Nightsister Tamith Kai, who had betrayed their world of Dathomir.

All together, the Jedi companions escaped in a special Imperial ship stolen from the Shadow Academy. Before the New Republic space fleet could arrive to deal with the Imperial station, though, Brakiss powered up the engines and the cloaking generators, and the Shadow Academy vanished into the vast emptiness of space.

Returning to Coruscant to spend time with Han and Leia Organa Solo, the young Jedi Knights recovered from their ordeals. They explored the lower levels of the huge planetary city with Zekk, an orphaned street scamp the twins had known for years. Zekk often felt ill at ease around his high-class friends, since he came from a disadvantaged upbringing. Jacen and Jaina invited Zekk to a formal dinner of state, but the evening ended in a social disaster, and Zekk fled in misery—only to be captured by Tamith Kai. The Nightsister and others from the Shadow Academy had gone to Coruscant's underworld to gather new recruits for the dark training center. They had already taken the members of a rough street gang known as the Lost Ones.

Zekk was brought to the hidden Shadow

*Shadow Academy revealed*

Academy, where Brakiss showed him how to tap into his own unsuspected Jedi potential. Suddenly, Zekk found himself in control of great powers he had never dreamed of—and he became an easy mark for Imperial brainwashing. He resented his friends for how they had abandoned him, and soon he became one of the greatest of the new Dark Jedi.

Jacen, Jaina, and their friends discovered that Zekk had been taken captive, and that the Imperial station was secretly in orbit around Coruscant itself. Using giant solar mirrors in space, they were able to burn out the Shadow Academy's cloaking systems and expose the station to New Republic military forces. When Zekk was offered the opportunity to come back with Jacen and Jaina, he refused, insisting on staying with the Second Imperium. The Shadow Academy vanished into hyperspace, once again foiling pursuit.

Over the following weeks, Zekk received his own lightsaber and devoted himself to intensive training. Other members of the Lost Ones gang became stormtroopers or Dark Jedi students. During an assembly to describe future plans for conquest, Zekk watched a transmission from the hidden leader of the Second Imperium—and witnessed the cowled visage of Emperor Palpatine himself! Once again, Palpatine appeared to have returned.

Zekk battled other students training at the Shadow Academy, and in a life-or-death duel in zero gravity, he killed the best student, thus becoming Brakiss's Darkest Knight. Zekk was horrified at the blood he had shed, but Brakiss remained supportive, insisting that only the strong would survive.

Faced with the threat of the Shadow Academy and evil plans of the Second Imperium, Luke Skywalker decided that his students must build their own lightsabers. He gave Jacen and Jaina, Tenel Ka, and Lowbacca stern warnings that such weapons were dangerous and not to be used for games, and the young Jedi Knights set to work. When finished, the students trained first against remotes and then each other, but in a tragic accident, Tenel Ka lost her arm when her weapon failed in a sparring match against Jacen Solo.

Recuperating, but deep in despair, Tenel Ka went home to be pampered on the wealthy world of Hapes, home of her father, Isolder. She had always relied on herself and her own abilities, and refused to be fitted with a prosthetic arm. When her friends joined her to lend their support, they learned of the political dangers in the royal court of Hapes. They barely survived an assassination attempt that was designed to overthrow Tenel Ka's grandmother, Queen Mother Ta'a Chume, but the Jedi Knights—including the one-armed warrior girl—worked together and proved stronger than their enemies.

They all returned to Yavin 4, still vowing to be a team, and soon departed for Lowbacca's homeworld, Kashyyyk. While the Jedi trainees stayed in the high-tech Wookiee tree cities and computer fabrication plants of Thikkiiana City, agents of the Second Imperium struck again, this time with the intention of raiding the New Republic stores of powerful new computer units. This was to be a final stage before the launching of their battle to retake the galaxy, and the Imperial commando team was led by Zekk himself.

Back at the Shadow Academy, Brakiss learned that the Emperor himself was coming to the cloaked station. An armored ship dropped out of hyperspace and docked. Brought aboard in a giant isolation tank carried by repulsorlifts, Palpatine refused even to see Brakiss—which caused the leader of the Shadow Academy to be concerned that the

Emperor's health might be fading. So far, Palpatine had offered no explanation as to how he had survived the destruction of all his clones, years earlier.

The Emperor was attended by his red-armored Royal Guards, who blocked all of Brakiss's inquiries. The presence of the guards was a mere show. The last true Royal Guard had been Kir Kanos; Major Tierce had been a clone. The Royal Guards present aboard the Shadow Academy were former stormtroopers, symbolically promoted to Guardsman status during Admiral Daala's rule.

During Zekk's raid on the Kashyyyk manufacturing centers, the Jedi trainees fought against the intruders, but the Shadow Academy had sent stormtroopers, evil Nightsisters, and other Dark Jedi trainees. Zekk pursued his former friends deep into the dangerous forested underworld. Jacen, Jaina, Tenel Ka, and Lowbacca defeated most of the Imperial troops, but Jaina faced off with her former friend Zekk deep in the shadowy jungle. Zekk couldn't bring himself to hurt her, though; instead, he warned her to stay away from Yavin 4, because the jungle moon would soon be destroyed, and all the Jedi with it. Then he departed from the Wookiee planet; the Second Imperium troops had stolen the equipment they needed.

From his isolation chambers, the mysterious Emperor made an important announcement; impatient for the reign of the Second Imperium, he decreed that it was time to move on the Jedi academy. They had all the might they needed to begin his conquest.

The young Jedi Knights raced back to Skywalker's training center, sounded the alarm, and prepared to fight. New Republic forces were called in while Luke Skywalker and the Jedi rallied their own defenses. Soon, the Shadow Academy appeared in the sky over the jungle moon, and Imperial assault teams dropped to the surface: TIE fighters, stormtroopers, and swarms of Dark Jedi. The Dark Jedi attackers were led by Zekk and the Nightsister Tamith Kai, while Brakiss, receiving orders from the holographic projection of Emperor Palpatine, directed the battle from the station itself.

Skywalker's Jedi trainees defended themselves admirably. Tenel Ka sabotaged the floating battle platform from which Tamith Kai directed ground forces, and the structure crashed into the river, killing the Nightsister. Jaina Solo stole a downed TIE fighter and used the Imperials' own firepower against them.

While the New Republic fleet engaged the space cruisers of the Second Imperium, Brakiss once again faced Luke Skywalker, student to master. But when Skywalker defeated the leader of the Shadow Academy, Brakiss pulled out a final trick and succeeded in escaping back to the orbiting station. He barely made it aboard his dark training center.

As the tides of battle turned against him, Brakiss demanded to see the Emperor. Two of the Imperial guards tried to block his way, but Brakiss cut them down with his lightsaber, then used the energy blade to chop through the thick door of Palpatine's armored isolation chamber. Inside, he found a third Imperial guard working a bank of controls, computer screens, and holographic generators. The Emperor had never actually come back to life. It was merely an illusion, promulgated by the red guards to restore themselves to a position of power in the Second Imperium. The last guard escaped from Brakiss's outrage and flew away, then used his

"Emperor's" override controls to detonate the Shadow Academy's self-destruct systems. The giant station turned into a fireball in space.

On the surface of Yavin 4, the Imperial fighters witnessed the destruction of the Shadow Academy and knew the battle had been lost. Still, another Imperial soldier slipped inside the Great Temple, the headquarters of the Jedi academy, and planted a bomb, setting the timer. When Skywalker's remaining Jedi fighters, including Jacen, Jaina, and their friends, gathered around the Temple, Zekk reappeared, blocking their way.

He was a broken young man now, realizing what damage he had caused, how he had betrayed everyone. Jaina thought he intended to fight her to the death, but in truth Zekk meant to prevent anyone from entering the pyramid. The hidden bomb exploded, destroying much of the Great Temple. No one was seriously hurt, but if Zekk had not stopped them from going inside, they would all have died.

The Second Imperium had been quashed, the Shadow Academy destroyed, and the remaining Imperials and Dark Jedi were taken prisoner.

## THE DIVERSITY ALLIANCE

**23–24 A.B.Y.**

Skywalker's trainees set to work rebuilding the academy, using the Force as well as their own muscles. Standing in the rubble of the Massassi temple, Luke Skywalker spoke to his students, urging them to continue their training and prepare for new challenges. Defensive measures, shields, and New Republic guardian forces in orbit were implemented so that the Jedi academy would not be so vulnerable to external attack. Though Skywalker would have preferred to be more private, he recognized the necessity.

While Zekk recovered from injuries received during the explosion, he was haunted by nightmares stemming from his deep involvement with the dark side. He had many deaths on his conscience, and many in the New Republic wanted him imprisoned for his crimes. However, Skywalker recognized Zekk's Force talent and wanted to train

him to forsake the dark side and become a talented Jedi. Ultimately, since Zekk had been brainwashed by Brakiss, Skywalker received a special dispensation for him.

But Zekk never wanted to use the Force again. He had brought his friends too much pain, inflicted too much damage. He left Yavin 4 in search of his home, in search of peace, while the other trainees rebuilt the temple. Eventually, he decided to use his talents to become a bounty hunter.

During the repairs, Han Solo arrived with a grim message for student Raynar Thul, a prince of the surviving highborn family that had escaped Alderaan. Raynar's father, Bornan Thul, a wealthy merchant and shipping magnate, had disappeared while en route to an important trade meeting with the Twi'lek Nolaa Tarkona, leader of the radical Diversity Alliance, an "aliens first" political movement.

Nolaa Tarkona was the embittered half sister of

*Nolaa Tarkona, demagogue*

the dancing girl Oola whom Jabba the Hutt had fed to his pet rancor. Vicious and skillful, Nolaa had succeeded in becoming the first female leader of her species. She gave many charismatic and enthusiastic rallies, whipping up support for her all-alien alliance, whose ultimate goal was to punish humans for the horrors of the Empire and past excesses. From the Twi'lek world, Ryloth, she offered a huge reward for Thul, and most especially for the mysterious cargo he carried. Thul had meant to sell his cargo to the Diversity Alliance, but had never arrived for his appointment. Her huge bounty attracted numerous bounty hunters, including the great Boba Fett.

Meanwhile, in order to collect a unique gift for their mother, the Solo twins traveled to the Alderaan system to search through the rubble of the planet that had been blasted by the Death Star. The Jedi trainees landed on a barren asteroid and secured a special shard from what was once the metallic core of Alderaan.

There, Boba Fett ambushed the young Jedi Knights and crippled their ship. He meant to interrogate them, or at least use them as bait in his search for Bornan Thul. While Jacen, Jaina, Tenel Ka, and Lowbacca worked to outwit the bounty hunter, Han Solo raced to respond to their distress call. Before Fett could attack from his hiding place, though, the former Dark Jedi Zekk reappeared in his own ship, drawn to his friends and their danger.

With a surprise barrage of firepower, Zekk drove off Boba Fett and helped Solo rescue his children. Jaina tried to convince Zekk to come back with them, but he was more determined than ever to make his own life as a bounty hunter. Later, he, too, decided to search for Bornan Thul.

Still desperate for news about his missing father, Raynar received a message from his mother Aryn and his uncle Tyko, a powerful merchant running the droid-manufacturing facilities on Mechis III. Afraid they would become targets for the criminals looking for Bornan, the Thul family went into hiding within their mobile merchant space fleet. They requested that Raynar join them, and the young man was escorted by Master Skywalker, Jacen, Jaina, Tenel Ka, and Lowbacca. Until they found Bornan Thul and resolved whatever mess he had gotten into, the whole family would live in fear.

Hoping to track down Thul themselves, the young Jedi Knights searched the man's last known locations, from ancient ruined worlds to Mechis III. They found a female Wookiee named Raaba, a close friend of Lowbacca's who had disappeared years before. Raaba had joined the Diversity Alliance, seeing it as a way to claim repayment for all the excesses humans had committed against aliens during the dark Imperial years. In her opinion, humans had never atoned for the devastation wrought by the horrific New Order. When Lowbacca grew uneasy at hearing the propaganda, Raaba accused him of having been around humans too long. Eventually, she convinced Lowbacca to leave his friends and come with her to Ryloth, so he could learn more about the Diversity Alliance.

On Thul's trail, Zekk went to a small and isolated human colony, only to find that the entire population had been wiped out by a devastating plague. He found evidence that the colony might have been intentionally destroyed, and somehow the signs pointed to Nolaa Tarkona. Shortly thereafter, he was secretly contacted by a disguised Bornan Thul and entrusted to deliver a message to Thul's family that he was safe, but that he had to remain in hiding. Thul had stumbled upon the location of an abandoned asteroid, one of the Emperor's secret biological labs, which held stockpiles of terrible plagues that could wipe out the human race. This deadly research center had been the scientific headquarters of the evil Imperial scientist Evir Derricote, who had unleashed the devastating Krytos virus in the early days of the New Republic. Though Derricote was long dead, his legacy of disease and death remained sealed on the lab asteroid.

In her political fervor, Nolaa Tarkona indeed sought to exterminate humanity, and the dead colony Zekk had found was her first test case. She was pursuing Thul to find the location of the Emperor's plague storehouse and had already used her one small sample to wipe out the colony. She needed enough of the plague to spread it across the galaxy, and Thul couldn't allow such information to fall into the hands of the Diversity Alliance. Nor could he trust the New Republic, because the alien-rights movement had spies everywhere.

Terrorist acts against humans escalated, including several assassination attempts, and Jacen and

Jaina uncovered further evidence of the Diversity Alliance's dark plans. They were especially concerned because Lowbacca had gone to the Twi'lek homeworld to join the movement, without suspecting its true purpose. The young Jedi Knights vowed to go to Ryloth and take their Wookiee friend back, but when they attempted to slip undetected into the Twi'lek tunnels, they were captured and sent to work deep in the ryll mines; Lowbacca was never informed of their presence, since Nolaa Tarkona wanted to convert him to their political cause. When the young Wookiee discovered the deceit, though, he turned entirely against the Diversity Alliance and helped his friends escape. They barely survived the rigors of the harsh Ryloth environment, but did get away, spreading alarms about the insidious plans of Nolaa Tarkona.

The Diversity Alliance was too clever to let their plans be exposed so easily. Thanks to alien political leaders in the senate, the testimony of the Solo twins and their friends was dismissed as the imaginings of children. Master Skywalker, however, spoke on their behalf and requested an inspection tour, composed of humans and aliens, be sent to Ryloth. The team set off, while Tarkona frantically covered her tracks.

Understanding the complexity of the plot, Zekk took Raynar to meet his father in hiding. The young Jedi Knights, still stinging from the disgrace that had been orchestrated for them in the senate, met them in space. Once they realized that Tarkona would stop at nothing to gain possession of the Emperor's plague storehouse, the group decided that they themselves had to go to the isolated asteroid and destroy the secret biological laboratory.

Boba Fett had also succeeded in tracking down the location of the plague storehouse and, per contract, reported it to the Diversity Alliance. Nolaa Tarkona left troops behind to fight against the New Republic inspection team, and set off with her own forces to obtain the Emperor's human-killing plague. When Skywalker and the inspectors pried too deeply into the hidden workings of Ryloth, the Diversity Alliance loyalists opened fire, and many died in the skirmish in the Twi'lek tunnels before the New Republic soldiers finally quelled the disturbance. But Tarkona had other priorities and knew if she could obtain the plague stockpiles, she would easily seal her ultimate victory.

As Bornan Thul, Zekk, and the other Jedi trainees set to work planting explosive charges throughout the asteroid depot, Diversity Alliance warships arrived. The companions split up in a race against time, trying to set their bombs before Tarkona could get her hands on the deadly containers.

Summoned by the young Jedi Knights, the New Republic emergency fleet arrived, led by Han Solo. The fleet engaged the Diversity Alliance ships in orbit, while the commandos planetside set off explosions to wreck the Imperial weapons depot. Bornan Thul sealed himself inside the central containment chamber that held the tanks of disease solution, trapped with Nolaa Tarkona and several of her henchmen. When they fired upon him, several of the plague cylinders cracked, and Thul was infected. While the rest of the laboratories and storehouses were destroyed around them, Thul died, hoping he had succeeded in denying the Diversity Alliance access to such a horrible weapon.

Nolaa Tarkona barely escaped, never realizing she herself had been infected by one of the alternate strains of Derricote's plagues, until she died alone in quarantine on an asteroid not long afterward.

# THE RESURGENCE OF BLACK SUN

**24 A.B.Y.**

Finally, after confronting his dark past, Zekk agreed to spend time at the Jedi praxeum to learn Force skills and to control his anger. He exhibited many talents and undeveloped potential, but once he turned his studies to emphasize his strengths, he became a crack pilot who assisted the other Jedi Knights. He won the famous Blockade Runners' Derby held at Ord Mantell, a classic race that was judged by Han Solo, one of the previous champions. One of the sponsors of the race, Czethros, was an old enemy of Solo's who claimed to be a respectable businessman.

*An ambush foiled*

On Ord Mantell, Solo—accompanied by his children and their friends—was nearly killed by space mines planted in the path of his ship. When evidence from the incident was brought back to a docking bay to await inspection, a group of chameleon creatures crept in and fought to steal all the debris. The creatures were driven off by the Jedi companions, with the timely assistance of a mysterious young woman, Anja. She had her own lightsaber, but no Jedi training, relying instead on large doses of spice to enhance her senses. When the exhausted friends asked her who she was, Anja announced that she was the daughter of Gallandro, a man she claimed Han Solo had murdered back in his early smuggling days; Anja had vowed her revenge.

Solo insisted that Anja Gallandro had her facts

wrong, and promised to prove to her he was a good man by going to help in the civil war that ravaged Anja's planet, Anobis. Anja reluctantly joined them on the *Millennium Falcon*, and they traveled to her war-torn world.

In reality, Anja worked for Czethros, and he was a secret leader of the Black Sun criminal organization. Black Sun had kept a low profile for years, but continued to work behind the scenes, infiltrating their loyal workers into positions of political and economic power throughout the New Republic. Czethros had addicted Anja to spice in order to keep her under his thumb, and he had sent her out on a mission to lead Han Solo into mortal danger.

When the *Falcon* arrived on Anobis, Solo met with the two factions in the long civil war, trying to learn each side of the story, though both tried to kill him and the Jedi trainees—as well as each other. Thanks to Jedi powers and Solo's fast thinking they survived and managed to broker an uneasy peace in the years-long war. Anja could barely believe what he had done, and began to wonder if her long hatred might have been misplaced. She agreed to join Jacen, Jaina, and the others back at the Jedi academy to see what she could learn from Master Skywalker.

Though the students tried to help her settle in, Anja remained restless and impatient with the slow progress of Jedi training. Skywalker found that she had no true potential, but owing to her hidden addiction to spice, she was able to fight well with her lightsaber. Though her certainty had been shaken, Anja's secret intention was to harm Solo in whatever way she could, and that included harming his children, despite the fact that she found herself warming to Jacen and Jaina's overtures of friendship.

During this time Lando Calrissian, who still owned *GemDiver Station* around Yavin, had repurchased a controlling interest in the spice mines of Kessel, using dividends from a more successful mining operation on Varn. He had invested the substantial spice profits in a new commercial venture, SkyCenter Galleria, an amusement park on Cloud City. He and his business partner Cojahn wanted the Solo twins and their friends to act as test subjects before the new attraction could be opened. Learning that Anja was herself a smuggler and rough around the edges, Calrissian invited her along, too, thinking she might be a kindred spirit.

When they all arrived at Cloud City, though, Calrissian learned that his partner Cojahn was dead; apparently, he had flung himself off one of the balconies on the city in the clouds. Appalled, Calrissian couldn't believe it was a suicide, and the group used their skills to investigate. The trail led them to the underlevels of the levitating city and to the bayous of Clak'dor VII. They uncovered the manipulations of Black Sun.

Czethros had sent his spies to the gambling centers on Cloud City, secretly taking over while maintaining normal appearances. Black Sun was interested in controlling the casinos and gambling, much as they had orchestrated gunrunning on Anobis and other embattled worlds, and worked in skimming the products from the spice mines of Kessel. On Bespin, he had attempted to extort cooperation from Cojahn, but when Calrissian's partner had refused, Czethros had murdered him.

Since Black Sun had bribed most of the Cloud City police force, they weren't inclined to investigate the crime too closely. When Calrissian and the young Jedi Knights poked around too much, Czethros sent in teams of assassins, including the chameleon creatures that had attacked them on Ord Mantell. But when the assassins and political traitors on Cloud City were exposed, the entire Black Sun plot began to unravel. A warrant for the arrest of Czethros went out to all planets.

Already disturbed by the near deaths of the people she had grudgingly begun to think of as friends, Anja Gallandro was even more anxious when she learned that Czethros, her mentor and drug supplier, had vanished. New Republic investigatory teams searched the galaxy, but he had gone to ground, hoping to set in motion the final stage of his plot for a government takeover.

When they returned to Yavin 4, Anja realized she was deeply addicted to spice, and without Czethros she had no supply of the controlled substance. Skywalker suspected her addiction, but knew that he should not use his Jedi powers to wipe away the problem; Anja had to find her own solution. Desperate, she slipped away from the academy, stole Zekk's personal ship, and flew to Kessel, where she hoped to get enough spice to control her need.

There in a guarded docking bay she encountered one of Czethros's hireling smugglers, who reluctantly gave her a few doses and told her about a larger stash hidden under the ice caps of Mon Calamari. Anja quickly departed to retrieve that shipment for herself.

The mousy Sullustan Nien Nunb, Calrissian's longtime manager of the Kessel mines, barely survived an "accident" in the carbon-freezing sections of the processing facility. Black Sun had also infiltrated there, and Nien Nunb knew he was in great danger. His own workers were turning against him.

When Zekk and his friends discovered Anja was missing, along with his ship, they went after her. Arriving too late on Kessel, they learned that Anja had already departed for Mon Calamari. Because of

Nien Nunb's fears, though, Jaina and Lowbacca remained at the spice mines to help, while Jacen, Zekk, and Tenel Ka raced off to the ocean world.

They traced Anja to the polar seas of Mon Calamari, where she had landed on a floating resort city known as Crystal Reef. They confronted her as she tried to lease a minisub to explore the ice caps, expressing their disappointment and feelings of betrayal.

Anja, too, felt betrayed—by her own mentor. She'd learned that Czethros had been secretly behind gunrunning to her war-torn homeworld, that he and Black Sun were responsible for the devastating battles and suffering. By now she had also admitted her terrible addiction to spice, and she meant to get her revenge on Czethros by destroying the valuable stockpile he had accumulated on Mon Calamari.

Reluctantly giving her another chance, the Jedi trainees followed her to the ice caps, where she did destroy the stashed spice. They were attacked by a huge sea creature, however, and barely escaped by running their minisub into an iceberg labyrinth. The ice ground together, nearly crushing the vehicle, and the Jedi had no choice but to go into the arctic water with their lightsabers to cut the vehicle free. During the worst part of the ordeal, her friends used desperate Jedi healing techniques to free Anja of the chemical addiction of spice, though she would have to deal with the mental part herself.

Not long after Jacen, Zekk, and Tenel Ka departed from Kessel, a nondescript supply ship crept to the mine's shipping center, then disgorged mercenary troops led by Czethros himself. Black Sun took over the spice mines of Kessel, setting up Czethros in command. Nien Nunb was taken prisoner, but Jaina and Lowbacca managed to hide in the tunnels, from which they could eavesdrop and strike out against the criminals.

They learned that Black Sun had established loyal infiltrators in many important positions throughout the New Republic government and military, on numerous allied planets and industrial stations. From his headquarters on Kessel, Czethros planned to send a coded signal that would call them to arms. Thousands of traitors in thousands of key positions could cripple the galactic government. Though their numbers weren't great enough to withstand a concerted resistance from the military, their overthrow attempt would happen simultaneously and be so widespread that the New Republic could not hope to resist.

However, Czethros didn't count on sabotage from within. Jaina and Lowbacca destroyed the transmitter before Black Sun could send its signal. They also freed the prisoners in the spice mines and drove back the mercenaries who had taken over Kessel. Nien Nunb rallied his troops and chased Czethros through the tunnels to the carbon-freezing facility. Rather than allow himself to be captured, Czethros fell into a vat of carbonite, where he was flash-frozen. Later, Chief of State Leia Organa Solo supervised his unthawing and interrogation and uncovered the names of the Black Sun infiltrators who remained in key positions throughout the New Republic. Black Sun was effectively crushed.

After their numerous successes, Master Luke Skywalker declared that his group of young trainees—Jacen and Jaina Solo, Tenel Ka, Lowbacca, Zekk, and Anakin Solo—could now consider themselves apprentice Jedi Knights. One day soon, they would form a new generation of defenders for the Republic.

# AFTERWORD

The preparation of this chronology has been a long and difficult process, requiring teams of historians and scholars. However, we can by no means consider this to be a comprehensive history of the galaxy. Thanks to the very nature of time, once this work has been completed, it is already out of date.

So the work continues. Processing droids are currently sifting through the enormous archives of the Imperial Information Center in search of records hidden, altered, or damaged during Palpatine's numerous purges. Evidence technicians and data restorers have spent years combing through the rubble of Mount Tantiss, with frequent discoveries that shed light on the Emperor's crimes and plans.

Archaeologists have only begun to discover the vast storehouse of knowledge buried in the ruins of the great Jedi library of Ossus. Existing Jedi Holocrons containing the lost knowledge of legendary Masters have barely been tapped. Ancient records from numerous isolated planets, such as Toola and Dathomir, are still being translated.

Much of the new information even now coming to light relates to the dark transition years at the birth of the Empire, when Palpatine overthrew the crumbling government of the Republic. Actual eye-witnesses to these events remain alive, though many of the participants are reaching advanced age. We continue to make a concerted effort to locate these precious sources of information and debrief them for the historical record—before it is too late.

Even now, historic events are in motion. Borsk Fey'lya, a member of the Rebellion since its early years, has overcome several dark scandals in his past and finally ascended to the coveted office of chief of state. Master Luke Skywalker's new Jedi Knights have become the galaxy's patrol officers, but Skywalker now sees a need to oversee the Jedi. Consequently, he is seeking approval to reestablish the Jedi Council, which would unite twelve leading Jedi into a governing body not seen since the days of the Old Republic.

Of course, trouble spots remain. A few inter-species rivalries have been simmering ever since the Hand of Thrawn incident, and professional firebrand Nom Anor—the mysterious figure involved with Carnor Jax's Interim Council—has resurfaced to stir up trouble on the planets of Rhommamool and Osarian. But these are localized controversies, representing no imminent danger. With the remnants of the Empire content to rule their pocket of the Outer Rim, there seem to be no corners from which a new threat can arise. Historians can only hope that the galaxy will at last settle into an era of peace and stability.

It is our continuing job to preserve and present the epic events of the long saga of life's struggle across the galaxy. For only by knowing our history can we understand ourselves—and history never ends.

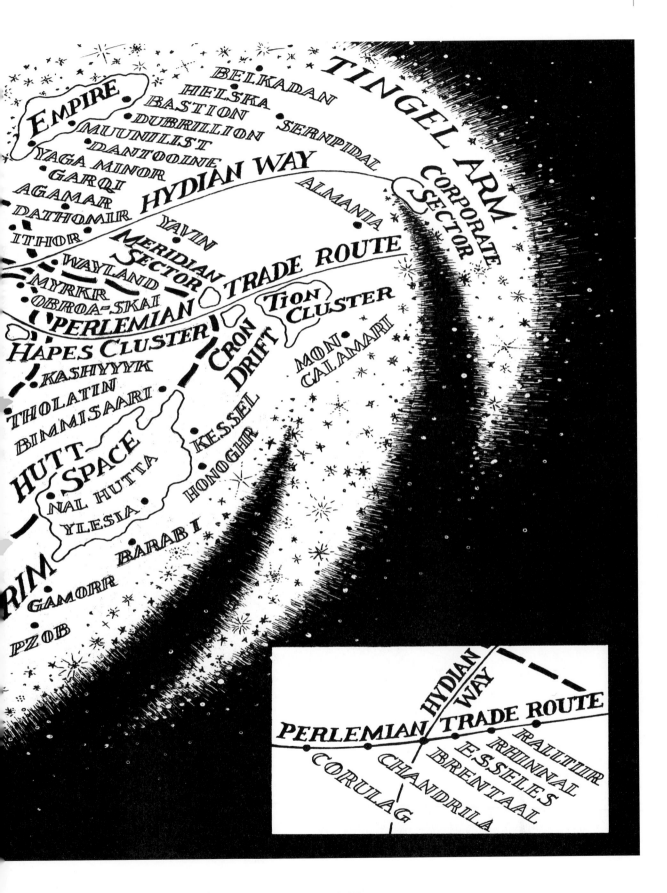

# TIME LINE

For readers who wish to explore the historical events of the *Star Wars* galaxy in greater detail, the following time line presents the films, major novels, comics, and computer games in sequence. As befits a historical chronicle, only those sources that have had a significant impact on galactic events and on the lives of key personalities are listed here.

Some portions of the *Essential Chronology*, particularly ancient Republic history, were drawn from historical details in novels set much later in the time line. For ease of reference these novels are only listed once, under the time period where the bulk of their story takes place.

Whether you're looking for information on a particular era or simply trying to read the major *Star Wars* stories in approximate chronological order, this time line makes a handy reference tool.

## PART I—
## TALES OF THE ANCIENT JEDI KNIGHTS

### EMERGENCE OF THE SITH

**5000 B.B.Y.**

THE GOLDEN AGE OF THE SITH
- *Tales of the Jedi: The Golden Age of the Sith* comics #0, 1–5

THE GREAT HYPERSPACE WAR
- *Tales of the Jedi: The Fall of the Sith Empire* comics #1–5

### LEGACY OF THE SITH

**4400 B.B.Y.**

THE SHADOW OF FREEDON NADD

**4000 B.B.Y.**

TRIALS OF THE JEDI
- *Tales of the Jedi: Knights of the Old Republic* comic collection

**3998 B.B.Y.**

### THE NADDIST REVOLT
- *Tales of the Jedi: The Freedon Nadd Uprising* comics #1–2

**3997 B.B.Y.**

### THE COMING RUIN
- *Tales of the Jedi: Dark Lords of the Sith* comics #1–6

**3996 B.B.Y.**

### THE SITH WAR
- *Tales of the Jedi: The Sith War* comics #1–6

**3996 B.B.Y.**

### THE DEVASTATION OF OSSUS

**3986 B.B.Y.**

### THE REDEMPTION OF ULIC QEL-DROMA
- *Tales of the Jedi: Redemption* comics #1–5

**4000–3000 B.B.Y.**

### REPERCUSSIONS THROUGH THE REPUBLIC

**2000–1000 B.B.Y.**

### THE NEW SITH

**600–400 B.B.Y.**

### JEDI VALIANCY

## PART II—
## THE EMPIRE AND THE NEW ORDER

**APPROX. 50–18 B.B.Y.**

BIRTH OF THE EMPIRE
- *Star Wars Episode II*
- *Star Wars Episode III*

**32 B.B.Y.**

- *Star Wars:* Episode I: *THE PHANTOM MENACE* film/screenplay/novel/radio drama novel/radio drama/juvenile and comic adaptations

**APPROX. 18–0 B.B.Y.**

DAWN OF DISSENT
- *Droids* television cartoon
- *Droids: The Kalarba Adventures* comic collection
- *Droids: Rebellion and Season of Revolt* comics #1–8
- *The Protocol Offensive* comic
- *Jabba the Hutt: The Art of the Deal* comic collection
- *Boba Fett: Enemy of the Empire* comics #1–4
- *X-Wing* computer game
- *Dark Forces: Soldier for the Empire* graphic story album #1

## PART III—
## PROFILES IN HISTORY

THE SKYWALKERS
- *Star Wars Episode IV: A New Hope*

HAN SOLO AND LANDO CALRISSIAN

**10 B.B.Y.**

YLESIA
- *The Paradise Snare* volume one of the Han Solo trilogy

**10–5 B.B.Y.**

THE ACADEMY

**5–2 B.B.Y.**

### THE LIFE OF A SMUGGLER
- *The Hutt Gambit* volume two of the Han Solo trilogy

**4 B.B.Y.**

### THE SHARU AWAKEN
- *Lando Calrissian and the Mindharp of Sharu*

**3 B.B.Y.**

### THE BATTLE OF NAR SHADDAA
### BACK TO THE OSEON
- *Lando Calrissian and the Flamewind of Oseon*
### FORTUNE WON, FORTUNE LOST

**3–2.5 B.B.Y.**

### TO SAVE THE THONBOKA
- *Lando Calrissian and the Starcave of ThonBoka*

**2–1 B.B.Y.**

### CORPORATE SECTOR BLUES
- *Han Solo at Stars' End* novel/comics #1–3
- *Han Solo's Revenge*

**2.5–0 B.B.Y.**

### ENTREPRENEURISM

**1–0 B.B.Y.**

### DESTITUTE IN THE TION
- *Han Solo and the Lost Legacy*

**0 B.B.Y.**

(months before the Battle of Yavin)
### RETURN TO YLESIA
- *Rebel Dawn* volume three of the Han Solo trilogy
(immediately prior to the Battle of Yavin)
### "THE LAST SPICE RUN"

**0–3 A.B.Y.**

### "THE RESPECTABLE ONE"

# PART IV—
# REBELLION AGAINST THE EMPIRE

## THE REBELLION BEGINS

**3–0 B.B.Y.**

THE DEATH STAR CONSTRUCTION
- *Dark Forces: Soldier for the Empire* graphic story album

**0 B.B.Y.**

PREPARATIONS FOR BATTLE
THE CAPTURE OF PRINCESS LEIA
A NEW HOPE
- *Star Wars Episode IV: A New Hope* film/screenplay/novel/radio drama/juvenile and comic adaptations
- *Tales from the Mos Eisley Cantina* anthology

**0–0.5 A.B.Y.**

IMPACT AND CONSEQUENCES
- *Vader's Quest* comics #1–4
- *Boba Fett: Salvage* comic #1/2
- The Bounty Hunter Wars trilogy (flashbacks)

REBEL TRAP
- *Classic Star Wars* newspaper strips/comics #1–17
- *Shadow Stalker* comic serial/comic
- Marvel *Star Wars* comics #1–38

**0.5–2 A.B.Y.**

IMPERIAL COUNTERSTRIKE
- *Galaxy of Fear #1: Eaten Alive*
- *Galaxy of Fear #2: City of the Dead*
- *Galaxy of Fear #3: Planet Plague*
- *Galaxy of Fear #4: The Nightmare Machine*
- *Galaxy of Fear #5: Ghost of the Jedi*
- *Galaxy of Fear #6: Army of Terror*
- *Galaxy of Fear #7: The Swarm*
- *Galaxy of Fear #8: Spore*
- *Galaxy of Fear #9: Doomsday Ship*
- *Galaxy of Fear #10: Clones*
- *Galaxy of Fear #11: The Hunger*
- *Dark Forces* computer game
- *Rogue Squadron* computer game
- *River of Chaos* comics #1–4
- *Classic Star Wars: The Early Adventures* newspaper strips/comics #1–9

**2 A.B.Y.**

CIRCARPOUS JOINS THE RESISTANCE
- *Splinter of the Mind's Eye* novel/comics #1–4

**2–3 A.B.Y.**

HOME IN THE ICE
- *Classic Star Wars* newspaper strips/comics #17–20
- *Rebel Mission to Ord Mantell* audio adventure

**A LIGHT ECLIPSED**

- *Star Wars Episode V: The Empire Strikes Back* film/screenplay/novel/
radio drama/juvenile and comic adaptations
- *Tales of the Bounty Hunters* anthology
- *TIE Fighter* computer game
- *Rebel Assault II: The Hidden Empire* computer game
- Marvel *Star Wars* comics #39–80

**3 A.B.Y.**

THE BATTLE OF HOTH
A NEW JEDI

**3.5 A.B.Y.**

PRINCE XIZOR AND BLACK SUN
- *Shadows of the Empire* novel/juvenile adaptation
- *Shadows of the Empire* comics #1–6
- *Shadows of the Empire* computer game
- *Battle of the Bounty Hunters* pop-up comic
- *X-Wing Alliance* computer game

**4 A.B.Y.**

**ALLIANCE TRIUMPHANT**

- *Star Wars Episode VI: Return of the Jedi* film/screenplay/novel/radio drama/juvenile
and comic adaptations
- *Tales from Jabba's Palace* anthology
- *The Mandalorian Armor* volume one of the Bounty Hunter Wars trilogy
- *Slave Ship* volume two of the Bounty Hunter Wars trilogy
- *Hard Merchandise* volume three of the Bounty Hunter Wars trilogy
- *The Jabba Tape* comic

THE REBELLION REGROUPS

THE BATTLE OF ENDOR

THE TRUCE AT BAKURA

- *The Truce at Bakura*
- Marvel *Star Wars* comics #81–107
- *Classic Star Wars: The Vandelhelm Mission* comic

### 4–5 A.B.Y.

ONWARD TO SSI-RUUVI SPACE

## PART V—
## BIRTH OF THE NEW REPUBLIC

### 4–4.5 A.B.Y.

IMPERIAL FRAGMENTATION

- *X-Wing* comics #1–20

BLACK NEBULA

- *Mara Jade: By the Emperor's Hand* comics #0, 1–6
- *Shadows of the Empire: Evolution* comics #1–5

ISARD'S ASCENSION

- *X-Wing* comics #21–35
- *Boba Fett: Twin Engines of Destruction* comic serial/comic
- *The Glove of Darth Vader*
- *The Lost City of the Jedi*
- *Zorba the Hutt's Revenge*
- *Mission from Mount Yoda*
- *Queen of the Empire*
- *Prophets of the Dark Side*

### 5–5.5 A.B.Y.

GENERAL SKYWALKER

- *Jedi Knight* computer game
- *Dark Forces: Rebel Agent* graphic story album
- *Dark Forces: Jedi Knight* graphic story album

### 6 A.B.Y.

THE LAST GRAND ADMIRAL?

### 6.5–7 A.B.Y.

THE BATTLE FOR CORUSCANT

- *X-Wing: Rogue Squadron*
- *X-Wing: Wedge's Gamble*

**7–7.5 A.B.Y.**

THE KRYTOS VIRUS
- *X-Wing: The Krytos Trap*

**7.5 A.B.Y.**

THE BACTA WAR
- *X-Wing: The Bacta War*

**7.5–8 A.B.Y.**

THE HUNT FOR ZSINJ
- *X-Wing: Wraith Squadron*
- *X-Wing: Iron Fist*
- *X-Wing: Solo Command*

**8 A.B.Y.**

THE HAPANS AND THE DATHOMIR NIGHTSISTERS
- *The Courtship of Princess Leia*

THE DEATH OF ZSINJ

**8.5 A.B.Y.**

PICKING UP THE PIECES

## PART VI— EMPIRE RESURGENT

**9 A.B.Y.**

### THE DEPREDATIONS OF GRAND ADMIRAL THRAWN
- *Heir to the Empire* volume one of the Thrawn trilogy novel/comics #1–6
- *Dark Force Rising* volume two of the Thrawn trilogy novel/comics #1–6
- *The Last Command* volume three of the Thrawn trilogy novel/comics #1–6

TALON KARRDE AND THE SMUGGLERS

THE NOGHRI SWITCH SIDES

THE KATANA FLEET AND THE CLONE TROOPERS

THRAWN'S FALL

**9–10 A.B.Y.**

### THE RETURN OF ISARD
- *X-Wing: Isard's Revenge*

**10 A.B.Y.**

THE RESURRECTION OF EMPEROR PALPATINE
- *Dark Empire* comics #1–6
- *Mysteries of the Sith* computer game
- *Boba Fett: Death, Lies, and Treachery* comic collection

OPERATION SHADOW HAND
- *Dark Empire II* comics #1–6

**11 A.B.Y.**

PALPATINE VANQUISHED
- *Empire's End* comics #1–2

JAX, KANOS, AND THE RULING COUNCIL
- *Crimson Empire* comics #0, 1–6
- *Crimson Empire II* comics, 1–6

## PART VIII—
## THE RETURN OF THE JEDI KNIGHTS

**11 A.B.Y.**

SKYWALKER'S JEDI ACADEMY
- *Jedi Search* volume one of the Jedi Academy trilogy
- *Dark Apprentice* volume two of the Jedi Academy trilogy
- *Champions of the Force* volume three of the Jedi Academy trilogy
- *I, Jedi*

MAW INSTALLATION

POLITICAL TROUBLES

EXAR KUN'S REVENGE

THE RECAPTURE OF MAW INSTALLATION

**12 A.B.Y.**

THE EMPEROR'S HAND AND THE SENEX LORDS

THE EYE OF PALPATINE
- *Children of the Jedi*

THE DARKSABER THREAT
- *Darksaber*

THE HUTT PLAN

ADMIRAL DAALA RETURNS

DURGA'S FOLLY

ASSAULT ON YAVIN 4

**12–13 A.B.Y..**

THE EMPIRE REGROUPS

**13** A.B.Y.

MISSION TO ADUMAR
- *X-Wing: Starfighters of Adumar*

THE DEATH SEED PLAGUE
- *Planet of Twilight*
- *The Leviathan of Corbos* comics #1–4

## PART VIII—
## UPRISING AND INSURGENCIES

**14** A.B.Y.

THE "EMPIRE REBORN" MOVEMENT
- *The Crystal Star*

**16–17** A.B.Y.

THE BLACK FLEET CRISIS
- *Before the Storm* volume one of the Black Fleet Crisis trilogy
- *Shield of Lies* volume two of the Black Fleet Crisis trilogy
- *Tyrant's Test* volume three of the Black Fleet Crisis trilogy

MASTER SKYWALKER AND THE FALLANASSI

THE TELJKON VAGABOND

**17** A.B.Y.

UPRISING AT ALMANIA
- *The New Rebellion*

SMUGGLER'S RUN

**17–18** A.B.Y.

IMPERIAL SKIRMISHES

**18** A.B.Y.

THE CORELLIAN INSURRECTION
- *Ambush at Corellia* volume one of the Corellian trilogy
- *Assault at Selonia* volume two of the Corellian trilogy
- *Showdown at Centerpoint* volume three of the Corellian trilogy

## PART IX—
## A LASTING PEACE

**19** A.B.Y.

THE CAAMAS DOCUMENT
- *Specter of the Past*
- *Vision of the Future*

THE HAND OF THRAWN

## PART X—
## GENERATIONS OF JEDI KNIGHTS

**22** A.B.Y.

### THE GOLDEN GLOBE AND KENOBI'S LIGHTSABER
- *Junior Jedi Knights #1: The Golden Globe*
- *Junior Jedi Knights #2: Lyric's World*
- *Junior Jedi Knights #3: Promises*
- *Junior Jedi Knights #4: Anakin's Quest*
- *Junior Jedi Knights #5: Vader's Fortress*
- *Junior Jedi Knights #6: Kenobi's Blade*

**23** A.B.Y.

### THE SHADOW ACADEMY AND THE SECOND IMPERIUM
- *Young Jedi Knights: Heirs of the Force*
- *Young Jedi Knights: Shadow Academy*
- *Young Jedi Knights: The Lost Ones*
- *Young Jedi Knights: Lightsabers*
- *Young Jedi Knights: Darkest Knight*
- *Young Jedi Knights: Jedi Under Siege*

**23–24** A.B.Y.

### THE DIVERSITY ALLIANCE
- *Young Jedi Knights: Shards of Alderaan*
- *Young Jedi Knights: Diversity Alliance*
- *Young Jedi Knights: Delusions of Grandeur*
- *Young Jedi Knights: Jedi Bounty*
- *Young Jedi Knights: The Emperor's Plague*

**24** A.B.Y.

### THE RESURGENCE OF BLACK SUN
- *Young Jedi Knights: Return to Ord Mantell*
- *Young Jedi Knights: Trouble on Cloud City*
- *Young Jedi Knights: Crisis at Crystal Reef*

# INDEX

Ackbar, Admiral, 46, 52, 53, 67, 70, 88, 106, 113, 145
   at Battle of Coruscant, 72–73
   at Battle of Endor, 60, 63
   in Corellian insurrection, 142
   Darksaber attack on, 115
   and financial scandal, 86, 87
   in *Lusankya* rescue mission, 90
   retirement of, 102
   and warlords, 82
Adumar mission, 118, 178
*Agave*-class warships, 98
Akanah Norand Pell, 131
Alderaan, 35, 43, 50, 53, 55, 79, 160
   destruction of, 48–49
*Alderaan*, 124
Aleema, 10–11, 14, 15–16
Alliance of Free Planets, 65, 67
Allya, 20
Almania uprising, 132–36, 178
Amanoa, Queen of Iziz, 9, 10
Ambria, 10
Amidala, Queen of Naboo, 22
Amisus, 33
Ammuud, 32
Anobis, 162–63
Anor, Nom, 98, 165
Antilles, Wedge, 20, 53, 85, 88, 113
   Adumar mission of, 118
   and Almania uprising, 135
   in Bacta War, 75–76
   at Battle of Coruscant, 73, 91
   at Battle of Endor, 61, 63
   at Battle of Orinda, 117
   Darksaber attack on, 115
   as *Lusankya* commander, 98, 117
   Wraith Squadron of, 76–77
Arca Jeth, Master, 9, 10, 11, 12, 18
Argazda, 18
Aruk the Hutt, 29, 33–34
Ashgad, Seti, 25, 118–19, 121
Atzerri, 131
Augwynne, 80
Auyemesh, 134

Bacta War, 75–76, 176
Badure, 28, 32
Bakura
   fleet of, 140
   Ssi-ruuk invasion of, 63–65
   truce with, 63
Bane, Darth, 20
Bast Castle, 153, 154
Batch, Grand Admiral, 72
Battles
   in Corellian insurrection, 141–42
   for Coruscant, 72–73, 175
   of Dathomir, 80
   of Derra IV, 55

of Doornik–319, 128, 129
of Endor, 42, 60–63
of Ession, 77
of Gravlex Med, 143
of Hoth, 55–56, 174
of Milagro, 71
of Mindor, 71–72
of Mon Calamari, 91–93
of Nam Chorios, 121
of Nar Shaddaa, 30, 31, 37, 172
of N'zoth, 130, 131
of Onderon, 97
of Orinda, 117
of Ruusan, 18–20, 23
of Sluis Van, 85
of Storinal, 82
of Taanab, 42
of Taung-Zhell, 1
of Vontor, 1
of Yavin, 26, 42, 50
of Yavin 4, 116–16
Behn-kihl-nahm, 127
Beldorian the Splendid, 20, 120–21
Bel Iblis, Garm, 26, 53, 86, 137, 145
Belsavis, 25, 108
Bengat, 31
Beruss, Doman, 129
Besadii Hutts, 28, 29, 34
Bespin, 99
Big Bunji, 31
Black Fleet Crisis, 127–30, 178
Black holes of Maw, 1, 29, 35, 45, 100, 101, 102, 104
Black Nebula, 68, 175
Black Sun criminal syndicate, 58–59, 68, 98, 111, 162–64, 174, 179
Black Sword Command, 70, 127
Blockade Runners' Derby, 161
Blue Max, 31, 32–33
Bollux, 31, 32–33
Bonadan, 32
Borleias, capture of, 72
Bothans, 144, 145, 147
Bothawui, 58
Bounty Hunters Guild, 51, 56
Bounty Hunter Wars, 51–52, 58
Bpfassh, 24
Brakiss
   and Almania uprising, 132, 134, 135–36
   Shadow Academy of, 155–58
Brand, Empatojayos, 95, 97
Brentaal, capture of, 68–69
*Bria*, 29, 31
Briggia, 26
Brill, Foga, 122, 132
Brotherhood of Navigators, 3
Byss, 89, 91, 93, 94, 95, 130

Caamas, 25
Caamas Document, 144, 145, 147, 149, 179
Callista

as *Eye of Palpatine* saboteur, 109
in *Knight Hammer* explosion, 115–16
loss of Jedi powers, 110–11, 113
Skywalker's search for, 120–21
Calrissian, Lando, 27, 35–42, 171–72
at Battle of Coruscant, 91
at Battle of Endor, 61, 63
at Battle of Nam Chorios, 121
at Battle of Nar Shaddaa, 37–38
and Bothan incident, 145
in Cloud City, 42, 56, 57, 71, 163
combat with Gepta, 41
and drug bust, 38, 39
escape from Kessel, 101
as gambler and con artist, 31, 35, 38, 41–42
and Han Solo, 29, 31, 34, 35, 41, 42
in Maw Installation assault, 105
mining operation of, 84, 87, 130, 138, 155, 163
on Myrkr, 84, 85
in Oseon system, 35–36, 38–39
in Oswaft defense, 39–41
in Rafa system, 36–37
in Smuggler's Run, 137
in space battle with *Eclipse II*, 97
on Teljkon vagabond, 132
and Thrawn impersonator, 144
used-spaceship lot of, 31, 37, 41
wife hunt of, 138
in Ylesian assault, 34, 42
Captison, Gaeriel, 63, 65, 140, 141–42
Captison, Yeorg, 63, 65
Carida, 28, 103
Carivus, Xandel, 98
C'baoth, Joruus, 84, 87
Celchu, Tycho, 71, 75
Centerpoint Station, 138–39, 140
Chewbacca, 32, 57, 58, 79, 85, 86, 88, 91, 100, 108, 115, 124
in Corellian insurrection, 139, 140
escape from Death Star, 50
marriage of, 31
in Maw Installation assault, 104, 105
rescued by Han Solo, 28–29, 31
rescues Han Solo, 130
as smuggler, 34–35
in Smuggler's Run, 136, 137
*Chimaera*, 67, 83, 86, 89, 98, 143, 145
Chiss, 65–66, 149
*Chu'unthor*, 20, 56, 79, 80
Cilghal, 102, 106, 111
Cinnagar, 14
Circarpous IV, 54
Circarpous V (Mimban), 54, 55
Ciutric Hegemony, 89, 90
Cloaking device, 88, 156
Clone soldiers, 84, 87–88, 147, 176
Clone Wars, 24
Cloud City, 42, 56–57, 71, 163
Cojahn, 163
Commission for the Preservation of the New Order (COMPNOR), 25
Corellia, 1, 27

Corellian insurrection, 138–42, 178
Corellian Treaty, 26, 48
Corporate Sector Authority (CSA), 31–32
Coruscant
Battle for, 72–73, 175
Great Hyperspace War on, 5, 6
Imperial blockade of, 88
Imperial Center, 25
Imperial recapture of, 90–91
Jedi headquarters, 21
Krytos virus in, 73, 75
Republic advance against, 70
Taung-Zhell battle on, 1
Xizor's fortress, 58
Crado, 11, 12, 15–16, 17
Croke, 41
Crseih Research Station, 124, 125–26
*Crynyd*, 71, 82
Crynyd, Arvel, 63
C-3PO, 48, 49, 65, 79, 86, 91, 125, 135
Czethros, 161, 162, 163, 164

Daala, Admiral
at Battle of Nam Chorios, 121
flagship of, 111, 116, 137
at Maw Installation, 46, 100–101, 105
in Mon Calamari assault, 102
retirement of, 117
Sun Crusher attack on, 103, 104
as warlords leader, 121–22, 130
in Yavin 4 assault, 113, 115–17, 177
Dagobah, 60, 113, 152, 154
Dantooine, 11, 26, 48
Daragon, Gav, 2–4, 5
Daragon, Jori, 2–5
Darksaber, 112, 113–15, 177
Darth Vader. *See* Vader, Darth
Da Soocha, 91
D'Asta, Baron, 98
Dathomir, 20, 79, 155–57
Battle of, 80
Nightsisters of, 80, 155–56, 176
Death Seed plague, 119, 178
Death Star, 27, 100
Alderaan destroyed by, 48–49
design and construction of, 45–46, 173
destruction of first, 50
destruction of second, 60–63
prototype, 104–5
second, 51, 57, 60, 72
site of, 45
theft of plans for, 46–47, 48, 111, 113
Declaration of a New Republic, 67
Declaration of Rebellion, 48
Deep Core, 89, 91, 93, 97, 98, 111, 113, 115
*Defender*-class warships, 98
Dela, 39
Dellalt, 33
Dellalt Project, 33
Delvardus, General, 90, 111
Denarii Nova, 7

Deneba, 12
Dequc, 68
Derra IV, Battle of, 55
Derricote, Evir, 73, 75, 160
Desilijic Hutts, 29, 33–34, 42, 60
Despayre, 46
*Devastator*, 47
Dewlanna, 27
Disra, Moff, 143–44, 145, 147
Diversity Alliance, 158–61, 179
Djo, Teneniel, 80
Dodonna, Jan
    joins Rebel Alliance, 47–48
    in *Lusankya* prison, 53, 75, 76
    rescue of, 89–90
    at Yavin, 50, 52
Dolph (Kueller), 132, 134–35, 136, 137, 155
*Dominant*, 64
Doneeta, Tott, 9, 10, 11, 14, 15, 16
Doole, Moruth, 35, 100
Doornik-319, Battle of, 128, 129
Dorsk 81, 100, 111, 113, 115
Dracmus, 139
Drago, Vyyk (alias of Han Solo), 28
Drall, 138, 139, 140, 141, 142
Drayson, Hiram, 127
Droid factories, 134, 135, 137
Drommel, Gaen, 67, 137
Durane, Giles, 43–44
Durga the Hutt, 29, 34, 111, 113–15, 177
Durron, Kyp, 100, 111, 113, 150
    on dark side, 102–3
    at Jedi Academy, 102, 106
    in Maw Installation assault, 104–6
    as spy in Deep Core, 115
Duskhan League, 127, 129–30
Dxun moon
    beasts of, 7, 8
    and Naddist revolt, 10, 11
Dzym, 119

Ebrihim, 139, 140
Echo Base, 55, 76, 95
*Eclipse*, 82, 94
*Eclipse II*, 96–97
*Emancipator*, 82, 93
*Eminence*, 41
Empire
    attacks on Rebel bases, 53, 55–56
    in Bacta War, 75–76
    birth of, 21–25, 171
    blockade of Rebel base, 52, 53
    in Bounty Hunter Wars, 51–52
    Daala's command, 101–2, 103, 104, 111,
        113
    defeat at Endor, 60–63
    destruction of Alderaan, 48–49
    fall of Coruscant, 72–73
    final collapse of, 96–98, 106
    fragmentation of, 67–68, 76, 175
    Ghorman Massacre, 25

guerrilla-style strikes against, 54
and Hutt smugglers, 29, 31, 37
Interim Council of, 97–98
Isard's ascension in, 68–70, 175
and *Katana* fleet, 86–87
Mutiny, 90–91
Oswaft attack by, 40–41
Pellaeon's command, 117, 137
and Pellaeon's peace offer, 143–45, 178
recapture of Coruscant, 90
Renatasia invasion by, 39
resistance to. *See* New Republic; Rebel Alliance
resurrection of Palpatine, 90–96
Ssi-ruuk invasion of, 63–65
Tarkin Doctrine, 46
under Thrawn, 83–89, 176
truce with Rebel Alliance, 63
war machine of, 25–26
weaponry of, 88, 92, 93, 95, 101, 103.
        *See also* Death Star
Zaarin's plot against, 59
Zinj campaign of, 77
    *See also* Vader, Darth
Empire Reborn movement, 123–26, 178
Empress Teta system, 10, 11, 12, 14
Endor, Battle of, 42, 60–63
*Endurance*-class warships, 98, 117
Eol Sha, 99
Ession, Battle of, 77
EV-9D9, 42
*Executor*, 52–53, 59, 63
Exis Station, 17, 99–100, 154
*Eye of Palpatine*, 25, 108, 109–10

Falanthas, Mokka, 121, 124
Fallanassi, 130–31
*Falleen's Fist*, 58–59
Fardreamer, Cole, 135
Fel, Soontir, 28, 31, 69, 145
Female-dominated societies
    of Dathomir, 20
    Hapes Consortium, 18
Fett, Boba, 29, 35, 42, 51, 56, 58, 160, 161
Fey'lya, Borsk, 54, 67, 86, 88
Fiolla of Lorrd, 32
Flamewind, 38
Flim, 143, 145, 147
Force, 1, 7, 9, 71, 93, 95, 99, 110
Furgan, 101, 103, 106

Galaxy Gun, 95, 96, 130
Galia, Queen of Iziz, 9, 10
Gallandro (gunman), 32, 33
Gallandro, Anja, 33, 162–64
Gantoris, 99, 102
Gavrisom, Ponc, 142
Geith, 109
*GemDiver Station*, 155, 156
Gepta, Rokur, 36, 38, 41
Getelles, Moff, 119, 121, 122

Gethzerion, 80
Ghorin, 53
Ghorman Massacre, 25
Glottalphib, 137
Golden Globe of Exar Kun, 20, 152, 179
Gra'aton, Master, 20
Grant, Grand Admiral, 72
Gravlex Med, Battle of, 143
Great Hyperspace War, 2, 5–7, 169
Greelanx, Admiral, 29, 31
Griff, Admiral, 53
Grigmin's Traveling Airshow, 32
Grunger, Grand Admiral, 72
*Guardian*, 137
Guri, 59, 68

*Hajen*-class warships, 98
Halcyon, Nejaa, 75
Hand of Thrawn, 34, 148, 149, 179
Hapes Consortium, 18, 79, 80, 82, 157, 176
Harrsk, Admiral, 67, 90, 97, 111
Hethrir, Lord, 123–24, 125–26
Hoffner, Captain, 86
Hoggon, 17
Holocron, Jedi, 93, 95, 154
Honoghr, 86
Horn, Corran, 75, 100, 106
Horuz system, 46
Hoth, 53, 54, 55, 76, 95
   Battle of, 55–56, 174
Hoth, Lord, 18
Human League, 139
Hutts
   in Battle of Nar Shaddaa, 30, 31
   in Battle of Vontor, 1
   Besadii clan, 28, 29, 34, 111
   Desilijic clan, 29, 33, 42, 60
   illicit activities of, 28, 29
   theft of Death Star plans, 111, 113
Hydian Way, 18

Ikrit, 20, 152, 154
Il-Raz, Grand Admiral, 72
Imperial Center, 25
Imperial City, 1, 75
Interim Council, Imperial, 97–98
*Intimidator*, 70, 127
*Invidious*, 106
*Invincible*, 26
*Iron Fist*, 76, 78, 79, 80
Isard, Ysanne
   ascendancy of, 68–70, 175
   in Bacta War, 75–76
   and fall of Coruscant, 73
   as head of state, 75
   and Krytos virus, 75
   return of clone, 89–90, 176
Ismaren, Irek, 108, 109
Ismaren, Roganda, 106, 108
Isolder, Prince of Hapes, 79, 80, 82, 157

Isoto, Admiral, 69
Ithor, Great Meet on, 107, 108
Ivpikkis, 63, 64, 66
Iyon, 123
Iziz
   beast riders attack on, 9
   Sith sorcery in, 11
   walled city of, 7–8

Jabba the Hutt, 29, 34, 34–35, 42, 57, 60, 71, 79, 160
Jade, Mara, 150, 151
   in cloning facility sabotage, 87
   in Corellian insurrection, 139–40
   as Emperor's Hand, 68, 85, 106
   Force abilities of, 99, 105
   in Hand of Thrawn, 147–49
   marriage to Luke Skywalker, 149
   with smugglers, 84–85
*Jade's Fire*, 139, 147, 149
Jax, Carnor, 94–95, 96, 97, 98, 177
Jedi Academy
   advanced trainees, 149–50
   Gantoris in, 102
   and Jedi search, 99–100, 106
   and Shadow Academy, 155–58
   under Streen, 130
   under Tionne, 151
   younger students in, 149, 151
Jedi Knights
   Daala's attack on, 113, 115–17
   *Jensaarai*, 25, 106
   Kun's spirit possession of, 103
   new generation of, 151–64, 179
   Purge of, 25, 43
   Skywalker's restoration of, 71, 79, 95
Jedi Knights, ancient, 169–70
   achievements of, 20
   in Beast Wars of Onderon, 7–8, 9
   convocation of, 12, 154
   exiles in Sith Empire, 2–7
   fallen, 14, 15, 16–17, 20
   in Great Hyperspace War, 5, 169
   and Lorell Raiders, 18
   meditation technique of, 10, 14
   and Naddist revolt, 10–11, 170
   origins of, 1
   and resurgence of Sith sorcery, 11–15
   revolt of, 2
   at Ruusan, 18–20
   in Sith War, 15–16
   training of, 10
   trials of, 8–10, 169
Jedi Masters, 1
   Arca Jeth, 9, 10, 11, 12, 18
   C'baoth, 84, 87
   Gra'aton, 20
   Hoth, 18
   Ikrit, 20, 152, 154
   Jinn, 22–23
   Mace Windu, 24

Ood Bnar, 16, 95
Thon, 9, 10, 12, 15
Vima-Da-Boda, 93, 95, 99, 100
Vodo-Siosk Baas, 10, 11, 12, 15, 103
Vulatan, 20
Yoda, 20, 23, 56, 60, 79, 149, 154
*See also* Kenobi, Obi-Wan
*Jensaarai*, 25, 106
Jerec, 71
Jiliac the Hutt, 29, 34
Jinn, Master Qui-Gon, 22–23
J't'p'tan, 131
Juvex Lords, 108

Ka, Tenel, 154, 155, 156, 157, 160, 164
Kaan, Lord, 18
Kai, Tamith, 155, 156, 157–58
Kaiburr Crystal, 54, 55
Kaine, Ardus, 67, 84, 117
Kallea, Freia, 18
Kamar, 31
Kanos, Kir, 98, 157, 177
Kanz disorders, 18
Karrde, Talon, 84, 85, 86, 87, 88, 137, 147, 176
Kashyyyk, 31, 72, 86, 157
*Katana* fleet, 21, 86–87, 176
Katarn, Kyle, 47, 53, 71, 99, 100, 115
Keldor, Ohran, 45, 108
Kenobi, Obi–Wan, 99, 102
  death of, 50
  lightsaber of, 154
  mission to deliver Death Star plans, 49, 50
  Skywalker twins hidden by, 43
  spirit of, 54, 56, 63, 113
  training of Anakin Skywalker, 23, 24, 102
Kessel, 1, 29, 100, 104, 163, 164
Kessel Run, 29, 34–35, 45, 100
Keto, Satal, 10–11, 14
Khabarakh, 86
Kirrek, Great Hyperspace War on, 5
*Knight Hammer*, 111, 115, 116
Koornacht Cluster, 70, 127, 129
Korriban
  civil war on, 3
  Daragons' journey to, 3–4
  Kun's psychic outcry from, 12
  Palpatine's journey to, 96
Kossak the Hutt, 1
Kothlis, 58
Krennel, Admiral, 70, 89, 90
Kressh, Ludo, 3, 4, 5
Krytos virus, 73, 75, 160, 161, 176
Kuat, 77, 82, 126
Kueller. *See* Dolph
Kun, Exar
  alliance with Ulic, 14–15
  battle with Vodo, 15
  as Dark Lord of Sith, 14
  entombment of, 17
  Golden Globe of, 20, 152, 179
  in Sith War, 15–17

and specter of Nadd, 11–12, 14
spirit of, 102, 103


*Lady Luck*, 141
Lamuir IV, 41
Lars, Owen and Beru, 43
Lehesu of the Oswaft, 39, 40
Leia, Princess. *See* Organa Solo, Leia
Lemelisk, Bevel, 91, 101, 126
  and Darksaber construction, 111, 113, 114
  and Death Star construction, 45, 46, 51
  execution of, 115
Leth, Umak, 45, 93, 95, 101
*Liberator*, 82, 91
Lightsider, 95
Lobot, 42, 132
Lorell Raiders, 18
Loronar Corporation, 119, 121
Lorrd, 18
Lowbacca, 154, 155, 156, 160, 161, 164
Lucazec, 131
Lur, 32
Lusa, 124
*Lusankya*
  attack on Imperial City, 74, 75
  in Bacta War, 75–76
  in New Republic command, 98, 117
  prisoners of, 53, 71, 76
  rescue of prisoners, 89–90
Lyn, Arden, 106

Mace Windu, Master, 24
Madine, Crix, 53, 113, 114, 115
*Majestic*-class warships, 98
Mallatobuck, 31
Marcha of Drall, 140, 142
Marr, Nichos, 109, 110
Massassi warriors, 3, 5, 7, 12, 14, 17
  spirit of, 152
Maul, Darth, 23
Maw black hole cluster, 1, 29, 35, 45, 100, 101, 102, 104
Maw Installation, 45–46, 100–101, 104–6, 177
Micamberlecto, 138
Milagro, Battle of, 71
*Millennium Falcon*
  in Battle of Coruscant, 91
  Calrissian's ownership of, 29, 35, 36, 37, 38, 39
  in Corellian insurrection, 141
  on Dathomir, 79
  escape from Cloud City, 57
  escape from Corellia, 139, 140
  escape from Death Star, 50
  escape from Hoth, 56
  escape from Kessel, 100, 101
  in Maw Installation assault, 105
  in smuggling activities, 35
  Solo's rescue from N'zoth, 130
  Solo's winning of, 31, 41
  in Ssi-ruuk invasion, 63, 64

stolen on Dellalt, 32–33
in Yavin 4 defense, 115
Milvayne, 53
Mimban, 54, 55
Mindharp of Sharu, 36–37, 38
Mindor, Battle of, 71–72
Mingla, Cray, 109, 110
Mole miners, 84, 85
Mon Calamari, 31, 102, 163–64
Battle of, 91–93
*Mon Remonda*, 76–77
Mos Eisley, 35
Mothma, Mon
and Almania uprising, 134
and Bakura defense, 63
at Battle of Milagro, 71
as chief of state, 97, 104, 134, 135
and Corellian insurrection, 140
dispute with Bel Iblis, 53
evacuation of Pinnacle Base, 95
formation of Rebel Alliance, 25–26, 34
and Hapan alliance, 79, 82
and Jedi academy, 99
and Krytos virus, 75
poisoning of, 101, 102, 106
on Provisional Council, 67
and Rebel headquarters, 47–48, 54, 55
Ssi-ruuk invasion force of, 65
and theft of Death Star plans, 46–47
Mrlssi, 45
Munto Codru, 123
Mutdah, Bohhuah, 38
Myrial, 18
Myrkr, 84–85
Mytus VII, 31

Naboo, invasion of, 22
Nadd, Freedon, 169
as King of Onderon, 7–8
specter of, 11–12, 12, 14
tomb of, 8, 10
Naddist Revolt, 10–11, 170
Nadill, Memit, 5
Nam Chorios, 20, 25, 118–21
Nandreeson, 137
Nar Shaddaa, 29, 34, 41, 93, 95
Battle of, 29–31, 37, 172
*Nebula*-class warships, 98, 126
Nereus, Wilek, 63, 64
Nespis VIII, 95
New Cov, 86
*New Hope*, 71
New Republic, 175
and Adumar mission, 118, 178
and Almania uprising, 132–36, 178
and Black Fleet Crisis, 127–30, 178
and Bothan incident, 144, 145, 147
and Corellian insurrection, 138–42, 178
in Coruscant liberation, 72–73
Daala's threat to, 101–2, 103, 104, 111, 113,
115–17

Darksaber threat to, 112, 113–15, 177
evacuation of Pinnacle Base, 95–96
fleet of, 82
government-in-exile of, 91
guerrilla attacks by, 90, 91
and Hapes Consortium, 79, 82
and Hutts, 111, 113
and *Katana* fleet, 86–87
and Krytos plague, 75, 176
in *Lusankya* rescue mission, 89–90
in Maw Installation assault, 104–6
and Noghri, 86
Palpatine's strike against, 91–97
and peace accord, 143–45, 147, 178
Pestage's defection to, 70
Provisional Council of, 67, 89
Senate Hall bombing in, 132, 133, 136
Senate Planetary Intelligence Network (SPIN), 71
Senex/Juvex plot against, 106, 108
Skywalker's command in, 71–72, 175
Ssi-ruuk invasion force of, 65–66
victory over Palpatine, 97
and warlords, 76–78, 82, 137
warship development program of, 98, 126
*See also* Jedi Academy; Jedi Knights
Nightcloak, orbital, 80
*Night Hammer*, 111
Nightsisters of Dathomir, 80, 155–56, 176
Nikto, 1
Ninx, Shug, 29, 93
Nirauan, 147–49
Nkllon, 84
Noghri, 86, 89, 176
Nomad City, 84, 87
Nunb, Nien, 164
N'zoth, 127, 129–30
Battle of, 130, 131

Obroa-skai, 24
Odan-Urr
death of, 15
in Great Hyperspace War, 5, 10
at Jedi convocation, 12
Ooroo's prophecy about, 7
Odumin, 32
Ommin, King of Iziz, 10, 11
Onderon
Battle of, 97
Beast Wars in, 8, 9
and Naddist revolt, 10–15
Nadd's rule of, 7–8
Solos hideout on, 96
Ood Bnar, Master, 16, 95
Ooroo, Master, 5, 7, 15
Operation Shadow Hand, 94, 98, 117, 177
Operation Skyhook, 35
Operation Strike Fear, 26
Ord Cantrell, 98
Ord Mantell, 55, 161–63
Organa, Bail Prestor, 25–26, 43, 46–47, 48, 53
Organa Solo, Leia, 18, 27

and Almania uprising, 134–35
and Bakura truce, 63
Belsavis visit of, 108
birth of Anakin, 95
birth of twins, 87
and Black Fleet Crisis, 127, 129–30
and Bothan incident, 144
capture of, 48–49, 50, 54, 56, 58, 64, 93, 108, 119, 139, 173
as chief of state, 106, 108, 111, 113, 118, 121, 129–30, 132, 134, 135, 142
Corellia visit of, 138, 139
and defection of Pestage, 70
escape from Cloud City, 57
escape from Corellian insurrection, 139–40
escape from Hoth, 56
escape from Nam Chorios, 120–21
escape from Palpatine, 93–94
and evacuation of Hoth, 55
flagship of, 76, 82
and Hapans, 79
lineage and upbringing of, 43–44
marriage to Solo, 80–82
as minister of state, 97
on Nal Hutta, 111, 113
Nam Chorios visit of, 118–19
and Noghri, 86, 89
peace talks with Pellaeon, 145
rescues brother from dark side, 93, 94
rescues kidnapped children, 123–24, 126
and restoration of Jedi Knights, 95
revelation of true identity, 60, 61, 63
in Senate Hall bombing, 132, 133
Solo's kidnapping of, 79
spirit of father before, 63
theft of Death Star plans, 47, 48
and Thrawn's kidnapping attempt, 84
in Waru's spell, 126
Orinda, Battle of, 117
Orloc, Mage, 154
Oron Kira, 9
Oseon system, 35–36, 38–39
Ossilege, Admiral, 141
Ossus
    museum city on, 7, 10
    origins of Jedi Knights on, 1
    ruins of, 95
    in Sith War, 16
Oswaft, 39–41
Outbound Flight Project, 21, 23
Overden, 139

Palace of Woolamander, 151–52
Palpatine, Emperor, 37, 40, 41, 58, 60, 157
    admirals of, 72
    ascension to power, 22, 23, 25
    consolidation of power, 25–26
    death of, 61, 63
    and Death Star construction, 45, 46, 51
    disbanding of Senate, 48
    and *Eye of Palpatine*, 109

final defeat of, 96–97, 177
    resurrection of, 90–96, 177
    as senator, 21
    and Senex Lords, 106
    spirit of, 68, 89
Parck, Voss, 149
Pedducis Chorios, 67, 84, 117
Pellaeon, Gilad, 67, 83, 89, 98, 113, 130, 137
    exposure of false Thrawn, 147
    Imperial command of, 117
    and peace accord, 143–45, 147
    in Yavin 4 assault, 115, 116–17
Pentastar Alignment, 67, 84, 117
*Peremptory*, 82, 87
Perlemian Trade Route, 2
Pestage, Sate, 68, 69, 70
Phaeda, 98
Pinnacle Base, 91, 94, 95
Pitta, Grand Admiral, 72
Plawal rift, 108, 109
Plett, 108
Ploovo Two-For-One, 31
*Priam*, 26
*Pride of the Senate*, 31
*Pride of Yevetha*, 129, 130
Priole Danna festival, 41
Project Starscream, 42
Prophets of the Dark Side, 71
Pydyr, 134

Qel-Droma, Cay, 9, 10, 11, 12, 14, 15, 16
Qel-Droma, Ulic, 85, 110
    alliance with Kun, 14–15
    and droid attack, 12
    infiltration of Cinnagar, 14
    and Naddist revolt, 10, 11
    in Onderon mission, 9
    redemption of, 17, 170
    rescue of, 16
    trial of, 15
Qella, 132
Qom Jha, 147
Qom Qae, 147
Qorl, 155, 156
*Queen of Ranroon*, 32
Qui-Gon Jinn. *See* Jinn, Master Qui-Gon
Q-Varx, 121

Raaba, 160
Rafa system, 36–37
Ragnos, Marka
    death of, 3
    prophecy of, 7
    spectre of, 14–15
Ralltiir, 26
Ram's Head Mission, 54
Raynor, Dominic, 42
*Reaper*, 117, 122
Rebel Alliance, 173–74
    attack on Yavin base, 53

Battle of Endor, 60–63
Battle of Hoth, 55–56
Battle of Yavin, 26, 42, 50
blockade of Yavin base, 52–53
Bria Tharen in, 34, 35, 47
Declaration of Rebellion, 48
Dodonna's defection to, 48
financed by Circarpous business leaders, 54, 55
formation of, 26
headquarters of, 50, 52–53, 54, 55
Operation Skyhook, 35
Ram's Head Mission, 54
Rogue Squadron of, 53
and Ssi-ruuk invasion, 63–65
theft of Death Star plans, 46–47, 58
in Ylesian assault, 34, 42
*See also* Alliance of Free Planets; New Republic
*Rebel Dream*, 76, 82
Renatasia, 39
Rendar, Dash, 58
Renthal, Drea, 39, 41, 42
Republic, Old
contact with Sith, 2–4
decline and fall of, 21–25
in Great Hyperspace War, 2, 5–7
growth of, 1
Jedi guardianship of, 8–10, 20, 21
and Naboo invasion, 22
and Naddist revolt, 11
regional conflicts in, 18
in Sith War, 15–17
threat from Sith followers, 11–15, 18
*See also* New Republic
Rieekan, Carlist, 55, 95, 106, 121
Rillao, 123, 124
Risant, Tendra, 138
Rogriss, Admiral, 77, 78, 82
Rogue Squadron, 53, 67, 70, 71, 88
in Bacta War, 75–76
in Battle of Coruscant, 72, 73
in Battle of Orinda, 117
in *Lusankya* rescue mission, 89–90
Royal Guards, 72, 97, 143, 147, 157
R2-D2, 48, 49, 91, 93, 97, 108, 135, 149, 151
Rukh, 86, 89, 143
Ruling Circle, 68
Ruusan
Battle of, 18–20, 23
Valley of the Jedi, 71

Sacorria, Triad of, 138, 139
Sadow, Naga
exile of, 7
flagship of, 15–16
in Great Hyperspace War, 5
holocron of, 15
rivalry with Ludo Kressh, 3–4
Salis D'aar, 63, 64
Sal-Solo, Thrackan, 27, 139, 140–41
Second Imperium, 135–36, 155–58

Sedriss, Executor, 94, 95
Selonia, 138, 139, 140
Senate, bombing of, 132, 133, 136
Senate Planetary Intelligence Network (SPIN), 71
Senex Lords, 106, 108, 177
Shadow Academy, 155–58, 179
Shadowspawn, Lord, 72
Sharu, 36–37, 172
Shild, Moff Sarn, 29
Shrike, Garris, 27, 28, 32
*Shriwirr*, 63, 64
*Sibwarra*, 65, 66
Sibwarra, Dev, 63–64, 65, 71
Sidious, Darth, 22
Si'klaata Cluster, 1
Singing Mountain Clan, 79, 80
Sith Empire, 169
civil war in, 3, 4
Daragons' voyage to, 2–4
exile of Naga Sadow, 7
in Great Hyperspace War, 2, 5–7
legacy of sorcery, 7–8, 10–12, 41
origins of, 2
Sith order
in hiding, 20
at Ruusan, 18–20
Sith War, 15–17, 170
Sivron, Tol, 45, 46, 104, 105
SkyCenter Galleria, 163
Skynx, 33
Skywalker, Anakin
death of, 61
hidden children of, 43
Jedi training of, 22–23, 24, 102
revelation of children's identity, 57, 60, 61, 63
spirit of, 63
*See also* Vader, Darth
Skywalker, Leia. *See* Organa Solo, Leia
Skywalker, Luke, 17, 25, 27
and Almania uprising, 134–35
and Bakura invasion, 63–65
at Battle of Nam Chorios, 121
at Battle of Onderon, 97
Black Sun plot against, 58
as blockade runner, 53
and Bothan incident, 147
and Callista, 110–11, 113, 116, 119–20, 121
captured by Darth Vader, 57, 60–61
captured by Karrde, 84–85
captured by Palpatine, 91
clone of, 87
on dark side, 91, 93–94
on Dathomir, 80
delivery of Death Star plans, 50
destroys Death Star, 50
destruction of Tatooine home, 49–50
discovery of Leia's message, 49
duel with Darth Vader, 54
escape from Cloud City, 57
escape from Hoth, 56
escape from Kessel, 101

on *Eye of Palpatine*, 109–10
and Fallanassi, 131
generalship of, 71–72, 175
in Hand of Thrawn, 147–49
Jedi academy of, 99–100, 102, 106, 130, 138, 149–50
and Jedi restoration, 71, 79, 95
Jedi training of, 56, 60
and Kaiburr Crystal, 54, 55
Kun's spirit possession of, 103
lineage and upbringing of, 43
marriage to Mara Jade, 147
on retreat, 130–31
revelation of father's identity, 57, 60
revelation of sister's identity, 60
and Rogue Squadron, 53
in Tavira rescue mission, 106
and Teljkon vagabond, 132
in Waru's spell, 125, 126
Slice, 18
Sluis Van, Battle of, 85
Smugglers
in Battle of Nar Shaddaa, 29–31, 37, 172
and Hutt politics, 29
under Karrde's command, 84–85, 88
in Kessel Run, 34–35
in Smuggler's Run, 29, 136–37
Solo, Anakin
birth of, 95
in Corellian insurrection, 139, 140–41, 142
Furgan's attack on, 103, 106
in Jedi academy, 150
as Jedi Knight, 151–54
kidnapped by Hethrir, 123, 124, 125–26
Palpatine's plot against, 96, 97
Solo, Han, 27–35, 171–72
and Anobis civil war, 162–63
and Bakura invasion, 64
at Battle of Milagro, 71
at Battle of Nam Chorios, 121
at Battle of Nar Shaddaa, 31
at Battle of Onderon, 97
Belsavis visit of, 108
and Bothan incident, 145
and bounty hunters, 55
captured by Darth Vader, 56, 57
carbon-frozen body of, 57, 58
childhood and youth, 27
in Corellian insurrection, 139, 140
in Corporate Sector, 31–32, 172
on Dathomir, 79, 80
and Diversity Alliance, 161
escape from Death Star, 50
escape from Hoth, 56
escape from Jabba the Hutt, 60
escape from Maw Installation, 100
escape from Moruth Doole, 100
escape from Palpatine, 93–94
kidnaps Leia Organa, 79
marriage to Leia Organa, 80–82
in Maw Installation assault, 105

at military academy, 28
*Millennium Falcon* won by, 31, 41
on Myrkr, 84, 85
prisoner of Spaar, 129, 130
rescued from N'zoth, 130
rescues Chewbacca, 28–29, 31
rescues children, 160
rescues Leia Organa, 50, 56, 64
and restoration of Jedi Knights, 95
smear campaign against, 136
and smugglers, 29, 34–35, 136–37, 162, 171
and Thrawn's kidnapping attempt, 84
in Tion Hegemony, 32–33, 172
on Ylesia, 27–28, 33–34
in Ylesian assault, 34, 42
in Zsinj campaign, 76, 77–78
Solo, Jacen, 91, 95, 103
birth of, 87
in Corellian insurrection, 139, 140–41
as Jedi Knight, 154–58, 160–61, 163, 164
kidnapped by Hethrir, 123, 124
Solo, Jaina, 91, 95
birth of, 87
in Corellian insurrection, 139, 140–41
as Jedi Knight, 154–58, 160–61, 163, 164
kidnapped by Hethrir, 123, 124
Solo, Leia. *See* Organa Solo, Leia
Solusar, Kam, 95, 99, 115, 150
Sorcerer of Tund, 36, 38, 41
Sorcery, Sith, 7–8, 10–12, 41
Spaar, Nil, 70, 127, 129, 130
Spince, Mako, 28, 29
Ssi-ruuk
and Alliance invasion force, 65–66
Bakura invasion of, 63–64
*Starbreaker 12*, 2–3, 4
*Star of Empire*, 35
Stars' End prison, 31
Stele, Maarek, 106
Storinal, Battle of, 82
Stormtroopers, 25, 53, 72
Streen, 99, 130, 150
Sulamar, General, 111, 114
Sun Crusher, 101, 103, 104, 105
Sunrider, Andur, 9
Sunrider, Nomi, 11, 12, 15, 17, 99, 154
Jedi training of, 10
ordeal of, 9–10
and rescue of Ulic, 14, 16
Sunrider, Vima, 16, 17
Survivors cult, 33
Susevfi, 24–25
Sylvar, 11, 12, 17
Syn, Grand Admiral, 72

Ta'a Chume, 79, 80, 82, 157
Taanab, 42
Tahiri, 151–52, 154
Takel, Grand Admiral, 72
Tallon, Adar, 90

Talus, 138, 140
*Tantive IV*, 47
*Tarkin*, 57, 113
Tarkin, Grand Moff, 25, 45, 46, 48–49,
    50, 100, 104, 121
Tarkin Doctrine, 46
Tarkona, Nolaa, 158–60, 161
Tatooine, 22, 23, 35, 43, 48, 49–50
Taungs, 1
Taurill, 113–14
Tavira, Leonia, 106
Teljkon vagabond, 131–32
Telti droid factory, 134, 135, 137
Temple of Pomojema, 55
Teradoc, Admiral, 67, 82, 90, 98, 111
Terrik, Booster, 75, 76, 145
Teta, Empress
    in Great Hyperspace War, 5
    *See also* Empress Teta system
Tethys, Moff, 122
Teyr, 131
Thanas, Commander, 65
Thanta Zilbra, 139
Tharen, Bria, 28, 29, 34, 35, 42, 47
Thila, 54
Thon, Master, 9, 10, 12, 15
ThonBoka, 40, 172
Thrawn, 23, 33, 66, 72, 176
    cloaking devices of, 88
    clone of, 149
    clone soldiers of, 84, 87–88
    death of, 89
    false, 143, 144, 145, 147
    Hand of, 33, 148, 149, 179
    reorganization of fleet, 83–84
Thul, Bornan, 158, 160, 161
Thul, Raynar, 158, 160, 161
Thyferra, 75, 76
Tierce, Grodin, 89, 143, 145, 147, 157
Ti, Kirana, 100, 115
Tion, Lord, 26, 46
Tion Hegemony, 1, 32–33, 172
Tionne, 99, 100, 110, 115, 150, 154
Toka, 36, 37
Toprawa, 35, 47
*Trader's Luck*, 27
Tralus, 138, 140
Triad of Sacorria, 138, 139, 141–42
TriNebulon News, 42
Trioculus, 71, 72
Tusken Raiders, 49, 110
*Tyrant*, 76
Tyris, Nikkos, 106


Uldir, 152, 154


Vader, Darth, 23, 42, 152
    and Black Sun criminal syndicate, 58, 59
    and bounty hunters, 51–52
    capture of Han Solo, 56, 57
    capture of Luke Skywalker, 57, 60–61
    death of, 61
    and Death Star construction, 46
    at Derra IV, 55
    duel with Luke Skywalker, 54
    heirs of, 43, 44, 50
    at Hoth, 55–56
    in Jedi Purge, 25, 43
    murder of Obi-Wan Kenobi, 50, 154
    and Noghri, 86
    pursuit of Death Star plans, 47, 48
    Super Star Destroyer of, 52–53
    at Yavin, 50
    *See also* Skywalker, Anakin
Valley of the Jedi, 71
Valorum, Finis, 22
Varn, 31, 144
*Varn, World of Water*, 31
Veila, Tryst and Cassa, 152
Vergere, 24
*Victory*-class Star Destroyers, 98, 130, 135
Vima-Da-Boda, 93, 95, 99, 100
Vjun, 153, 154
Vodo-Siosk Baas, Master, 10, 11, 12, 15, 26, 103
Vodran, 1
Vontor, Battles of, 1
Vorn, Liegeus, 120, 121
Vortex, 101–2
Vuffi Raa, 36, 37, 38, 39, 40
Vulatan, Master, 20


Warriors of the Shadow (Taungs), 1
Wars
    Bacta, 75–76
    Beast Wars of Onderon, 7–8, 9
    Bounty Hunter, 51–52, 58
    Clone, 24
    with Duskhan League, 129–30
    Great Hyperspace, 2, 5–7, 169
    Sith, 15–17
    *See also* Battles; Rebel Alliance
Warship development program, New Republic, 98,
    126
Waru, 124, 124–26
*Watchkeeper*, 140, 141
Wayland, 84
Weapons, Imperial, 88, 92, 93, 95, 101, 103
    *See also* Death Star
Weequay, 1
Wessiri, Iella, 90
White Current, 130
Willard, Vanden, 90
Witches of Dathomir, 79, 80, 99
Worldcraft, 126
World Devastators, 92, 93
Wraith Squadron, 76–77


Xaverri, 29, 125

Xim the Despot, 1, 33
Xizor, Prince, 34, 51, 58–59, 68, 174
Xux, Qwi, 45, 101, 103, 104

Yaga Minor, 145, 147
Yag'Duhl space station, 76
Yane, 135
Yavin 4, 7, 12, 15, 20, 50
   Daala's assault on, 115–17, 177
   Imperial blockade of, 52, 53
   Jedi Academy on, 100, 103
Yavin, Battle of, 26, 42, 50
Yevetha, 127–30, 131
Yinchorr, 97, 98

Ylesia, 27–28, 29, 33–34, 42
Yoda, Master, 20, 23, 56, 60, 79, 149, 154
Ysanna, Jem, 95
Ysanna, Rayf, 95, 97

Zaarin, Grand Admiral, 59, 72
Zekk, 156–57, 158, 160, 161, 163, 164
Zend, Salla, 29, 31, 93
Zhell, 1
Ziost, 3
Zonama Sekot, 24
Zorba the Hutt, 71
Zsinj, 67, 76–78, 80, 176

# AUTHORS' BIOS

**Kevin J. Anderson** has written a total of fifty-four novels, comics, short stories, and other *Star Wars* works for Lucasfilm, and is best known for his Jedi Academy trilogy and the Young Jedi Knights series (with his wife Rebecca Moesta). He is also the international bestselling author of three *X-Files* novels and a new trilogy, with Brian Herbert, that is a prequel to Frank Herbert's classic *Dune*. In 1998 he also set the Guinness World Record for "Largest Single-Author Book Signing in History."

**Daniel Wallace** plans mass media communication stategies for one of the world's largest advertising agencies. He is the author or coauthor of numerous *Star Wars* projects, including Episode I *What's What, C-3PO: Tales of the Golden Droid*, and two previous entries in the *Star Wars* Essential Guide series: *Planets and Moons* and *Droids*. He lives in the Detroit area with his wife, two sons, and a minor menagerie.